Frederick Albion Ober

**In the Wake of Columbus**

Frederick Albion Ober

**In the Wake of Columbus**

ISBN/EAN: 9783743324435

Manufactured in Europe, USA, Canada, Australia, Japa

Cover: Foto ©ninafisch / pixelio.de

Manufactured and distributed by brebook publishing software (www.brebook.com)

Frederick Albion Ober

**In the Wake of Columbus**

# IN THE
# WAKE OF COLUMBUS

ADVENTURES OF THE SPECIAL COMMISSIONER SENT
BY THE WORLD'S COLUMBIAN EXPOSITION
TO THE WEST INDIES

BY

FREDERICK A.

Author of "TRAVELS IN MEXICO,"
"MONTEZUMA'S GOLD MIN[ES]"

With above two hundred illustrations
Author, and sketches by

BOSTON
D. LOTHROP
1893

### Respectfully Dedicated

AS A PERSONAL TRIBUTE

TO

## HARLOW N. HIGINBOTHAM

PRESIDENT OF THE WORLD'S COLUMBIAN EXPOSITION

AND

## WILLIAM ELEROY CURTIS

CHIEF OF THE LATIN–AMERICAN DEPARTMENT

---

AND TO

ALL OFFICIALS, NATIONAL AND LOCAL

WHO HAVE CONTRIBUTED TO THE SUCCESS OF THE

GREATEST EXPOSITION OF THE WORLD'S HISTORY

BY THE

SPECIAL COMMISSIONER TO THE WEST INDIES

# PREFACE.

SIXTEEN years ago, while sailing between Dominica and Martinique, those verdure-clad islands lying midway the Caribbee chain, I first looked upon land discovered by Columbus.

I will not deny that I was strangely thrilled; nor shall any scoffer put me down as a sentimental voyager because I attached to those islands an importance not implied in the Admiralty charts.

In the two succeeding years I had threaded the chain of the Caribbees, explored all the islands discovered by the Admiral in his second and third voyages, hunted in the forests in which he and his men had encountered the cannibal Caribs, and had lived for months with the descendants of those same fierce Indians so graphically described by the pen of the great Discoverer.

In 1880 I re-visited the West Indies, and added other islands to those already investigated, my object (as on the previous voyage) being the ornithological exploration of the Lesser Antilles. Birds and woods — the *avi-fauna* of the islands and the great forests — were the subjects I particularly studied; but, from being constantly on the trail of the great Genoese, I at last became interested in the story of his voyagings, and began to collect information regarding the places identified with his life and labors.

In 1881, on the coast of Yucatan, I was reminded of his last voyage in the year 1502, when he encountered that great canoe laden with chocolate beans, copper utensils and cotton, and guided by mariners of a higher order of intelligence than any other of these new peoples he had seen. Seven years later, in the Bahamas, I saw that island on which Columbus landed — San Salvador or Guanahani — rising ghost-like from the sea; the first landfall of the eventful voyage of 1492. The south coast of Cuba gave me the emerald " Gardens of the Queen," and the " Bay of the Hundred Fires."

## PREFACE.

Wherever I have wandered, it will be seen, I have met with reminders of Columbus; and, having viewed with so keen an interest these jewels of his gathering, with which he adorned the crown of Spain, was it strange that I was impelled to seek that Mother Country, and that when there I found no more precious relics than those of the Admiral of the Ocean Sea?

Having followed the fortunes of Columbus, in a desultory manner, for nearly fifteen years, it was extremely gratifying to have offered me the opportunity for further investigation afforded in the appointment as Columbian Commissioner to the West Indies. It was purely fortuitous, as I had no previous acquaintance with any of the officials; but, being specially charged to search out every spot and relic of the discovery, I was thus enabled to carry out my own explorations and complete an exhaustive study of the subject.

In this work, which I have called "In the Wake of Columbus," I aim to present what may be termed the environment of the Admiral; giving scenes with which he was identified, starting with the inception of the enterprise in Spain, carrying the action across the Atlantic to the first landfall, through the Bahamas to Cuba, thence to the scene of the first wreck and the first fort, on the coast of Haiti, the first settlement at Isabella, the initial attempts at discovery in Española, showing where the gold was found and the first cities started — in fact, following him through all his voyages, writing every description from personal observation, and using the historical events merely as a golden thread upon which to string the beads of this Columbian rosary.

Whether my work has been well done or badly done, such as it is I now offer it — a tribute to our great Exposition; to the genius that conceived, the courage that continued, the energy that executed, and the faith that sustained to a triumphant conclusion, this the grandest work of its kind the world has ever seen; the crowning event of a century filled with wonders and miracles of man's invention.

WASHINGTON, April, 1893.

# CONTENTS.

| CHAPTER | | PAGE |
|---|---|---|
| I. | THE BRIDGE THAT SPANNED THE WORLD | 1 |
| II. | AT THE NEW WORLD'S PORTAL | 23 |
| III. | IN GUANAHANI WITH COLUMBUS | 52 |
| IV. | WHERE WAS THE ADMIRAL'S LANDFALL? | 85 |
| V. | THROUGH THE BAHAMA ISLES | 104 |
| VI. | THE COMMISSIONER'S MISSION TO CUBA | 121 |
| VII. | NORTH COAST OF CUBA TO HAITI | 148 |
| VIII. | THE HAITIAN CIVILIZATION | 173 |
| IX. | THE BUCCANEERS AND THE BLACK KING | 192 |
| X. | THE FIRST AMERICAN CHRISTMAS | 217 |
| XI. | ROUND ABOUT ISABELLA | 235 |
| XII. | WHERE THE FIRST GOLD WAS FOUND | 259 |
| XIII. | THE PORT OF THE SILVER MOUNTAIN | 277 |
| XIV. | SAMANA AND THE BAY OF ARROWS | 292 |
| XV. | THE HOLY HILL OF SANTO DOMINGO | 302 |

CONTENTS.

| | | |
|---|---|---|
| XVI. | The Earthquake-buried Towns | 321 |
| XVII. | In Santo Domingo City | 338 |
| XVIII. | Where is the Tomb of Columbus? | 363 |
| XIX. | Puerto Rico and Ponce de Leon | 388 |
| XX. | Among the Saints and the Virgins | 413 |
| XXI. | An Island quite out of the World | 426 |
| XXII. | The Second Voyage to the New World | 448 |
| XXIII. | Carib Islands and Lake Dwellers | 471 |
| XXIV. | Jamaica and the Wreck of Columbus | 492 |

# ILLUSTRATIONS.

| | |
|---|---:|
| Columbus received by the Catholic kings after his first voyage . . *Frontis.* | |
| In the Convent Garden . . . . . | *3* |
| Doña Carmen and Carmencita . . . . | *5* |
| The Atalaya of Arbolote . . . . . | *8* |
| Distant view of the Alhambra . . . . | *9* |
| The marble head of the Moor at Santa Fé . . | *11* |
| City gate of Santa Fé . . . . . | *12* |
| The Bridge of Pines . . . . . . | *13* |
| Santa Fé across the Vega . . . . . | *15* |
| Entrance to the Bridge of Pines . . . . | *18* |
| The taking of Moclin . . . . . | *19* |
| The crosses of Zubia . . . . . . | *21* |
| A corner of my garden at Granada . . . | *22* |
| Moorish arch at Palos . . . . . | *23* |
| The Mosque of a Thousand Columns at Cordova . | *25* |
| Church of St. George, Palos . . . . | *27* |
| Seville, with the Tower of Gold in the foreground | *31* |
| The Convent of La Rabida . . . . | *37* |
| The Mirador of La Rabida . . | *39* |
| In the Convent Court . . . . . . | *41* |
| The Columbus Room, Convent of La Rabida . | *45* |

## ILLUSTRATIONS.

| | |
|---|---|
| *Alabaster tomb at Burgos* . . . | *49* |
| *Cross at La Rabida* . . . . . | *51* |
| *Crossing the Sargasso Sea* . . . . . | *52* |
| *Map showing the route of the first voyage of Columbus* . . . . . | *55* |
| *A salt heap on Fortune Island* . . . | *58* |
| *Windmill for pumping salt water* | *60* |
| *My "Turtler"* . . . . . . . | *64* |
| *Looking across the lagoons on Watling's Island* . | *66* |
| *The landing-place of Columbus* . . . | *69* |
| *Skull of Bahama Indian* . . . . | *75* |
| *Indian antiquities from the Bahamas* . | *78* |
| *Carved seat of lignum-vitæ from the Bahamas* | *82* |
| *Map of Watling's Island* . . . . . | *85* |
| *The headland coast of Watling's Island* | *90* |
| *Green's Harbor, Watling's Island* . . | *93* |
| *The coast of Watling's Island* . . . . | *97* |
| *Map, showing route from Watling's Island to Cuba* . . . . . . . | *99* |
| *Indian celt, from Cat Island* . . . | *102* |
| *Indian chisel found in the Islands* . | *103* |
| *Stone axe, Turk's Island* . . . | *103* |
| *Natives of Watling's Island* . . . . | *105* |
| *Pushing through the canal, Watling's Island* . | *106* |
| *Cave on Cat Island* . . . . . . | *108* |
| *On the beach of Watling's Island* | *110* |
| *The silk-cotton tree, Nassau* . . | *114* |
| *Statue of Columbus, front view* . . . | *116* |
| *Statue of Columbus, rear view* . . . . | *117* |
| *Guanahani, or Watling's Island — Lady Blake's Aquarelle* . . . . . . | *119* |

## ILLUSTRATIONS.

| | |
|---|---|
| Tablet bust in cathedral at Havana, in memory of Columbus | 121 |
| Palm Avenue | 125 |
| Cathedral St. Maria de la Concepcion, Havana, Cuba | 130 |
| The Morro | 133 |
| Les Cabanas | 135 |
| Morro Castle, Harbor of Havana | 137 |
| At the Market | 138 |
| On the Pasco | 141 |
| Belem | 142 |
| Real Acadamia, Havana | 144 |
| A bit of old Havana | 147 |
| Royal Palms | 148 |
| Selling plants in Havana | 150 |
| Plaza de Armas, Havana | 152 |
| "Morning mist," Yumuri Valley from the Cumbres | 155 |
| Yumuri Valley, from the hill of Guadeloupe | 158 |
| Mountains of Zibara | 160 |
| North coast of Cuba | 163 |
| Baracoa | 166 |
| In the Volante, Cuba | 169 |
| Frederick Douglas | 173 |
| Hyppolite | 175 |
| Hyppolite and staff | 177 |
| Abandoned estate, coast of Haiti | 181 |
| D. F. Legitime | 183 |
| A view from the residence of the English consul, Haiti | 186 |
| Tortuga, the pirates' paradise | 193 |

## ILLUSTRATIONS.

| | |
|---|---:|
| *Old Buccaneer watch-tower, coast of Haiti* | *199* |
| *Sans Souci, the Black King's palace* | *205* |
| *Sans Souci, ruins of the Black King's palace* | *206* |
| *The Black King's castle* | *209* |
| *Old mortars in the Black King's castle* | *213* |
| *Broken arch, the Black King's castle* | *214* |
| *Beauty and the beasts, found at Millot* | *216* |
| *A religious procession at Cape Haitien* | *218* |
| *The Santa Maria, the flag-ship of Columbus* | *220* |
| *The wrecked caravel* | *223* |
| *In Petit Anse* | *227* |
| *Soldiers of the guard at rest* | *230* |
| *The anchor of Columbus, found at Petit Anse* | *231* |
| *St. John and the Agnus Dei* | *232* |
| *The old convent* | *235* |
| *Huckster's shanty, on the river Yaqui* | *236* |
| *The Bajo-Bonico* | *242* |
| *On the bluff at Isabella* | *244* |
| *Site of Isabella* | *249* |
| *Map of Isabella* | *252* |
| *The cactus-covered ruins of Isabella* | *254* |
| *Coco's idol* | *257* |
| *View on the Bajo-Bonico near the Hidalgos' pass* | *262* |
| *The American ferry across the Yaqui* | *264* |
| *In the valley of the Yaqui* | *265* |
| *"They built a wooden tower"* | *268* |
| *View of Santiago across the Yaqui* | *270* |
| *The site of the tower of Santo Tomas* | *273* |
| *The bed of the river Yaqui* | *275* |
| *Loading a bull cart* | *279* |
| *View of the Plaza and church at Puerto Plata* | *284* |

## ILLUSTRATIONS.

| | |
|---|---:|
| *Girl on bullock's back, Puerto Plata* . . . | 287 |
| *The typical beast of burden* . . . . | 288 |
| *Washerwomen of Haiti* . . . . . | 290 |
| *Coaling station, Samana Bay* . . . . | 293 |
| *Scene of the first encounter with the Indians* . | 295 |
| *A typical washerwoman of Samana* . . . | 297 |
| *The approach to Sanchez* . . . . . | 300 |
| *A relic from Old Vega* . . . . . | 302 |
| *In the Savannas of Santo Domingo* . . . | 303 |
| *The manager's house at Sanchez* . . . | 306 |
| *View of the Royal Plain* . . . . . | 309 |
| *Santo Cerro Church and the aged tree* . . | 313 |
| *The shrine of the Virgin worshiped in the time of Columbus* . . . . . . | 315 |
| *A view of Santo Cerro* . . . . . | 317 |
| *Along the river Yuna* . . . . . | 318 |
| *Window in Rosario Chapel, Santo Domingo* . | 320 |
| *Ruins of the church built by bequest of Columbus* | 322 |
| *Ruins of Fort Concepcion* . . . . . | 324 |
| *A precious relic* . . . . . . | 327 |
| *One of the most interesting spots of Jacagua* . | 329 |
| *The cemetery at Santiago* . . . . | 333 |
| *Site of the old church at Jacagua* . . . | 335 |
| *Used by the early Spaniards* . . . . | 336 |
| *The whistling jug* . . . . . . | 337 |
| *A Santo Domingo seaport town* . . . | 339 |
| *Homenage, the oldest castle in America* . . | 341 |
| *The house of Columbus* . . . . . | 344 |
| *The sun-dial to be seen in Santo Domingo* . | 346 |
| *Columbus in chains* . . . . . . | 349 |
| *The cathedral, western entrance* . . . | 351 |

## ILLUSTRATIONS.

| | |
|---|---:|
| *Inscription on an old tombstone* | *354* |
| *View of the cathedral high altar and retable* | *356* |
| *The portal of the Mint, Santo Domingo* | *359* |
| *The Homenage* | *362* |
| *Bronze statue of Columbus before the door of the cathedral in Santo Domingo city* | *369* |
| *The Columbus vaults in Santo Domingo cathedral* | *373* |
| *The Columbus casket, end view* | *375* |
| *The Columbus casket, front view* | *376* |
| *Fac-simile of old baptismal book* | *378* |
| *Fac-simile of inscriptions* | *379* |
| *The tablet and the vault at Santo Domingo* | *384* |
| *Arms of Puerto Rico* | *388* |
| *General Heureaux* | *391* |
| *The harbor of San Juan seen from the Casa Blanca, or home of Ponce de Leon* | *395* |
| *A sugar lighter in Puerto Rico waters* | *399* |
| *Native huts and dove cotes* | *402* |
| *Along the river* | *404* |
| *Sentry box and cemetery gate at San Juan* | *406* |
| *The Casa Blanca* | *408* |
| *The last of him who sought eternal youth* | *410* |
| *Arches of San Francisco Convent, Santo Domingo City* | *412* |
| *The harbor from the fort* | *415* |
| *Old fort at St. Thomas* | *419* |
| *Buccaneer cannon, St. John's* | *424* |
| *The ladder* | *430* |
| *Town of Bottom, Island of Saba* | *433* |
| *A tropical sunrise* | *437* |
| *Cacao fruit* | *442* |

## ILLUSTRATIONS.

| | |
|---|---:|
| *Bread-fruit* | *443* |
| *St. Patrick's Rock, Saba* | *447* |
| *The island of St. Eustatius, seen from St. Kitt's* | *449* |
| *Washerwomen of Nevis* | *452* |
| *Great trees of the high woods* | *458* |
| *Banyan-tree, Guadeloupe* | *460* |
| *The waterfall out of the clouds* | *463* |
| *Volcano on St. Lucia* | *467* |
| *Negro boys of Martinique* | *469* |
| *The diamond rock off Martinique* | *472* |
| *The pitons of St. Lucia* | *474* |
| *Kingstown, capital of St. Vincent* | *475* |
| *Palms of the leeward coast, St. Vincent* | *477* |
| *The ten little caribs* | *479* |
| *Beach near the Boca, Trinidad* | *483* |
| *The pitch lake, Trinidad* | *485* |
| *Sunset on the Venezuelan coast* | *488* |
| *Ploughing under the palms* | *489* |
| *Washing clothes at Curacao* | *490* |
| *The heart of the cocoa palm* | *495* |
| *Carib carvings on a rock in the island of St. John's* | *505* |
| *Don Christopher's Cove, where Columbus's caravels were wrecked, 1503* | *511* |
| *The bay of St. Ann's, Jamaica* | *514* |

# IN THE WAKE OF COLUMBUS

I.

THE BRIDGE THAT SPANNED THE WORLD.

GARDENS of Granada are famous throughout Spain, and of them all, perhaps none more fascinating than the *Karmen del Gran Capitan.* The Arabs called them *Karmenes*, those hillside vineyards lying abreast the sun of Spain and Africa, and this particular garden received its name from having belonged to the Great Captain, Gonsalvo de Cordova. It was given him by King Ferdinand for his assistance at the siege of Granada; this ancient vineyard of a luckless Moor.

All these particulars were set forth upon a tablet let into the wall above one of the fountains that supplied water for the household. Centuries old, as was the dwelling attached, yet it did not present an appearance of antiquity, for annual coats of whitewash kept fresh its thick stone walls, while the roofing-tiles were rich in reds and mellow tints of age-imparted browns.

Perhaps I may never attain more nearly to an earthly paradise than I did in my residence in this beautiful garden; and it was by the merest chance that I became aware of its existence, and possessed it during the space of a month. In Seville one day, where I had quarters in the house of a priest, I encountered an English artist whose eccentricities were a constant wonder to the dwellers there. At the time of our meeting he was engaged in kicking his slippers from the pavement of the *patio* to the roof-tiles of the house, a feat which he performed to his own entire satisfaction and the openly-expressed astonishment of his Spanish spectators. As he was going to Granada, it happened we traveled together, and when there he introduced me to the owners of the garden, who consented to take us as dwellers therein for whatever time we might elect to remain. The nominal head of the establishment was Don Nicolas, a small asthmatic gentleman who did business in the city of Granada; the actual and authoritative Presence was Doña Carmen, his wife: tall, stately, magnificent; but the real ruler, the resident queen of Carmen del Capitan, was little Carmencita, their joint possession and pride. Rosalie, the smiling maid-of-all-work, completed the family circle which, from center to circumference, was so entirely at our service that it seemed as though it must have been specially created

IN THE CONVENT GARDEN.

for us, and made only to revolve in anticipation of our needs.

This, then, was the garden in which I had ensconced myself for an attack upon the outposts of American history.

I have chosen it as vantage ground, as a base of operations; for, in our little journeys in and about the world, we all need a starting-point; a place to keep in mind for retreat, or a deposit for our plunderings. One may wander, and gather things new and old, but if one has no home to return to where he may accumulate the products of his toils and contemplate their values, what good, then, his gatherings? I felt almost as secure in my garden as the old father of Boabdil, who fought Ferdinand so gallantly, must have felt in his mountain fortress in the Alpujarras; and, like him, I made many a foray into the historic fields around me, returning always well-laden with richest spoil. My companion in these adventures was José, the gardener, whose duties permitted him a day off whenever he liked, and whose poverty made him gladly accept an opportunity for adding a few dollars to his scant salary. He knew all the country round about and its traditions, and, with the help of Washington Irving's "Conquest," which I carried in my pocket, we visited and identified all the places of interest in the Vega.

As I have said, I went to Spain to study the beginnings of American history, and as the central figure of that history is Christopher Columbus, we shall visit all the most important places connected with his life after he became interesting as the Personage with a purpose. We shall take him at the outset of his career of discovery and follow him to the end. And in assuming that Columbus is the hero of America's initial appearance upon the stage of history, I do not deny the great Norsemen anything; only that the Genoese made his discovery known, while the first visitors did not, and through Columbus the way was opened whereby America was peopled with those who brought the blessings of civilization.

Leaving this question of honors to the historian, let us inquire a little into the conditions prevailing in Spain at the close of the fifteenth century, in the last decade of which her star was in the ascendant. Following the successive invasions of the Phœnicians, the Carthaginians, the Vandals and the Goths, came the Moors, at the opening of the eighth century. The power of the Goths terminated with the fall of Roderick, their last king, who was overwhelmed beneath the Arab flood

DOÑA CARMEN AND CARMENCITA.

from Africa. For nearly seven hundred years, the Moors possessed the better part of Spain; they built mosques and palaces, and intended their descendants should own this fair land forever. They gave to Spain a distinctive people, as well as Oriental forms of speech and of architecture. The Moorish invasion had been almost miraculous in its wide-spread conquests; but finally came the time when they, too, must succumb, and to the prowess of northern arms. Down from the mountains of the North, from the Asturias and the Pyrenees, swept the Castilian armies, wave after wave, until were wrested from the Africans the soil and cities they had won with so much bloodshed, and the conflict of centuries culminated in the fall of Granada, in 1492. Toward the close of the fifteenth century, the only strongholds remaining to the Moors lay in Andalusia, called by the Spaniards the "Land of the most Sacred Virgin," because of its delightful climate, its fruitful fields, and its natural advantages as a dwelling-place for man. When at last the union of Isabella and Ferdinand joined the forces of Leon and Castile, then appeared possible the long-deferred, long-hoped-for scheme of universal conquest, and the ultimate expulsion of the Moors from their territory. The most fascinating episodes of that final period of warfare occurred in the Vega of Granada, and among the hills surrounding this beautiful plain.

Standing conspicuously upon every hill-crest overlooking the Vega are the remains of Moorish watch-towers, their *atalayas*, from which the watchful sentinels flashed blazing signal-fires at the appearance of an enemy. Even to-day, they may be seen in various places, lone and solitary landmarks, though useless now, around the fruitful valleys they were built to guard. Centuries have slipped by since the danger-signals flamed from their summit-platforms, and they are now fast going to ruin and decay. One such *atalaya* rose above the hill of Elvira, always visible from the Alhambra at sunset, black sentinel against the brilliant sky. This tower I took as the objective point of my first foray; and one May morning, guided by José, I left the Karmen, passed through the beautiful grove of elms to the Alhambra, and thence down the Darro, through the half-sleeping city of Granada, seeking the distant hills. Fain would I linger by the way to describe the beauties of the palace we left behind, and the elm-grove in which I have heard the nightingales singing at midnight, as well as the golden-sanded Darro, down the right bank of which we strolled. It was delightfully cool in the grove, where the birds were twittering preparatory to their matin music, and until we were well out upon the plain beyond Granada, we did not feel the heat of the sun. Three hours later we were reclining at the foot of the tower, which is locally known as the *Atalaya of Arbolote*, whence we had a view outspread that well rewarded the long and somewhat dusty walk. Nearly all the Vega lay before us. At our feet were the remains of old Roman Illora, dating from a period near the birth of Christ; beyond, Granada, dark in the valley, with the Hill of the Sun crowned by the Alhambra, above it; and behind, the shining crests of the Sierra Nevada, broadly breasting the sun;

"Like silver shields new burnished for display."

As in the time of Columbus, so now: smiling plain, dark masses of olive-trees, silver threads of streams coursing emerald meadows, frowning battlements capping the Alhambra hills, and glistening snow-peaks lying against the sky. Columbus saw all this, and, though he has left no description of it, its beauty impressed him, for in his voyagings through the island-dotted seas—on which we shall follow him—he constantly recurs to the charms of Andalusia.

THE ATALAYA OF ARBOLOTE.

But Granada and the Alhambra we have left behind. Before us lies a city seldom visited by strangers; a city sleeping in the memories of the past, and with no tie connecting it with the present. Four centuries agone — and three years more — the armies of Isabella and Ferdinand had advanced their line of conquest to the mountain wall around the Vega. One after another the Moorish towns and cities had fallen before the implacable Ferdinand: Zahara, Antequera, Alhama, Loxa, Illora, Moclin; until, in 1490, Granada stood alone; isolate, crippled, yet proudly defiant.

In April, 1491, the Spanish army, horse and foot, fifty thousand strong, poured over the hills and into the Vega, intrenching themselves upon the site of Santa Fé, as a situation strategically important, in the center of the plain.

Granada lay full in sight before them. Where to-day rise the towers of its great cathedral, the minaret of a Moslem mosque towered skyward, and from its summit the muezzin called the faithful to prayers: "*Allah il Allah!* Great God! great God! Come to prayer! come to prayer! It is better to pray than to sleep!" So near were the soldiers of Ferdinand to the object of their desires, that they could almost hear the summoning cry of the muezzin.

Upon the site of the fortified camp, which was first of tents, then huts of wood and stone, was founded, in the year 1492, the town of Santa Fé, or the City of the Holy Faith. It may now be seen as I saw it that hot day in May, scarcely lifting itself

DISTANT VIEW OF THE ALHAMBRA.

above and beyond broad fields of barley, wheat and alfalfa. A semi-somnolent city is Santa Fé; completely walled about, with most picturesque gates facing the cardinal points. If the term "dead-and-alive" may be applied to any place, it certainly may be to this. Yet its history is interesting, and no student of the conquest of Granada can afford to pass it by without at least a peep into its past.

Although we are dealing with Columbus, yet we may not neglect the historical accessories that make his story worth the telling. A hundred books, at least, will give us the tale of his life and adventures, but they only repeat what is already familiar; and since a multitude of writers are even now on the search, hunting the victim from the cradle to the grave, as it were, we ourselves will not join in, but will lie quietly in ambush; perchance we may gain glimpses of the great man, unawares. Hence I will claim the privilege of digressing a while, merely to relate one of those exciting encounters that took place while the army was encamped at Santa Fé, and which, while it enlivened the monotony of camp life, kept up the spirits of the men.

Among the fiercest of the *caballeros* in command under the Spanish king, as the army lay before Granada, was, the historians tell us, Hernando del Pulgar. Casting about, one day, for an opportunity to distinguish himself, he espied the city gate of Granada but negligently guarded. Dashing in, he somehow evaded the Moorish sentinels, and reached to the great mosque in the center of the city. Losing not a moment, he rode his horse against the door, and there, with his poniard, affixed a bit of wood with *Ave Maria* printed on it. Then he wheeled about and darted through the gateway, with great clatter of hoof and clank of weapon, hurling cries of defiance at the astonished Moors, and escaped with a whole skin to the camp.

The Moors at first were puzzled to account for this foray; but when they finally found the *Ave Maria* pinned against the great door of the mosque, they were beside themselves with rage. And the next day an immense Moor, one of the most powerful and renowned of the Moslem warriors, insolently paraded before the Christian host, with the sacred emblem attached to the tail of his horse, and dragging in the dust. At the same

THE MARBLE HEAD OF THE MOOR AT SANTA FÉ.

time he defied any one of the cavaliers to meet him in single combat before the assembled armies.

Now, Ferdinand had forbidden any of his nobles to engage in this manner with the Moors, because their cavaliers were better horsemen, more skilled in the feats of the tourney, and generally came off victorious, thus greatly weakening the *esprit de corps*. But this insult to the Christian religion could not be borne, and the cavaliers all burned to avenge it. A fiery young Castilian, Garcilasso de la Vega, rushed before Isabella, and importuned her to allow him to defend the holy faith against this pagan Moor. Her permission reluctantly granted, he armed himself completely and went to meet the Moslem, who was almost twice his size, and mounted in a superior manner. And

CITY GATE OF SANTA FÉ.

yet, notwithstanding the apparent odds against him, young Garcilasso came out of the terrible combat triumphant. He killed the boastful Moor, rescued the emblem, and laid the head of his adversary at the feet of Isabella.

The site of this memorable encounter, and the spot where Isabella sat to witness it, is marked by a great stone cross, protected by an artistic canopy. Subsequently, a church was erected in Santa Fé, in which to-day the sacristan can show you a silver lamp presented by Isabella; but the most striking thing about this church stands between its two great towers: the marble head of the vanquished Moor, of heroic size, lies there placidly, and above him rises the lance which was used

to slay him, flanked with palm leaves, across which is the emblem of the faith. Thus, everywhere in Spain, are we reminded of the days of chivalry and their romances, and the scenes of the distant past brought vividly before us.

At the door of Isabella's silken tent another hero stands awaiting royal favor. He asks no boon of her, but only aid to carry out his schemes of conquest; he craves permission, like Garcilasso, to enter the lists against the infidel. The Moors are conquered, but mayhap there are other Pagans, in the world unknown beyond the sea.

He, Columbus, with his sovereigns' aid, and by the

SANTA FÉ ACROSS THE VEGA.

grace of God, would go forth single-handed to battle for the Crown.

It is the month of January, 1492. Briefly, the story of Granada's downfall may be told. That month Granada capitulated, and the last stronghold of the Moors in Europe passed from them forever. The year that saw the star of Spain in the ascendant, was the birth-year also of the history of civilization in America. The two great events are coeval, for, as the star of the Orient sank toward Africa, the star of the Occident rose upon the horizon. And this era of exploration and discovery was to be opened through the genius of an obscure, almost unknown individual, waiting humbly his sovereigns' pleasure in their camp at Santa Fé.

Spain's victories hitherto had been on land; for centuries she had been engaged in wresting from the infidel her own lost territory, foot by foot, city by city, until at last the great work was accomplished. Now, before their wearied soldiers had recovered breath, while their arms were yet tired with wielding the sword, and the blood of the slain was still fresh upon their weapons, the Spanish rulers were again importuned by that Genoese adventurer. He had gone away at last, disheartened, but had returned again at the solicitations of the queen's old confessor and at the instance of Isabella herself. He had returned as persistent, as calmly confident of ultimate aid from some quarter, as before. He abated no jot or particle of his ridiculous demands: he wanted ships and caravels, sailors, provisions, munitions, articles for barter. He demanded that he be made Admiral of the Ocean Sea; Viceroy over the regions discovered; the privileges of the aristocracy, and one tenth the revenue of that undiscovered country; in truth, there seemed no limit to his demands. And this from an unknown man whose only claims were to possessions yet to be possessed: nothing more or less than veritable "Castles in Spain." Perhaps, if the serious queen ever did take a humorous view of a situation, she may have seen the funny side of this one, and have yielded at last out of sheer weariness.

At first, however, notwithstanding the urgent solicitations of her respected confessor, she could not bring herself to accept the terms of Columbus, and he departed again, this time fully resolved to abandon the country. This, however, he was not allowed to do, for he had not accomplished more than two leagues of his journey back to the Convent of La Rabida, before he was overtakened by a courier from Isabella promising acquiescence to his demands.

Whether or not the queen did this of her own volition, whether her treasurer offered to find the requisite money for the outlay, or whether she proffered the pledge of her jewels, are matters for the historians to settle. The chances are, that Isabel did not offer to pledge her jewels, since they were, probably, already pledged to aid in furnishing the sinews of war for the siege of Granada. But let it suffice that she promised assistance, and, once embarked in the enterprise, gave the future admiral both pecuniary and moral support. All the more creditable is this to Isabella, since it was done at a time when the royal treasury had been completely exhausted by the drafts upon it for the Moorish wars, and when she might have been supposed to be already sated with the glory of conquest and not anxious for further exploits.

The place at which the royal courier overtook Columbus has been preserved in tradition ever since, and is pointed out to-day with unerring finger. He had reached a river flowing through the Vega, spanned then, as now, by the "Bridge of Pines." It is locally known as *Pinos Puente*, and was the object of another little journey by José and myself, after we had visited, and I had photographed, Santa Fé. We had noted it from our *atalaya* tower, and one day, through seas of scarlet and crimson poppies, had descended to the valley.

ENTRANCE TO THE BRIDGE OF PINES.

Although the discussion was carried on in Santa Fé, still this spot may be looked upon as that at which the career of Columbus really began; the turn of the tide in his fortunes, and the turning-point in his journey. For this reason, and in view of the far-reaching consequences of this departure, I have taken the liberty of calling this *Pinos Puente* the "Bridge that Spanned the World." It is a structure of stone and masonry, creditable to its designers, with a gateway and a turret, spanning the stream with two high arches, and is nearly always a scene of busy life. I rambled with my guide along the banks, and climbed the hill above, where are the remains of an ancient Moorish fort, finally resting at a *meson*, where the simple folk cheerfully served us with the best they had.

Another trip, on another day, was to Moclin, on the outer verge of the Vega, where the Moorish fortifications are exactly as left after being battered to pieces by the cannon of King Ferdinand, the year previous to the fall of Granada. Amongst the wood-carvings around the *silleria*, or choir-stalls, of Toledo cathedral, is one depicting the taking of Moclin; all the incidents of the siege of Granada, in fact, are there illustrated.

Again, we visited successively Loxa, Illora and Zubia, at which last place Isabella narrowly escaped capture by the Moors, and where a group of great stone crosses marks a religious shrine. Granada and its environs yet present a field for exploitation to the enthusiastic student of history, whether he be specially interested in the closing scenes of Moorish domination, the lives of Ferdinand and Isabella, or the dawn of discovery in America. Around Columbus, however, cluster the associations of Santa Fé and the Bridge of Pines, at the opening of this drama of the siege of Granada; thence, he followed the court as the army advanced to take possession of the city, and tradition relates, with an air of authenticity,

THE CROSSES OF ZUBIA.

that in the Alhambra itself Columbus was a visitor a while, pacing gloomily its columned corridors while the issue of his voyage was pending. Here, it is related, took place a memorable interview between the high contracting parties, in the beautiful " Hall of Justice," the *Sala del Tribunal*, which bounds one side of the famous "Court of Lions," and is a dream of beauty. Here, where the swart Moors reclined and dreamed away the noontide hours, and the stern caliphs sat, in days departed, the queen received Columbus.

During a month of most delightful days, I myself dwelt within the Alhambra walls, sallying forth upon excursions, as narrated; wandering through the palace by daylight and by moonlight, and weaving about the departed Moors, the Christian conquerors and the great Navigator, the tissue of a fabric I have herein attempted to unfold.

A CORNER OF MY GARDEN AT GRANADA.

## II.

### AT THE NEW WORLD'S PORTAL.

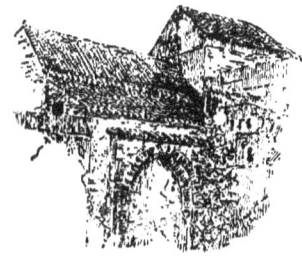

MOORISH ARCH AT PALOS.

AS we have seen, Columbus, crowned with success, departed for Palos, invested with all the rights and privileges he for years had been so anxious to obtain.

But two months after the surrender of Boabdil to Ferdinand and Isabella, the same hands that had received the emblems of their triumph over the Moors affixed the royal sign-manual to a paper confirming Columbus in titles in a yet undiscovered country beyond the unknown sea. A commemorative chapel on the bank of the Xenil marks the spot made famous by the surrender of the Moor; in the royal chapel attached to the cathedral of Granada the alabaster tombs of the king and queen are sacred shrines, to which pilgrims by thousands annually wend their way; but no monument rises above the spot where the great Navigator engaged to barter a world for prospective emolument and titular honors.

We know with what tenacity he clung to the scheme he had formulated for the enrichment and ennobling of himself and his family, preferring to abandon the country rather than to abate one iota of his project. And it was with doubtful pace that he followed the messenger from Isabella who had overtaken him at the Bridge of Pines, with the promise of her consent.

But at last he was on his way to Palos, triumphant. And while he is pursuing his way toward the coast, let us briefly review his history hitherto.

He was born in Genoa, the historians tell us, in the year 1435 — this may not be the exact date; and regarding his youth and early manhood there is the same obscurity; but about the year 1470, we find him residing in Portugal, the birthplace of his wife, and somewhat later engaged in correspondence with Toscanelli. According to his son's statement, in 1477 he "navigated one hundred leagues beyond Thule;" but in 1482 he is in the South of Spain, having vainly endeavored to enlist the king of Portugal in his plans, and is sent to Isabella by the Duke of Medina Celi, at the court in Cordova. He follows the court to Salamanca in 1486, and there has audience with the queen. In 1487 he is before the Council in the Dominican Convent; he returns to Cordova the same year in the train of Isabella, whence he is summoned to the military camp at Malaga. The year 1489 finds him before the walls of Baza, where he witnessed the surrender of the Moors under Boabdil the Elder, and doubtless conversed with the two monks who there came to the queen from Jerusalem. 1490 sees him in Seville and Cordova, whence he finally departs in disgust for the port of Huelva, on his way stopping at the Convent of La Rabida, where he attracts the attention of the prior, and subsequently has the

THE MOSQUE OF A THOUSAND COLUMNS AT CORDOVA.

famous conference with the friar, the village doctor of Palos, and Martin Alonzo Pinzon of Moguer.

This conference in the convent took place in the latter part of the year 1491; as the result, a messenger was dispatched to Isabella, then in camp at Santa Fé, who returned after fourteen days with royal orders for the prior to go to Granada; he departs in haste, and eventually returns with the queen's command for Columbus to appear before the court, and with the necessary money for the trip.

Columbus arrives at Santa Fé the first week in January, 1492, in good time (as we have seen) to witness the surrender of Granada. He has audience with his sovereigns, but cannot agree upon terms, so prepares to depart from Spain. He is overtaken by the queen's courier at the Bridge of Pines, returns, and is finally made happy with the royal consent.

The "Capitulation" for conquest and exploration is signed April 17, 1492, and the twelfth of May he sets out for Palos. Ten days later — the twenty-third — the royal command for the people of Palos to furnish men for the voyage is read in the church of St. George, and the Pinzon family come to his assistance. Preparations are hurried forward, and by the first of August the vessels drop down the Rio Tinto to the Domingo Rubio, where the final departure is taken at the Convent of La Rabida. This much for a chronological statement of events. We will now retrace our steps, and visit in person the scenes of the great Discoverer's weary wanderings and his final gladsome trip through Andalusia.

Memorials of Columbus are scattered throughout Spain, to-day; in Madrid, the royal armory contains his armor, the naval museum one of his charts; at Valladolid, in 1506, he died, and the house is still pointed out in which he drew his last breath; the convent, also, in which his remains were first deposited.

But though we may trace the wanderings of our hero over a great portion of Spain, it is in the South that the most interesting events occurred. Vastly rich is Seville, the queen city of the Guadalquivir, in Columbian

memories; for here we find that valuable library, the
Colombina, bequeathed the city by his son Fernando,
containing twenty thousand volumes, among them some
that once pertained to the great man himself; one with
marginal notes by his own hand, and one of his charts.
Those very islands of the Bahamas, which I myself
have seen, dim and shadowy, and shining in the sun,

CHURCH OF ST. GEORGE, PALOS.

are here outlined by the great Discoverer himself, upon
paper discolored and stained by sea-salt, as though it
had accompanied him on all his voyages.

That, however, which oftenest drew me and longest
held me was the marble slab in the pavement of the
great cathedral, that formerly covered the remains of
Columbus, and now marks the resting-place of his son
Fernando, with its world-famous inscription: *A Castilla*

*y á Leon, Mundo Nuevo dio Colon;* "To Castile and to Leon, a New World gave Columbus." Thus, although the remains of Columbus himself are now in the New World, many glorious memorials of him are to be seen in Spain, and mainly in Seville.

In the Lonja, containing the royal archives of the Indies, in the city of Seville, is a mass of material pertaining to the conquest of the West Indies and Mexico that has never been exploited. Inaccessible to the ordinary tourist, great bundles and packages of letters and documents lie securely intrenched behind glass doors. But affixed against the walls, at intervals, are certain letters that bear their history on their faces; they are open and can be read by every passer-by. They are well-nigh priceless; unique, at all events, for most of them are from the great *conquistadores* themselves. The first of these, in point of age, is one from Magellanes, dated at Seville, October 24, 1518.

Another, date October 12, 1519, is from Diego Velasquez, written from La Isla Fernandina (Cuba), giving notice of the disobedience of Cortez, who had taken possession of the ships and armament Velasquez himself had collected, and sailed away to what (as we now know) resulted in the conquest of Mexico.

Less than three years later, a letter is written by the indomitable Cortez himself to Charles V., announcing his great discoveries and acquisitions. It was written from Coyoacan (near the city of Mexico) May 15, 1522; one of those veritable *Cartas de Cortés* that have proved so valuable to historians.

Bearing date December 13, 1520, is a letter from

Diego Colon, son of Columbus, then in Santo Domingo as viceroy.

Another, the same year, addressed to the king, Charles I. (Charles V. of Germany), is from that fiery-hearted monk, Bartholomew de las Casas. Long before that letter was written, had the wrongs of the down-trodden Indians begun to cry for redress, through the good Bishop of Chiapas.

Next in sequence comes a letter from Juan Ponce de Leon, "Puerto Rico, February 10, 1521." He had then, doubtless, given up his search for the "Fountain of Youth," and was preparing for that last venture in which he lost his life. A confirmation of the statement by historians, that Francisco Pizarro, the conqueror of Peru, could not write his name, is found here; for the letter purporting to be his bears his sign-mark only.

With date 1526, there is a royal *cedula* of Charles I.; and another from the same king to Don Louis Colon, in 1537; another, by Phillip II., in 1560.

A letter written in July, 1539, from Hernando de Soto, touches Americans, surely, for it comes from the Puerto del Espiritu Santo, coast of Florida; Tampa Bay, it is called now; and De Soto was then disembarking his forces, preparatory to that terrible march through the Floridian wilderness that ended at the Mississippi, and brought him to his grave.

In 1556, that stout soldier and truthful historian, Bernal Diaz del Castillo, who fought all through the Mexican wars under Cortez, writes a letter to his sovereign. He was then governor of Guatemala, and his letter comes thence: "Guatemala, 10 *de Mayo*, 1556."

In these documents we have a history epitomized, and romance condensed, with suggestions enough to keep an elaborator busy for a lifetime.

But one more name, that of Columbus, is necessary to bring before us the conquest and discoveries of that period so rich in barbaric treasure, so red with Indian blood misspilt:

> "*No hay olla sin tocino,
> Ni sermon sin Agustino.*"

"No *olla* without its pork, no sermon without its saint," says the Spanish proverb. The saint in my sermon, these days, when the quadri-centennial lends an interest to everything American and Columbian, is Saint Colon; and it was to obtain information regarding his voyages, that I visited the Lonja and Columbian Library at Seville, and later the port of Palos and Convent of La Rabida.

At Seville, I dwelt in the house of a cleric, and my friend gave me a letter of introduction to the *cura* of Moguer, the town nearest to Palos. It was a bright morning in April when I left the city for a trip to Palos, and the valley of the Guadalquivir was bright in greenest fields of grain and of olive orchards. Seville is, in truth, of queenly aspect, sitting in the midst of the fertile plain, her towering *Giralda* rising far above the outline of distant hills. For two thirds the distance the railroad runs through a fertile and highly-cultivated plain, but the rest was mainly barren, though covered with sheets and beds of purple flowers in beautiful bloom. We passed the ruins of a Roman fortification of times most ancient, and then crossed a river flowing over iron-colored rocks, most curiously worn. The character of the soil was shown in its color, which was yellow and deep red; noting which I inferred, and rightly, that we had seen at last the historic Rio Tinto — the

SEVILLE, WITH THE TOWER OF GOLD IN THE FOREGROUND.

Wine-colored River, from which Columbus sailed four hundred years ago.

Just sixty years before me, in the spring of 1828, a man more famous than I traversed this same route, and with the same intent: gentle and genial Washington Irving. But there was no railroad in those days, and he was obliged to make the journey on horseback, taking as many days, perhaps, as I did hours; but enjoying it, every mile.

Leaving the railway at the station of San Juan del Puerto, I took the *diligencia*, an old carriage, for the town of Moguer, a league distant on a hill, where I found, contrary to my expectations, good accommodations: a *fonda*, or house of entertainment, with clean beds and an excellent table. I was soon served with a good breakfast, and "mine host" took quite a fancy to me; insisting on taking me to the places of interest, and telling me all the local news.

But he was lamentably ignorant respecting things Columbian, though intelligent and inquisitive. When I inquired about the scenes of interest to one studying Columbus, he excused himself, saying he was from another province, and not posted regarding the affairs of Palos.

"But this man, Columbus, when did he sail, Señor? and are you sure he sailed from Palos? No ship of any size has left there this many a year; the village, even, is half a mile from the river.

"But I'll find thee a boy to act as a guide to Palos; also a burro. It makes me impatient to have such a man about me."

The boy he secured must have been the surliest specimen in Spain; but the poor little fellow had lost an arm early in life, and I suppose that must have soured him; at any rate, he probably had a hard time of it in his struggle for bread.

He led up a donkey, hooked my valise on to his arm-stump, seized the rope attached to the donkey's nose, and then strode ahead without a glance at me. Don Pedro sent an emphatic Spanish word flying after him, that halted him instanter; at least long enough to allow me to scramble upon the burro's back; then he marched on again, pursued by the maledictions of my friend. "What a beast of a boy, to be sure; and to think that I, Pedro Val Verde, a respected householder of Moguer, should have been the means of putting a distinguished American traveler in his charge — one who has come all the way from America, too, just to see our little port of Palos. *Bien, Vaya con Dios, Señor* — God be with thee. You have a stick, let the burro feel the force of your arm."

Palos and Moguer are at least three miles apart. The road between them is broad and smooth, but traversed by carts only in the vintage season, when the wines are carried to the port of Palos. There was no saddle on the beast I rode, and I sat astride an enormous pack of old bags, using my cudgel as a balancing-pole; but was frequently obliged to bring it down upon the donkey's resounding sides, at which, much pleased, apparently, he would wag his ears and gently amble onward.

The boy was abstracted, and the donkey absorbed in meditation, so I gained little from their companionship; but after an hour I sighted the hamlet. Palos, the ancient port whence Columbus sailed on his first voyage to America, to-day consists of a few mean houses, scattered along a hillside, and one long straggling street. It is nearly half a mile from the river, but it was a port in the time of Columbus, and is called so now. There may be some eight hundred inhabitants, all told, and not one of them, that I could find, was aware that the hamlet had a history known to the world beyond its limits. Some of them had heard of Columbus; some remembered that it was said he had sailed hence, once upon a time, to a country called America; but no one could tell me anything, and I must see the *cura* — the parish priest — to know more. After an hour of waiting I found that he knew no more than the others, but the sacristan of the church, fortunately, was also the schoolmaster, and took an interest in my mission.

He took me to the church of St. George, the veritable one in which Columbus read the royal commands to the terrified sailors of Palos, and I found it as it doubtless stood then: a simple church of stone, guarding the entrance to the town. I photographed its eastern front, and also its rear, where there is a Moorish doorway (now walled up) draped in vines. The interior of the church is very plain, the chief ornament being an enormous wooden image of St. George, the patron saint of the church, slaying a terrible dragon. As St. George stood in a corner so dark that I could not obtain a photograph of his cheerful countenance, the sacristan and his boy obligingly trundled him out into the sunlight, where he was visible.

Sixty years ago, Washington Irving saw this same saint in the act of slaying this same dragon, and he particularly mentions that both had been recently repainted, and that the nose of the saint was as rosy-hued as the sunset. It is, even now, as gorgeous as ever, and the nose almost bright enough to guide the dragon in striking at his tormentor in the dark.

It was with great reluctance that I left the church and turned my face again toward Moguer; but the day was nearly ended, there was no accommodation of any sort for a traveler at Palos, and the boy and the burro were anxious to be away. Don Pedro of the inn received me cordially, spreading a table with fruit of his garden and wine of his vineyard, and afterward invited me to come forth and view the town. He first conducted me to the church, and then to the house of the Pinzon family, still in possession of a descendant of the great Pinzon who sailed with Columbus. Over the doorway is their coat-of-arms. I was delighted to learn that the present representative of the family is prosperous, and holds a position in the Spanish navy.

It was not my good fortune to be entertained, as Irving was, by a descendant of the great Pinzon, though I should have valued that attention more highly than any other in Spain; for it was to the two brothers Pinzon that Columbus was indebted for success. When he came here, penniless and without authority, they were prosperous citizens, men of influence over their neighbors, and we all know the part they took in that first voyage, furnishing money, men and vessels. Even the royal proclamation read in the church of St. George, was of less avail than their brave example. Badly treated, they were, by Columbus and by Ferdinand, yet posterity will not refuse them their meed of honor. In truth, the deeds of the Genoese pale before their steady glow of sturdy independence. The needy adventurer whom they befriended, and who treated them so basely, forgetting their noble friendship after his success was won, has left no direct descendants; but the sturdy

Pinzon stock still flourishes in the birthplace of its progenitors.

Our next visit was to the convent church of Santa Clara, where Columbus and his sailors fulfilled their vows after their return from the first voyage. You will recall, perhaps, that they promised their saints that if they were saved from a dreadful storm that threatened, they would spend their first night ashore in prayer. And it was in this very church that they performed their vows; Columbus, at least, kneeling here all night on the cold marbles, and before the altar.

As the church was then, it is now: with a magnificent altar-piece, fine statues and rich paintings. It was erected by the Puertocarreros, whose tombs and marble effigies lie in niches on either side. They were a noble family; and it was a Puertocarrero, you will remember, who was intrusted with the first vessel sent from Mexico to Spain, in 1519, bearing from New to Old Spain a portion of the rich treasure of Montezuma.

The day following, returning to Palos, a sturdy donkey boy attended me, not the one-armed brute of the day before, and we made the distance merrily, halting at the town only for a lunch.

As the place came into view, I drew up my donkey on the brow of the hill and looked long at the white-walled Palos, so silent before me, so lifeless, so sad. I need not put on paper the thoughts that possessed me as I gazed, nor the pictures that arose before my mental vision, for I am an American, and have a share in that common heritage left us by Columbus. Four hundred years only have passed since the great Genoese came here, to this very port of Palos, and sailed away with its sailor-citizens to the discovery of a continent, and though since then the cynosure of all eyes, little Palos has slumbered on, unmindful of its fame. One by one its prosperous men were gathered out of sight, one by one its houses fell to ruins, one by one its fleets were

THE CONVENT OF LA RABIDA.

depleted of its vessels, and to-day naught remains save the memory of its greatness.

About three miles beyond Palos, passing through scenery unattractive and sad, some clumps of trees appear and a hill rises against the sky. Then, slowly climbing, you bring the roofs and cupolas of a lone white building into view, which are found to pertain to a convent structure of the olden style. It is rambling, yet compactly inclosed within a high wall, and is extremely picturesque. I was very fortunate, later on, in securing a fine photograph of it, as clouds lay massed beyond, and a flock of sheep slowly grazed before it. And it was thus I found it, this Convent of La Rabida, at the gate of which Columbus halted to request refreshment for his son. How he came to such a secluded place as La Rabida no one has explained; but he probably made for the coast of Spain, thinking, perhaps, to obtain a vessel at Huelva, then, as now, a shipping port for copper ore to foreign parts. Indeed, this very spot is the ancient Tarshish of the Bible, and the Phœnicians came here more than two thousand years ago: those men of Tyre, who discovered a passage between the Pillars of Hercules. But Columbus came here, halted at the gate (the arched entrance at the right), and the prior of the convent, the good Marchena, chanced to see and to enter into conversation with him. Struck by his dignified appearance, and also by his evident learning, the prior invited him to tarry a while, and soon he had his visitor's story: of long-deferred plans, of wearisome waiting and crushing defeat. That very night he caused his mule to be saddled, and started for Granada, pursuing the same weary road through Palos and Moguer that I have traversed (only he was not favored by steam or stage) to the camp, perhaps two hundred miles away.

Meanwhile, Columbus waited, resting in the cool corridors, walking meditatively along the shore, and gazing wistfully out upon the scene from the arched and sheltered *mirador*.

The convent to-day is in excellent preservation, having been carefully restored and placed in the care of a faithful old soldier. I found the family in possession so simple, and so kindly disposed, that I craved permission to pass the day and night there, which they readily

THE MIRADOR OF LA RABIDA.
(*Looking out upon the stream down which Columbus sailed from Palos to the sea.*)

granted. So, paying my donkey boy double wages, and sending him back to Moguer with a kind message for the friendly landlord, I was soon placed in control of the convent, isolate from all the world. Not even Fray Perez could have possessed it more completely. I wandered at will through its corridors, its cloisters and vacant refectory, rambled over the hills back and beyond the convent; hills covered with artemisia and stunted pines, and indulged in solitary reverie to my heart's content.

Climbing the winding stairway to the *mirador*, I had before me broad vistas, through the arched openings, of the river and the sea. Directly beneath, the hills sloped rapidly to the half-submerged lands of the river and sound. Half-way down its slope was a date-palm, said to have been here in the time of Columbus; perhaps equally old are the gnarled and twisted fig-trees and two gray-green olives that keep it company. Extending southward, even to the mouth of the Guadalquivir, are the *Arenas Gordas*, or the great sands, that make this coast a solitary waste. Truly, it is a lonesome spot, this upon which the building is perched, and the soul of Columbus must have been aweary as he drew near the convent portal.

The Domingo Rubio, a sluggish stream tributary to the Tinto, separates from Rabida a sandy island, where there is an ancient watch-tower and a camp of carbineers on the watch for *contrabandistas*. A little to the west the Domingo Rubio meets with, and is lost in, the Rio Tinto, and the two join with the Odiel and flow tranquilly on to the ocean, where the foaming breakers roar with a sound that reaches even to La Rabida. Beyond their united waters again, is another sandy island, and another distant watch-tower, till the low coast fades away in the distance. Down this channel sailed, or floated, Columbus, bringing his boats from Palos, on his way to the sea. The landscape is of a dreary kind, flat, with distant woods, and farther on a hint of purple hills. Opposite, across the broad bay, lies Huelva, like a snowdrift, white upon a tongue of land between copper-colored hills and the sea. A dreary landscape, yet a bright sun in its setting might make it transiently glorious.

The old soldier in charge of the convent, Don Cristobal Garcia, the *concerge*, was evidently straitened in circumstances, yet he was cheerful, and his hospitality shone forth resplendently. He laughingly informed me that he rejoiced in the same name as Columbus—Cristobal; but, he added, he had never done anything to make it illustrious.

IN THE CONVENT COURT.

He and his family lived in a primitive and even pitiful state, at meal times gathering around a common platter; but my own meals they served me on snowy linen at a table apart. There were six of them: the old man, his wife, a little girl named Isabel, some twelve years old, and three boys. Isabel, poor child, pattered about the stone pavement with bare feet, but they were pretty feet, and with little brown ankles neatly turned. There was another member of the family, evidently an intruder, a little chap clad solely in a short shirt, who had squint eyes and a great shock of bristly black hair. Don Cristobal told me that he was a descendant of one of the Indians brought to Spain from America on the first voyage; and as the child's face was certainly that of an Indian, I was more than half-inclined to believe the story. The little people were delighted with the peeps I gave them through my camera, and capered about with delight at the sight of the court and its flowers spread out before them in miniature, and nearly jumping out of their clothes at the inverted image of the grave old *concerge* standing on his head, exclaiming, "Mira! Mira!" and gazing at me with awe and wonder.

They gave me a bed in one of the cloister-cells, the very one, Don Cristobal assured me, that Columbus occupied, and I slept well through the night. It was a disappointment to me that I did not dream, and receive a visitation from some steel-clad hidalgo, or from a girdled monk or two; but of dreams I had none worth preserving, and at six in the morning was awakened by the good *concerge*, who inquired if Don Federico would not like a little refreshment. Don Federico would, and well he did, for it was three or four hours before he received a hint of breakfast.

The eldest boy had gone to Palos for twenty cents' worth of meat and two eggs, making apparent the poverty of my host. He did not return until ten, and then we had breakfast; and there were the two eggs, which the mistress could not have regarded more proudly had they been golden, for they were very scarce at that time in Palos, and it was waiting on a hen's pleasure that caused the boy's delay. He had been told to bring back two eggs, and if two hens had not have happened along quite opportunely, I might have been waiting that boy's return to this day.

There were meat and bread and golden wine. And that wine! The product of Don Cristobal's own vineyard, true *vino de Palos*, sweet and yet sparkling. This wine is of a golden color, with fine bouquet, and celebrated at Seville. This rich, ocherous earth seems to have bestowed its fatness upon the wine-vat, for not on the plains of Xeres is wine produced of so rare a flavor as this made on the banks of the Rio Tinto. The rain had fallen all the forenoon and had made the convent cold and cheerless, so a fire was built in the fireplace of the ancient monks, and as it crackled and leaped up the huge chimney-throat we were warmed to our very hearts.

Then the old soldier told me bits of his past history and legends of the place, while the chubby children gathered around, chins on their hands, stretched before the fire like kittens, regarding us with wide-open, wondering eyes.

I said we had meat; it was not flesh of lamb or sheep, but of goat; and it was old, and it was tough. Don Cristobal remarked my desperate effort to carve it, vainly exerted, and observed that the market of Palos was never supplied with other than goat-meat, and that he doubted not that it was very old.

Now Don Cristobal had a way of ascribing everything ancient to the time of Columbus.

"Is this old?" I would inquire. And he would reply, "*Si Señor, es tiempo de Colon:*" "Yes, sir, surely. of the time of Columbus."

So I said, pointing to the goat-meat, "This is very old, is it not?" "Yes, sir," he replied; "I think so." "Very, very old?" "Yes, sir." "Well, then, do you think it is of the time of Columbus?"

The old man was slow at digesting this query at first, but when he did he nearly exploded with laughter, and hobbled outside to tell the Americano's joke to some old cronies who were sunning themselves at the door.

After the rain had ceased, and while the sun was struggling fiercely with the clouds, we ate our dinner in the corridor, which ran around a court, or *patio*, open to the sky. This court was filled with flowers, vines crept up the pillars, figs and oranges had possessed themselves of space enough for luxuriant growth, and altogether it was an attractive spot. From this court opened out many cloisters, but there was another, farther in, where the chamber-cells of the monks were very numerous. Vacant now, with doors ajar, and with no one to inhale the fragrance of oranges and roses in this inner court. Off at one side is the chapel where it is said Columbus knelt in prayer, and on the opposite side a passage leads to the refectory, the stone benches on which the good monks sat empty and chill.

Climbing a narrow stairway, you come to a corner room overlooking the Rio Tinto, a large square room, with floor of earthen tiles and ceiling of cedar, with dark beams overhead. This is the Columbus Room, where the great Admiral, the prior and the learned doctor held the famous consultation which resulted in the monk's intercession with Isabella. Many a painting has represented this historic scene, perhaps none more

THE COLUMBUS ROOM, CONVENT OF LA RABIDA

faithfully than the one hung in the room itself. An immense table, old but sturdy still, and around which the great men are said to have gathered, occupies the center of the room, and on it is the *tintero*, or inkstand, said to have been used by them. Around the wall are hung several excellent pictures; one representing the discovery of land, one showing Columbus at the convent gate, another the consultation, the embarkation at Palos, the publication of the king's commands in the church, and the final departure from La Rabida.

I had often thought that to be a monk, cloistered in cool corridors, would be an ambition it were well to gratify, and I must confess to a feeling of pity for the poor *frailes* who were turned loose from these quiet retreats and set adrift on an unfeeling world. I wonder if they enjoyed, as I did, the seclusion of the place and the sunset view from the *mirador?* In pleasant weather, when the hot sun shines, it must be supremely attractive, to one sitting in the shade and looking forth upon the sea. Drowsy insects hum outside, the half-suppressed noises of maritime life float in on the breeze, and lively swallows fly in and out, twittering to one another as they seek their nests. Ah! pleasant *mirador*, overlooking the historic Rio Tinto and the sea! The view afforded here comprises the scenes attendant upon the momentous departure; right before us, on the banks of the Domingo Rubio, it was, that Columbus careened his vessels and took aboard his stores, just before setting sail; somewhere near the mole he took his final farewell of the good prior, the last, best friend he had in Spain; and beyond the sand-spits glimmer the breakers on the Bar of Saltes. Down the stream, beyond the Tinto, glide lateen sails toward the bar the sailors crossed in 1492.

Don Cristobal went down to engage passage for me in a mystick, or little sloop, that was lading with ballast at the river bank, and soon I followed him to the mole, where a *carabinero* rowed me across the inlet. Once there, I found that the mystick would not leave till night; but the men were cheerful and chatty, and so I staid a while. It was on or near this very spot that Columbus cleared for his voyage; and what thoughts filled my mind as I tarried here!

But not a thought had the men for aught save their sand, which they would take to Huelva and sell for ballast. If I would wait, I was welcome to a passage; but they thought that by crossing the sands I could hail a fisherman in the main channel as he came in from sea. The *carabinero* thought so, too, and took me to an ancient tower where his companions were, two of whom rowed me in a boat to mid-channel, where I had the good luck to catch a fisherman bound for Huelva. He took me willingly, and we sailed away with a spanking breeze, arriving there in half an hour. Two men and a boy comprised the crew, and an immense fish the catch; and as we drew near the quay a boy drove down a mule-cart into the water, backed it up to the boat, and loaded us all into it, cargo and crew. Once on shore, a little urchin, with wide-extended mouth, seized my camera and valise and led the way to the railway station, where I spent the forty minutes till train-time in gazing wistfully at Palos and La Rabida.

ALABASTER TOMB AT BURGOS.

(*Alabaster Tomb in the Cartuja, Convent of Miraflores, in Burgos, the high altar of which convent church was gilded with the first gold brought from America by Columbus.*)

The convent lay against a bank of clouds, shining out like silver; Palos also and Moguer gleaming white against the hills. Two leagues away lay the sea; and I had just ploughed the channel crossed by the world-seeking caravels four hundred years ago. And so I left this historic triad of towns, which had evoked for me so many memories of the great century that joined the Old World with the New, left them shining against the barren hills, as they have shone in memory ever since.

CROSS AT LA RABIDA.

## III.

### IN GUANAHANI WITH COLUMBUS.

CROSSING THE SARGASSO SEA.
(*So named by the Spanish.*)

WE cannot but regard the first voyage of Columbus as a combination of favorable and fortunate events; for, barring a slight accident to the *Pinta*, nothing occurred to baffle his plans until the first land was in sight. The final departure may be said to have been taken from Gomera in the Canary Islands, and the last sight of land was off the Island of Ferro.

Two days after land was lost to sight, or on the eleventh of September, a floating mast was seen, and on the thirteenth, the most important discovery was made by Columbus. We may say, quoting a distinguished author, that Columbus made several discoveries before he discovered land. The first of these was the variation of the compass, the second the Sargasso Sea and the third the trade-winds of the tropics.

The variation of the magnetic needle of course disturbed him greatly; but he had the wisdom to keep his discovery to himself, until the change became so great that the pilots noticed it; then he gave them a plausible explanation.

It was about the first of October that they approached the region of the trade-winds, and noticed the peculiarities of that vast weedy expanse known as the Sargasso Sea. This seaweed, found floating on the surface of the ocean, bears globules like small grapes in shape. The Spanish sailors, fancying a resemblance between them and the grape grown in Portugal, called the sea-plant the *sargasso*, and the name was also given to that portion of the ocean where the weed is found.

We know that his astronomical knowledge was imperfect, and the nautical instruments very crude. He had a compass, and a rude instrument called the astrolabe, by which he determined his latitude; but he could only guess at his longitude, and he measured time by an hour-glass. "It has been said that he probably had no means for accurately calculating the speed of his vessels, as there is no mention of the log-and-line before 1519; and as to the telescope, it was first used in the year 1610. Having such a slight equipment, the sailors of that day, of course, were very timid about venturing far from land. The task that Columbus set himself was simply to go to the Canary Islands, in about latitude twenty-eight degrees north, and sail due west until he struck land." He was diverted from his course by the advice of the pilots and by the flight of birds to the southward, otherwise he might have landed on the coast of Florida, near the Indian River.

"When I think," said a celebrated writer, "of Columbus in his little bark, his only instruments an imperfect compass and a rude astrolabe, sailing forth upon an unknown sea, I must award to him the credit of being the boldest seaman that ever sailed the salt ocean."

After they had been a month at sea, the pilots reckoned they had sailed about five hundred and eighty leagues west of the Canaries; but by the true, though suppressed, figures of Columbus, they had made really over seven hundred leagues. It was about that time, or October 10, that the crew became mutinous; but later, signs of land, such as a branch with berries, and a piece of carved wood, changed gloom to hope, and strict watch was kept throughout the night. They were then on the verge of the great discovery. All seemed to have felt that some great event was pending; and on the night of October 11, Columbus claimed to have seen a wavering light. The next day, early in the morning, or that is about two o'clock of October 12, land was first sighted by a sailor on the *Pinta*. A landing was made the same day, and possession taken in the name of the Spanish sovereigns.

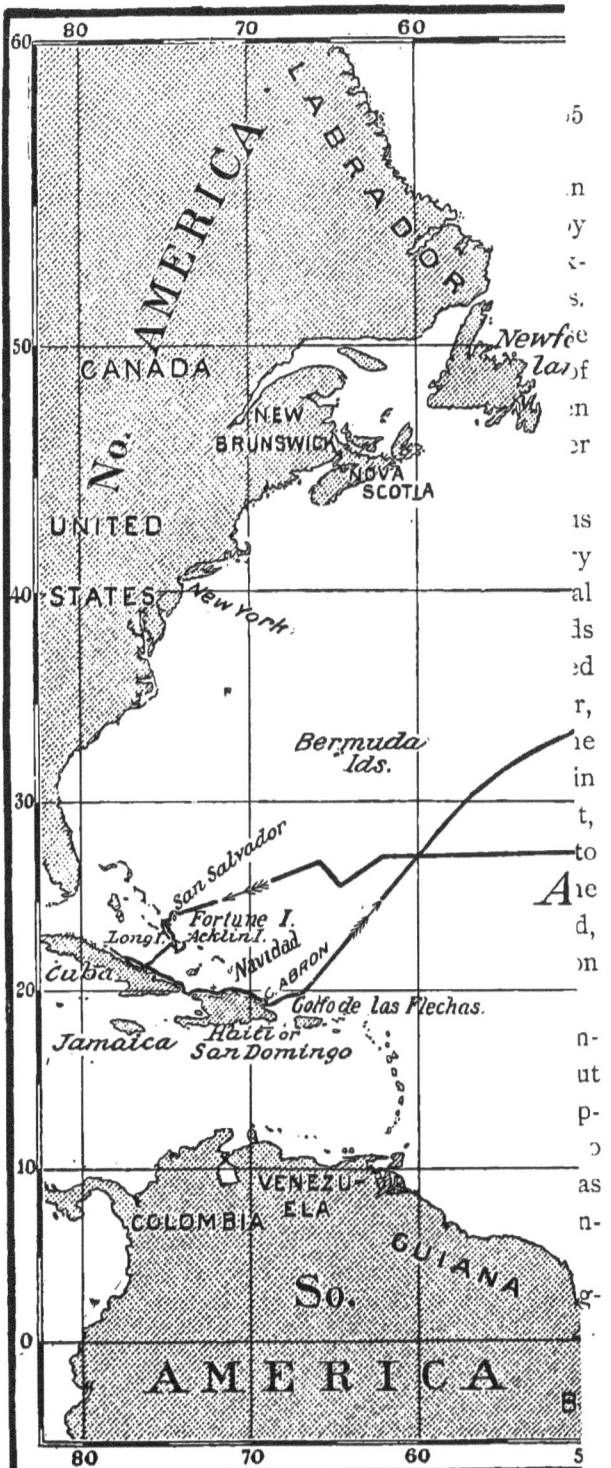

54

All these events, of course, we are familiar with in the works of many authors, notably in the history by Washington Irving, who first made the English-speaking world acquainted with the voyages of Columbus. But, although it is only four hundred years since these events took place, yet there is a great difference of opinion as to the island which may claim to have been the first land sighted on that memorable date, October 12, 1492.

One thing is certain: the first landfall of Columbus was an island in the Bahamas, although opinions vary as to which one, claimants having arisen for several others besides those mentioned. But although the islands claimed extend over a distance of some three hundred miles, yet, we may be justified in going a little farther, and saying that not only was the first island one of the Bahama group, but situate somewhere about midway in the chain. Since the time of Irving and Humboldt, several writers of distinction have given attention to this question, and though not all coming to the same conclusions, most of them agree upon Watling's Island, as the place where the Europeans first set foot upon soil of the New World.

Unfortunately for investigators, the journal of Columbus, which, as he informed the queen, at the setting out of the voyage, he should write day by day, has disappeared, and we have only a portion of it, alleged ɔ have been transcribed by a Spanish historian, Las Casas. And again, it is unfortunate that this transcription has apparently many discrepancies.

Since, however, the greater number of writers recognized as authorities are in favor of Watling's Island, it will be as well to grant that one the honor.

Whichever island it may have been, I myself can claim that I have seen it, as I have traversed the entire chain, from Turk's to Cat, and have studied them all carefully, with a view to giving an opinion on this vexed question. Years ago, it was my good fortune to bisect the group on my way to the south coast of Cuba, when I saw this island rising like a cloud, or rather a blue mound, above the horizon. But it was not until July, 1892, that I had the opportunity for visiting it. Being then in the West Indies as Commissioner for the World's Columbian Exposition, I received orders from the executives to investigate this question of the Landfall, and visit the islands in person.

I was then in Haiti, the Black Republic, and the first opportunity did not occur until a month after receiving my commands. Leaving the port of Cape Haitien early one morning on a steamer of the Clyde Line, called the *Ozama*, in a few hours we sighted the Island of Tortuga. The day before, from another port on the Haitian coast, we had scanned the leeward shore of this famous haunt of the buccaneers in times gone by, and now were on the bleak, iron-bound coast of the inward side.

Finally, the turtle-back Tortuga faded out of sight, and the next land, or rather indication of land, was the southwest point of Inagua, merely a shadowy semblance of *terra firma*, emphasized a few hours later by the flashing out of its revolving light from a high white tower. Its capital, Matthewstown, may be a prosaic place enough in broad daylight, but by the glamor of a summer's night it was transformed into a thing of exceeding beauty, as we lay a mile or so off shore, awaiting a little freight of Sisal hemp, mahogany logs that had floated over from Santo Domingo, in the last great storm, and some bags of smuggled coffee.

It had been my intention to land here, and take a chance vessel (should by good luck any such occur) for Watling's, in the center of the Bahama chain; but the agents of the steamer advised me not to risk it, as nothing promised for that island within a month. They assured me I would stand a better chance from Fortune Island, and if I could only reach it, be a hundred miles nearer my desired destination. As the steamer never touched at Fortune, and indeed at none of the Bahamas except occasionally, I felt myself in a predicament until gallant Capt. Rockwell, the master of the *Ozama*, came to my assistance, and promised that if I would take the chances he would drop me off the island, if the people there ashore would answer his signals and send out a boat.

Next morning at daylight we passed the light of Castle Island, and at ten o'clock were abreast the flashing surf of Long Cay, and could see the little settlement there that formed the only one on Fortune Island. Signals were set: "Passengers aboard; send off a boat," and shortly after we could see a movement on the beach about a mile away, where a boat was being launched. In a little while it came alongside, our engines having stopped, and after an interchange of salutations my luggage was quickly transferred to the boat below, and I left the comfortable *Ozama* and launched out into another unknown adventure. The steamer steered off, my friends waved me a last farewell, and by the time we reached the beach objects on board were indistinguishable.

I found myself a stranger in a strange land, but fortunately had my usual good luck, and obtained board and lodging at a house near the beach. Fortune Island, or Long Cay, is about eight miles in length and a mile or so in breadth, some eight hundred acres in area, with a population of seven hundred people, mostly black and colored. The chief production of the island is salt, which is raked out of the vast shallow salt ponds formed just over the sand-banks behind the reefs. The process of salt gathering is a primitive one; the ponds are divided into sections containing salt in various stages of crystallization, and the water is sometimes pumped from one to the other by means of a curious windmill. The great heaps of salt, containing many thousands bushels, are pyramidal in shape, white as snow, and glisten like silver in the sun. Formerly this island was a great rendezvous for the wreckers, and in yet earlier times

A SALT HEAP ON FORTUNE ISLAND.

perhaps for the buccaneers; but latterly their occupation has departed, owing to the erection of lighthouses and the substitution of steamers for the principal traffic to and through the islands instead of sailing vessels.

Now and then a steamer touches here going from New York to Jamaica and Central America, picks up a crew of laborers for the voyage, and drops them again at their homes on its return. It is a barren island as compared with the islands of the West Indies proper; and yet it is not unattractive, with its white sand beaches, its glistening salt heaps, and its half-tropical vegetation.

It was thought that I could readily get a vessel here to take me to Watling's Island, but it will show you how infrequently these islands are visited, even by coasting craft, when I tell you that it was nine days before I could secure a boat to take me over, a distance of only one hundred miles. Even then, although that day there happened four or five craft in port, the master of the dirty little "turtler" asked six pounds for a run of merely a night.

The old wrecker instinct is still strong in the residents of these coral islands, and when they get hold of a stranger they make him pay for long months of deprivation. This was well illustrated by the treatment I myself received at the hands of the man who had taken me from the steamer. He gave me accommodation in a large vacant house he had on the beach, but, although he is the accredited Commercial Agent of our Government at Fortune Island, and at least should have helped on my exploration, coming to him as I did, with letters from the Department of State, yet he did nothing for which I did not pay him the highest value. More than this; knowing well the urgent nature of my mission, he yet kept me practically a prisoner on Fortune, when he could easily have sent me over to Watling's, only one hundred miles away. For, lying at anchor inside the reef, during all my stay, was his fast schooner, the *Jane*, and a crew was at hand only too eager to earn a few dollars by a run. To be sure he did

WINDMILL FOR PUMPING SALT WATER.
(*Fortune Island*.)

offer to take me over at a most preposterous price — one hundred dollars — for the night's run, but that, as he well knew, was out of the question. Days wore away without the desired sail appearing; day by day I would pace the beach and climb the highest elevation, scanning vainly the horizon for a sign of rescuing sail in sight. To pass the time I made a boat excursion to Crooked Island, and thereby added to my increasing store of information respecting the conjectural isles first found by Columbus; for, in many respects, this one answers to the description given in his journal.

It was the Fourth of July when I arrived at Fortune, but the heat, I afterward learned, was not so oppressive as it was at the same time in our Northern States. The sun's rays may have been stronger, but all day long a refreshing breeze was blowing, which at night increased to a gale, and the only inconvenience during the day was from the terrific glare on the snow-white sands of the shore, and the unchanging blue of the sky. Solitude here reigned supreme, the few inhabitants being either within doors, at work on the salt pans, or with the steamers on distant coasts. The beauty of the moonlight on the pearly sands was something surpassing; but I had it all to myself, and finally tired of solitary strolls. My most refreshing diversion was sea-bathing, which I indulged in every morning before the sun got high, reveling to my heart's content in the sparkling brine, and under the shadow of the great black rocks stretching myself out in quiet enjoyment. But the delightful sense of security was one day rudely dispelled when, just as I was emerging from the water, I saw a shapeless something prowling warily among the coral ledges — a great gray ghost of a thing, which finally came near enough for me to see it was a shark. After that, when I went for a sea-dip, I took along a small boy to stand watch while I sported in the surf. The islanders had told me that no sharks ever came within the barrier-reefs of coral, which cropped out from some twenty yards to the distance of a quarter of a mile away; but the very day I saw the first shark two others came up directly in front of the house, immense fellows, each one over ten feet in length. Some fishermen had left fish-garbage on the sand, and in the death-like quiet of the burning noon these monsters stole boldly in, one after the other, and rolled over quite on the beach, their gray bodies entirely out of water in their efforts to snatch the refuse. This they repeated several times, even after the alarm was given and the people came flocking to the beach, and for several days after they followed the fishermen in from the sea. It is, even amongst the dwellers in these islands, a mooted question whether sharks will attack and kill a human being in water near the shore, and it is universally acknowledged that they will not snap at a black man if there is a white one near at the same time. Unlike the alligator, which likes nothing so well as a succulent negro, unless it may be a juicy porker, the discriminating shark always prefers white meat to dark; but whatever the fish's predilection, I for one shall give him as wide a berth as possible in his native element.

The name of the settlement at Long Cay, as the port of Fortune is locally called, is Albert's Town, a rambling collection of huts and houses, with a population composed mainly of negroes, there being but one person of undoubted white lineage in the place.

This was the Collector and Resident Justice, a very jolly Irishman, with a brogue as rich as the island itself is poor; a man extremely well-informed, with whom it was my delight to spend much of my spare time. He lived in a little house among the palms, all alone except for a small black boy whom he had in a way adopted, having found him, some years before, abandoned by his mother in a hut in a lonely place. Wherever the Collector went, little Joe went too, and the petting he got made him the envy of all the boys of the village. He was, I fancy, the only one of his kind on that island in danger of being spoiled by petting, and I have in mind two others particularly ill-treated. They were in the employ of my host, and the lashings he gave them were about his only diversion. Poor little chaps! Without the slightest provocation their master would lash them unmercifully with a stinging whip, and the sight of him set them to trembling so it was no wonder that they let things fall occasionally and broke the dishes. They were both of them orphans, and this brute had them entirely at his mercy. I often told him that it seemed to me burden enough for one to be black, and that he ought not to add to their misery. One would have thought that having himself a trace of black blood in his veins, he would have been more compassionate to those of his race; but it is strange, though true, that these are the ones who treat the negro worst. Once having risen in the world, they forget and despise their parents, and are harsh to their neighbors.

Although I regretted the loss of time in that island, yet I am thankful that I was not indebted to this man for any favors, and that he did nothing for which he was not fully compensated.

At last came the day of deliverance; the long-watched-for sails came in, three in one day, and in one of these unwashed "turtlers" I engaged a passage to the island of my desires. Captain and crew were black, and they lived on the windward coast of Crooked Island. We left Long Cay at dark, and in a few hours we were off the flashing light on Bird Rock, whence we took our departure for Watling's, and at daylight next morning

MY "TURTLER."

I saw a long low line of land against the sky. It was the island we were seeking. But the wind failed us for a while, and it was full noon before we could reach the roadstead of Riding-Rocks and the shelter of the island's only settlement of Cockburn Town. Having my consular flag with me, I had the captain hoist it, and we entered the harbor with the stars and stripes displayed in all their glory. This unexpected arrival at this quiet port, flying a flag that rarely was seen here, threw all the town into consternation; but no objection was offered to my landing, as the boat was mine for the time being, having been chartered by me, and I was entitled to fly the flag I liked best, of course. This was the view taken also by the Collector, a handsome Englishman, a retired officer of Her Majesty's navy, who was serving in this retired spot temporarily, in order to secure a "good-service" pension. He welcomed me most cordially, for strangers and news were equally scarce, and placed his services at my commands.

My arrival was most opportune, for the whole island was suffering from a drought, and many people were on the point of starvation. Fortunately, I had learned of their condition before leaving Fortune, and had brought a supply of provisions sufficient for a month. It proved in such demand that I had hardly any remaining at the end of the week. There was absolutely nothing to be had, not even milk or eggs, those last resorts of these needy people.

I had been recommended to the Resident Justice of the island, Captain Maxwell Nairn, as one who would attend to my wants; but recent and dangerous illness had rendered him unable to extend me the hospitality he would surely otherwise have done, and I could not obtain even a room in which to sleep. He and his family, however, were urgent in their endeavors to find me quarters, and finally secured a room in the thatched hut of an old black woman, who agreed to cook my meals. The stone walls of the apartment were white and clean, and the thatch overhead was neatly fastened to the rafters, while the old lady's cooking was at least endurable. Captain Nairn's was the only white family on the island, the other six hundred inhabitants being black and colored. The town consisted of a few score huts and houses, an English church, and a Baptist chapel. One road ran across to a central lagoon, a mile away, and a trail around the island; but the great highway is the ocean, their conveyances, boats and canoes. Watling's Island is egg-shaped; it is about twelve miles long, and from five to seven miles broad, with great salt-water lagoons in the center, and entirely surrounded with dangerous reefs. Once, it is believed, the coral rock, of which it is entirely composed, supported a fertile soil, but at present the rock is entirely denuded, and the only soil is found in pockets and depressions in the surface.

A Bahama farm, in fact, whether it be found in Nassau or Turk's Island, is always a surprise to one from the American States, because of its poverty. When the scant vegetation that covers the coral rock is removed,

LOOKING ACROSS THE LAGOONS ON WATLING'S ISLAND.
("*One road ran across to the central lagoon.*")

there remains only the white, glistening rock itself, gleaming out as bare and as devoid of plant life as a marble monument.

But these naked rocks, so pitifully suggestive of poverty, the natives regard with affectionate interest and speak of them as their "farms." The great drought of the past two years had deprived the farms of even the scant moisture of ordinary years, and induced a general failure of crops throughout the island.

Although the island lies just on the verge of the Tropics, in latitude twenty-four, yet its vegetation is by no means tropical in character, conveying rather a hint of nearness to the mid-zone than actual fertility. I am writing of the vegetation presumably natural to the island, as seen in the woods and in the fields, and not of the cultivated plants; for, indeed, all the fruits and vegetables of the Tropics can be raised here.

But we no longer note the luxuriant vegetation described by Columbus, who speaks of the orchards of trees, and of great forest giants, such as the present day does not produce. All the vegetal covering is now of the second growth, though there are evidences of the forest primeval in old stumps, long submerged, that still exist, showing that Columbus was probably correct in his descriptions.

It was my desire to examine every evidence that should help to establish the character of the people resident here at the coming of the Spaniards, and bring to light all the existing proofs of their residence; hence I devoted all my time to that end. The very morning after my arrival, the Collector accompanied me on a short exploring trip across the lagoon, where there was said to be a cave that had never been explored.

He placed the entire police force at my disposal, said police "force" consisting of one man, who, with his two sons, managed our boat and carried us over the shallow places in the lagoon. There were many shallow places, and also a small canal, so that their labor as carriers was somewhat arduous; yet the police force was equal to the demands upon him, and, all told, he "backed" the Collector and myself from the boat to the shore, and *vice versa*, eight times that day, and without apparent fatigue. As the Collector was a very large man, weighing at least two hundred pounds, this performance was very creditable to the "force."

After great difficulty, mainly experienced in cutting our way through the thorny and matted growth that everywhere covers the surface in all the Bahamas, we reached the cave in which tradition averred the ancient Indians used to dwell. It was merely a large opening in the limestone, forming a room of goodly proportions, the roof perforated in many places, and the floor covered with bat guano. It had not been investigated, the islanders told us, but we found nothing to reward our search, and so, late in the afternoon, we returned to the lagoon and the town.

The heat had been so intense that day, that the next I was unable to leave my hut, but the day after I went on the real exploring trip of the voyage, across the lagoon and up its entire length, to the north end of the island, where lies the conjectural landing-place of Columbus.

I had with me the two sons of the policeman, who ably managed the boat, and by noon we were at the head of the lagoon, where we left the craft in the mud, and trudged over land, or rather rock, to the lighthouse, which rose before us a mile or so away. Arriving there, heated and exhausted, I received a warm welcome from the head keeper, who placed a comfortable house at my service, and took me to the top of the tower for the view. Built as it is, upon the highest elevation in the island, this tower commanded the surrounding country and the sea adjacent, the whole of Watling's being visible, shaped like a pear, with its stem to the south.

There is little doubt in my mind that I was then looking upon the very spot at which Columbus landed just

THE LANDING-PLACE OF COLUMBUS.
(*Watling's Island.*)

four hundred years before. The reefs off shore threw up their sheets of foam as at the time of the discovery: the bright lagoons in the center of the island lay directly at my feet; the low hills scarce rising above the general level, the green trees, the sparkling beaches — all were spread before me, and the prospect was pleasing and beautiful in the extreme. Half a mile distant from the tower stretched a long continuous beach of silver sands terminated by promonotories, some two miles apart, breasting which the water is calm as in a pond, though broken by innumerable jagged reefs of coral. Beyond this calm space of water that encircles the island all around, lies a chain of barrier-reefs, that prevent the tumultuous waves from reaching to the shore, and where all is quiet and secure.

Bordering this beach, along its entire length, is a low growth of sea-grapes, dwarf palmetto, and sweet shrubs, just such as one may see on the southern coast of Florida. Scattered over its silvery surface are shells of every hue, and innumerable sprays of the Sargasso weed, such as the first sailors saw, coming here in 1492. Sea-birds hover over it, fleecy clouds fleck it with their shadows; but, other than the distant murmur of the breakers, no sound disturbs the eternal silence here.

It was at the southeast extremity of this beach, where a jutting promontory of honey-combed coral rock runs out toward the barrier-reefs, that we assume the first landing took place, in a beautiful bay, with an open entrance from the ocean. On the beach, the fierce sun beats relentlessly, but there are deep hollows in the rock, where, in the morning, we can find shelter from the heat; and, availing ourselves of one of these cool retreats, let us rest a while, and read what Columbus wrote respecting his landing on the sands before us.

Says that quaint old chronicler, Herrera: "It pleased God in his mercy, at the time when Don Christopher Columbus could no longer withstand so much muttering, contradiction and contempt, that on Thursday, the eleventh of October, of the aforesaid year, 1492, in the evening, he received some comfort by the tokens they perceived of their being near the land."

And the following, from the journal of the Admiral: "Two hours after midnight the land appeared, about two leagues off. They lowered all the sails, and lay to until Friday, when they reached a small island of the Lucayos, called Guanahani by the natives. They soon saw people naked; and the Admiral went on shore in the armed boat, also Martin Alonzo and Vincente Yanez Pinzon, commanders of the *Pinta* and *Niña*. The Admiral took the royal standard, and the two captains the two banners of the Green Cross, having an 'F' and a 'Y' at each arm of the cross, surmounted by its crown. As soon as they landed, they saw trees of a brilliant green, abundance of water, and fruits of various kinds. The Admiral called the two captains and the rest, as well as the notary of the fleet, to certify that he, in presence of them all, took possession of said island for the king and queen, his masters. Soon after a large crowd of natives congregated there. And what follows are the Admiral's own words, in his book on the first voyage and discovery of these Indies. 'I presented some of these people with red caps and strings of beads, and other trifles, by which we have got a wonderful hold on their affections. They afterward came to the boats of the vessels, swimming, bringing us parrots, cotton thread in balls, and such trifles, which they bartered for glass beads and little bells. All of them go about naked as they came into the world, their forms are graceful, their features good, their hair as coarse as that of a horse's tail, cut short in front and worn long behind. They are dark, like the Canary Islanders, and paint themselves in various colors. They do not carry arms, and have no knowledge of them, for when I showed them the swords, they took them by the edges, and through ignorance cut themselves. They have no iron, their spears consisting of staffs tipped with a fish's tooth and other things. . . . At dawn, of Saturday, October 13, many of the men came to the ships in canoes made out of the trunks of trees, each of one piece and wonderfully built, some containing forty men, and others but a single one. They paddle with a peel like that of a baker, and make great speed, and if a canoe capsizes, all swim about and bail out the water with calabashes. I examined them closely, to ascertain if there was any gold, noticing that some of them wore small pieces in their noses, and by signs I was able to understand that by going to the south, or going around the island to the southward, I would find a king who had large gold vessels, and also gold in abundance. At this moment it is dark, and all have gone ashore in their canoes. I have determined to lose no time, . . . but to wait till to-morrow evening, and then sail for the southwest, to try if I can find the Island of Cipango.'"

To this first land of the first voyage, Columbus gave the name San Salvador. By the Indians it was called Guanahani. By the "Indians," I say, for thus were termed these people found in possession, and who were here for the first time seen by Europeans. In the first day of their stay on shore, the Spaniards had added several new things to their discoveries: to the discovery of the variation of the compass, the Trades, the Sargasso Sea and weed, they now added the new people termed by their commander "Indians," the craft called by the Indians themselves canoes (*canoas*), new species of parrots, implements of bone and stone, and, later on, hammocks.

We would like to know what kind of people these were, who welcomed the first Europeans to America, and if any of their kind exist to-day. What they were we have seen; brown and bare, shapely, athletic, doing no harm, but gentle and loving. "I swear to Your Majesties," wrote Columbus, "there are no better people on earth; they are gentle, and without knowing what evil is, neither killing nor stealing."

And yet, what was their fate? We know, and it is true, that their lovable qualities availed them not, but rather hastened their extinction. That very year, in the closing decade of the fifteenth century, "was begun that historical tapestry, woven by the Spanish artisan-conquerors in the loom of the New World, the warp whereof was blood and tears, the woof the sighs and groans of a dying people."

One cannot but wonder why it was. We may find the key-note of the acts of Columbus in a quaint expression regarding him by Bernal Diaz, one of the conquerors who followed him: "He took his life in his hand that he might give light to them who sit in darkness, and satisfy the thirst for gold which all men feel." This thirst for gold was overpowering, it controlled all his actions, and caused him to inaugurate a system of slavery that eventually caused the extinction of all the Indians of the West Indies. Yes; it is a melancholy truth that of all the aborigines discovered by Columbus, in the Bahamas, Cuba and the larger islands, not a descendant lives to-day. In fact, hardly one remained alive fifty years after the discovery.

In the year 1508, Haiti having been depopulated of its Indians, the cruel Spaniards came to the Bahamas and deported the Lucayans to wear their lives away in the mines. They enticed them aboard their vessels under pretext of taking them to see their friends who had died. "For it is certain," says the historian Herrera, "that all the Indian nations believe in the immortality of the soul, and that when the body was dead the spirit went to certain places of delight." By these allurements above forty thousand were transported, never to return; and a few years later the islands, found teeming with inhabitants, were deserted and solitary. In Cuba were found other Indians, but a little better supplied with articles of adornment and subsistence, who had hammocks (*hamacas*), made fire by rubbing together two pieces of wood, raised maize, or Indian corn, and spun cotton, which grew everywhere in their fields. The only domesticated quadruped was found in Cuba, the *utia* or dumb dog; while in the Bahamas the people had domesticated only the parrot, from the wild life around them.

Having been so long extinct, let us say for three hundred years at least, little remains from which we may reconstruct their lives as led at the period of discovery. What little there is, I have seen it all, and will describe it. From the *disjecta membra* found at intervals in various places, we will try to evolve the Indian of the fifteenth century. In the first place, we have bones and skeletons, particularly crania, which undoubtedly pertained to the Lucayan, or Ceboyan, as he has been called. These have mostly been found in caves, and generally beneath the cave earth, or bat guano; and not one island alone has produced them, but many, throughout the Bahamas. I myself secured two, for exhibition at the Exposition, which illustrate the peculiar features of the Lucayan cranium. These have been described by Prof. W. K. Brooks, of the Johns Hopkins University, who says:

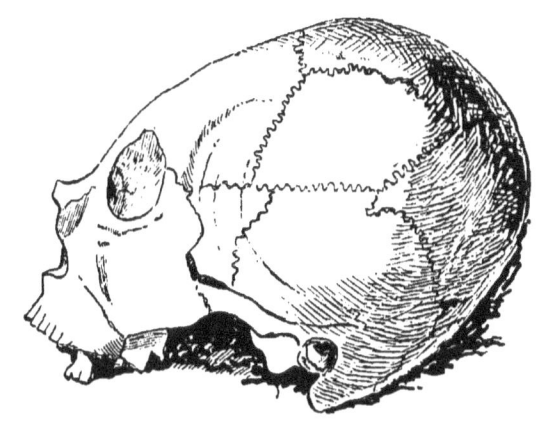

SKULL OF BAHAMA INDIAN.

"The skulls are extremely broad in proportion to their length, and are among the most brachycephalic (round-headed), of all human skulls, the greatest breadth being more than nine tenths of the greatest length. The brain was large, and the capacity of the cranium is about equal to that of an average Caucasian skull. The Ceboyans flattened their heads artificially in infancy, so that the vertical part of the forehead is completely obliterated in all adult skulls, and the head slopes backward immediately above the eyes."*

When I was in Cuba, in 1891, I saw and photographed, in the rooms of the Royal Academy, a couple of Indian skulls imbedded in lime-rock that had been found in a cave at Cape Maysi, the eastern point of Cuba. Their origin and their antiquity are undoubted, although, knowing, as we do, the rapidity of stalagmitic formation in limestone caves, we need not argue the extreme antiquity their surroundings might, at first glance, imply. Again, in Santo Domingo I found two crania,† in possession of a learned physician of Puerto Plata, which were undoubtedly of the native Ciguyans — the Indians living here at the arrival of Columbus.

The keeper of the Watling's Island light, Captain Thompson, kindly procured me trusty men for my investigation, and himself guided me to the nearest cave in which human bones had been found. It is only in the caves and hollows in the rocks that we now find human bones and skeletons; the deposition of the *humus* being so scanty that nothing extraneous deposited there has been preserved. To the caves, then, we went, for those of Watling's Island had already yielded valuable results.

In 1886, the United States steamer *Albatross* visited the island, and found many antiquities of value; and since then Sir H. Blake, while Governor of the Bahamas,

---

\* *Popular Science Monthly*, November, 1889.

† These three different types of the characteristic natives of these distinct groups of islands — Bahamas, Cuba and Haiti — I have had carefully drawn from my own photographs, and from them the Ethnologist may be able to deduce something of value to science.

thoroughly explored every island of his extensive province. Thus it will be seen that I myself could entertain but little hope of finding anything of importance, following in their wake. And, in truth, I do not make any claims that I did; but every contribution to science is welcomed by the earnest investigator, and the little I can add, together with a grouping of all the "finds," here for the first time given, cannot be otherwise than acceptable. We groped for hours, on that and succeeding days, in the dark and dismal caves, finding many disjected fragments of skeletons and moldering bones, but no skeleton in its entirety — as its owner left it when he shuffled off this mortal coil. If Columbus only could have known — if the Indians themselves could — what a value would now attach to an aboriginal skeleton in this quadri-centennial of their discovery, perhaps some of them might have kindly bequeathed their bones to the investigators of posterity. But the "Admiral" cared more for gold than for bones, and as for the poor aborigines, though many of them were eventually skeletonized by the Spaniards, it was not done in the interests of scientific investigation, but out of revenge; in the spirit of avarice, or lust. At all events, the three skulls I secured later, at Nassau, for the Exposition, and possibly one or two more, constitute all we have to work from.

The caves themselves are interesting, but as I had already made the "grand round" of our own Mammouth Cave, there was little here to attract, more than could be found in other limestone formations.

Subsequently, in Cat Island, I found other bones, and,

as these were added to those obtained here, and the whole given in charge of Prof. Putnam, of the Department of Ethnology, something of interest may eventuate. Yes, I must confess to grievous disappointment, and I really felt quite incensed at Columbus and the aborigines that they should have been so inconsiderately forgetful as to leave no vestige of their remains.

I did get on the trail of one (alleged) aboriginal skull; and though the recollection of the misadventure is by no means pleasant; still, a good story shall never be omitted because it reflects on me, and I will give it without comment, if only to illustrate a certain phase

INDIAN ANTIQUITIES, FROM THE BAHAMAS.

of negro character. It must be remembered that the people of Watling's Island were on the verge of starvation, and that my provisions and silver were, to say the least, very acceptable. It goes without saying, then, that if anything could have been obtained for money it was available then, at the time of my visit. More "guides" and laborers flocked around me than I could possibly employ, and more were really engaged than I had any use for.

They were honest enough, and faithful, especially

when the provision hampers were opened and the silver disbursed; but they didn't like work. I have a fellow-feeling for them there, but in view of the fact that they were in sore need of money, and that I offered to give them good prices for all the antiquities they could guide me to, it seemed to me they might have exerted themselves a little more to our mutual advantage. At last one of the negroes recollected that a boy had told him of a skull he had seen, deep down in a cave, only a few days before. Of course, I dispatched him for that boy, instantly.

The boy came; yes, he had seen the skull, and more than that, "dey was heaps ob bones, too, sah." I was afire at once; but as the hour was then late for the trip, I arranged for him to return next morning, which he promised faithfully to do. Morning came, but no boy. I sent one of the assistants in waiting to look him up, and as he did not return, another, until at last all the men had temporarily intermitted their entomological labors, and were scouring the fields for that boy. Night came, at last, but without the desired scientist, though the father of the delinquent came and told me a very doleful story of the disappearance of the skull.

"De head-bone, Massa, him done gone 'tirely, sah; when ma boy done go look fo' 'em, sah, dey wan' no head-bone dah. I spec some Jumbie gos' gut 'em, sah."

I looked at the man severely, and told him that was not true, which he admitted; but at the same time he said his son had cleared out, and that I had to admit. Finally the truth came out. It seems that some months previously the American artist, Bierstadt, had sojourned here while painting, or rather making, the sketches for his famous picture of the Landing-place of Columbus. All unconsciously, he had been the cause of my discomfiture. One of the negroes had brought him a skull, for which he had paid him a liberal price. But after the artist had departed, the officers of the chapel to which the negro belonged had hauled him over the coals, on the alleged offense of desecrating a grave. I do not suppose they for a moment entertained any scruples on the subject, but there was one thing they were unanimous on: and that was, that the quondam owner of those bones would sometime appear, in ghostly shape, and demand satisfaction. The poor fellow was frightened, as they intended he should be, but as he had already spent the money received he could not make a division with the chapel — which the unregenerate declared was the real object of the discipline — and he was put on probation.

This was the state of affairs when I entered into my negotiation, and it shows what a strong hold superstition still has upon those folk when, though in dire distress, they will not venture to relieve themselves at the risk of incensing the ghosts, or Jumbies. The boy did not appear during my stay, and I came away without the coveted cranium. As the black men themselves expressed it, "Dat was 'one' on the Buckra;" but I herewith respectfully submit: the "Buckra" did not suffer so much by it as they did.

But the bones are not the only remains the aborigines have left us by which to determine their status, for other objects are scattered throughout the West Indies.

Their houses, having been of perishable materials, such as reeds and palm-leaves, nothing remains to show us what they were; but some of the implements they used, and even some of their household furniture, have been found. The most numerous articles that have been recovered are those small stones carved and chipped in the shape of chisels, gouges, spear-heads, and even hoes and knives, known to collectors as "celts," and these have been found everywhere. And here again comes in the superstition and ignorance of the native, who, everywhere in the West Indies, calls these artificially-shaped stones "thunderbolts." The belief that they are of celestial origin is firmly planted and ineradicable, and I have even seen some men who declare they themselves have seen the "t'underbolts" descend from the skies. In Fortune Island I met one old negro who affirmed that he had seen the identical stone I bought of him drop out of the clouds during a thunder-storm. "Don' yo' mek no mistek," he said, "me see him drap wiv my own eye. One time da come t'under-storm an' da tree in da front ma house he done 'truck ba de t'under, an' ma wife he say, 'I 'clar I b'leve t'underbol' done drap in yander tree;' an' sho nuff, when me go look an' zamine da he be right in de crack ob de lightnum. Me mus' b'leve um ef me see um."

The name is universal; in the interior of Santo Domingo I found they go by the name of "*Piedras de Rayas*," which is the equivalent in Spanish of "Thunderbolt." One that I have in my possession, a beautiful green stone, of perfect shape, I obtained of an old goldsmith, in the historic region of gold where Columbus first found the precious metal. He employed it as a touch-stone, to indicate the purity of the gold brought him by the natives, by the streak left upon it after being rubbed with the gold. In color and texture, shape and workmanship, the celts of the Bahamas are exactly the same as those of the larger island far to the south; and, as there is no stone similar to that of which they were made throughout the whole Bahama chain, the natural

CARVED SEAT OF LIGNUM-VITÆ, FROM THE BAHAMAS.

inference is that the implements were imported, the Indians living in the southern islands bringing them here for barter. This is highly probable, for the Caribs of the southern isles are known to have made long journeys in their canoes, as well as the dwellers in the Bahamas.

The kinds of implements found here indicate that the aborigines were peaceful and agricultural, exactly what Columbus described them, and not warlike, for few war-weapons have been found. In addition to these celts we note mortars and pestles; the latter with carved heads that have been taken for idols; beads of stone and oyster shell and fragments of pottery. The Indians, it is believed, made fairly good pottery, and cooked their food by heating stones and throwing them into the water till it boiled.  Not alone the pottery, but all the articles yet discovered, indicate that these Indians were in a very low state of civilization, not far removed from barbarism, and it must have required a painful stretch of the imagination for Columbus to perceive in these simple people the rich and civilized inhabitants of Cathay, of whom he had dreamed of discovering.

There yet remain other articles to mention, which show that these barbarians did have among them, or were in communication with, skillful artisans who carved wonderful things in wood and stone, the like of which have not been found elsewhere.  Historian Herrera wrote that when the Indies were discovered, all the common people sat on the ground in the presence of strangers, but that their chiefs made use of low seats, of stone or wood, carved in the shape of a beast or reptile, with very short legs, its head and tail erect, and with golden eyes.  We believe this to have been the truth, because several such strange seats have been discovered, notably in the Caicos, and island of Grand Turk, in the southern Bahamas, where they may still be seen in the Public Library there.  The Spanish Consul at Grand Turk also has a very rare thing in the shape of an Indian axe, of stone, the head and handle being of one piece; and another axe is there shown: the head of stone, and fitted into a wooden handle; an object of extreme rarity.  Few of the many thousand implements hitherto found, of the ancient peoples of America, have possessed the interest that attaches to this, because of its completeness.

These, then, are about all that remain to us of the people discovered by Columbus, whose extinction he himself hastened by recommending and initiating their enslavement. Simple folk, without thought of harm, they early felt the evil effects of Spanish domination. Having no gold to tempt the cupidity of the conquerors, they for a time escaped their attention, but when slaves were needed for the mines of Haiti, then the Spaniards returned and snatched them from their homes. Even the very people whom Columbus praises as the most loving and gentle on earth, and who welcomed him and his crews as heaven-descended men, giving them all their possessions, were carried by these same men into a slavery worse than death.

Ah, well! We know not why it was that the strong should ever have oppressed the weak, and have stained their swords with innocent blood, in those first fierce days of America's beginnings.

They are gone, now, all of them. We know the Spaniards' fate; but no one can tell when and where and how perished the last of Guanahani's gentle tribe.

# IV.

## WHERE WAS THE ADMIRAL'S LANDFALL?

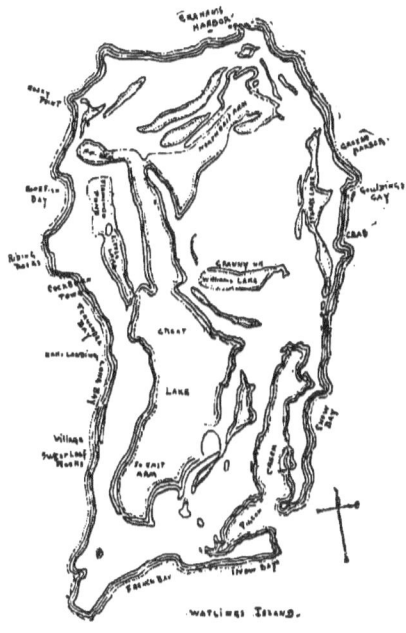

MAP OF WATLING'S ISLAND.

WHO can tell where it lies — that first land sighted by Columbus and his crew, after their weary voyage across the Atlantic?

We will ignore the light the Admiral claimed to have seen because it has not been proved that he saw one; there are those who think it was but in keeping with his character to affirm a light that never shone, in order to defraud that poor sailor, Rodrigo de Triana, of his reward. Let us ignore the light, and land with Columbus on the coast approached that memorable Friday, the twelfth of October, 1492. He landed, that is admitted; and he landed somewhere in the Bahamas; in all probability, as has already been stated, midway the chain. This much conceded, we turn to special investigators to ascertain upon which particular island of the group. Nearly every writer on the subject has a different theory; but fortunately there are a few who have given it exhaustive study, who have been over the ground in person, and who have received their impressions from actual observations.

It happens also that those whose opinions are entitled to consideration, have received their training in the naval service, either of this country or of England, and are qualified to write of the voyage as brother mariners. The recognized authorities on the subject are Capt. A. B. Becher, of the English Navy, and Capt. G. V. Fox, of the United States Navy. I am aware that others have written, and have written well; but all we need may be found in the pages of the two writers above named.

It was not until Capt. Becher's work, "The Landfall of Columbus," appeared, in 1856, that the question was agitated. Up to that time the conclusion of Washington Irving, that the landfall was Cat Island, had been generally accepted. The routes had been carefully worked out for Irving by an officer of the United States Navy, and had received the sanction and approval of so high an authority as Humboldt. Navarrete, from whom Irving drew much of the material for his history, assumed that Turk's Island coincided with

WHERE WAS THE ADMIRAL'S LANDFALL? 87

that described by Columbus; and in the year 1846 the late George Gibbs, for many years a resident of Grand Turk, ably supported this theory, in a paper before the New York Historical Society.

Capt. Fox wrote in support of Samana, or Atwood Cay; but his work, so thorough in its investigations, and honest in its conclusions, rather re-enforces the statements of Becher, who claims Watling's Island as the landfall. Capt. Becher is supported by Lieut. Murdock, who began on the coast of Cuba and traced the track of Columbus back to the island first sighted.

A summary of their conclusions, not only as to the conjectural landfall, but in regard to the islands subsequently discovered by Columbus, is herewith presented:

It will be noted that no

|   | Columbus | Navarrete | Irving | Becher | Murdock | Fox | Gibbs |
|---|---|---|---|---|---|---|---|
| 1. | Guanahani | Grand Turk | Cat Island | Watling's | Watling's | Samana | Grand Turk |
| 2. | S. Salvador | Caicos | Conception | Long | Rum Cay | Crooked | Caicos |
| 3. | Fernandina | Little Inagua | Great Exuma | Great Exuma | Long | Long | Little Inagua |
| 4. | Isabella | Great Inagua | Long | Crooked | Crooked Fortune Ragged Jibarra | Fortune | Great Inagua |
| 5. | Islas Arenas | | Mucarras | Ragged Port Nipe | | Ragged Port Padre | |
| 6. | Cuban Coast S. Salvador | Port Nipe | Cuba | Cuba | Cuba | Cuba | Cuba |

two investigators agree as to the first landfall without disagreeing as to the second; and if they happen to coincide on the third, it is only to fall out over the fourth. And the difference between the extremes, as represented by Cat Island in the north, and Grand Turk in the south, is something like three hundred miles. But this is not material; each writer had his own opinion, and perhaps a preconceived one, and by extracting a little truth here and a little there, we may approximate a correct result. There is a consensus of opinion decidedly in favor of Watling's as the first landfall, and so eminent an authority as Judge Daly, of the American Geographical Society, holds to this theory.

Says Major: "While agreeing with Capt. Becher in the identification of Guanahani with Watling's, I find that officer entirely at issue with the diary of Columbus in making him anchor near the northeast end of the island, and then sailing around its northern point. . . . The first anchorage of Columbus in the New World was off the southeast point of Watling's Island, a position which entirely tallies with all his movements as mentioned in his diary."

This is the opinion of a man who has never seen the island, but who has studied the subject so deeply that he thinks he knows all about it. His conclusions bear out the general statement, however, and are acceptable to the seeker after truth. Let us turn once more to the "Journal of Columbus," and question him again regarding his movements after he had landed.

I shall assume Watling's to be the island, having found no conclusive evidence to the contrary. We accept the courses of Columbus across the ocean (as worked out by the eminent navigators previously mentioned) which brought him, at least approximately, to the center of the Bahama group.

Hear, then, the evidence, presumably in his own words. I say presumably, because we have only an abstract from his journal, and not the original. The only evidence we have is in a manuscript copy of the "Diary of Colon," found by Señor Navarrete in Spain, in 1825; it is an abridgment of the "Journal of the First Voyage of Colon," made by the Bishop Las Casas, his famous contemporary, "the genuineness and authenticity of which copy have yet to be impeached."

According to the journal of Columbus, then; first, as his vessels approached the island, they "lay to," outside the reefs, and after the landing:

"This island is large and very level, has a very large lagoon in the middle, is without any mountain, and is all covered with verdure most pleasing to the eye;" all which is applicable to Watling's, and particularly the "lagoon in the center," which does not exist in Cat; a similar feature is found only in Crooked.

It was inhabited: "The people are remarkably gentle, have no iron, do not carry arms, and have no knowledge of them; are well-formed, of good size, and intelligent"—facts borne out by the remains discovered in modern times, such as crania, celts, agricultural implements and pottery. They had canoes, "made out of the trunks of trees, all in one piece." A canoe, or portion of one, was found in a cave near Riding-Rocks, the chief roadstead of Watling's Island. "They came to the boats, swimming, bringing us parrots, cotton" (which grows in the island), etc.

Cotton is indigenous here; parrots have been here within the memory of man, and are now found in flocks on Acklin Island, one hundred miles to the southeast; the second growth of forest on Watling's Island is not high enough to afford them shelter. "I have seen here no beasts whatever, but parrots only." There are no

THE HEADLAND COAST OF WATLING'S ISLAND.

indigenous quadrupeds larger than a rat, and few reptiles, the largest being the iguana, which he mentions later, as seen in another island.

After two days on the island — Sunday, October 14: "At dawn I ordered the boats of the ship and of the caravels to be got ready, and went along the island. . . . I was afraid of a reef of rocks which entirely surrounds that island, although there is within it depth enough and ample harbor for all the vessels of Christendom; but the entrance is very narrow. It is true that the interior of that belt contains some rocks, but the sea is there as still as a well." No more accurate description could be written of the great barrier-reef that surrounds this island, nor of the aspect of its inclosed waters.

In looking for a place to fortify, he found "a piece of land like an island, only it is not one, which in two days could be cut off and converted into an island." This was near the harbor, which in every particular answers to the sheltered Graham's Harbor, at the extreme end of the island; it is secure, though shallow, and ample for small vessels of the light draught of Columbus's time. As to the "piece of land like an island," this is found in "Cut Point," the eastern arm that protects Graham's Harbor from the open sea; it is a long neck of land cut in two by the erosion of wave-action; an island at high water, and part of the mainland at low tide.

Thus far, there is no discrepancy whatever, and it is only as the Spaniards leave the island that an apparent variance is noted.

"I observed all that harbor, and afterward I returned to the ship and set sail, and saw so many islands that I could not decide to which one to go first. . . . In consequence, I looked for the largest one, and determined to make for it, and am so doing, and it is probably distant five leagues from this of San Salvador, the others some more or less."

This is the one weak link in the chain of evidence in favor of Watling's. There are no large islands visible from this one; but the objection is equally applicable to

Cat, though not to Grand Turk. It is possible that the mariners may have been deceived, and mistook elevations and depressions of the same island for different cays. I myself, in approaching Watling's from Fortune, noted that the detached portions of the island gradually coalesced, until what appeared to be several islets were merged into one. But again: one island is visible from Watling's; this is Rum Cay, which, in clear weather, may be discerned from the extreme southern point. It is twenty miles distant; this agrees nearly with Columbus's estimate, for later he enters in his journal: "As the island was five leagues distant, rather seven, and tide detained me, it was about noon when I reached the said island, and I found that that side which is toward San Salvador runs North and South, and is five leagues in length, and the other, which I followed, ran East and West and contains over ten leagues."

The description applies exactly to Rum Cay, both as to situation with respect to the other and as to shape; but the same allowance must be made for errors of measurement as before, since the estimates of Columbus were made from his vessel's deck, and by the eye, and can by no means be regarded as accurate. Reckoning the Spanish league at two and one half miles, we must in nearly every case deduct at least one third from the estimates of Columbus, as due to unconscious exaggeration. Imperfect as the transcription of the journal may be, there is not one single feature of its description that is not applicable to Watling's. Having landed on its northeast shore, Columbus sailed around the north end, coasted the west shore its entire length and departed

GREEN'S HARBOR, WATLING'S ISLAND.
(Conjectural Landing-place.)

from the southern point, making Rum Cay, as related. His course was southwest to Rum Cay, thence due west to another island visible in the distance.

This was Long Island, and is accurately given, with the distance from the second island, or Rum Cay, the general trend of its shores, and configuration. "And from this island of Santa Maria to the other are nine leagues, east and west, and all this portion of it runs northwest and southeast. . . . And being in the gulf midway between these two islands, I found a man in a canoe, who was going from Santa Maria to Fernandina" (the large island), "who had a small piece of his bread" (probably cassava), "a calabash of water, a small string of beads, and two *blancas*" (small coins), "by which I knew that he came from the island San Salvador, had passed to Santa Maria, and was now going to Fernandina." This incident illustrates the boldness of these Indians, in venturing so far from land in their frail canoes, and explains the occurrence in these islands of articles that could only have been obtained from a great distance. This Indian also had "some dry leaves, highly prized, no doubt, among them, for those of San Salvador offered some to me as a present." This was, presumably, tobacco, which was afterward found in use in Cuba. The Admiral took the Indian aboard and treated him kindly; not because of any liking for the poor fellow, but that his friends "may give us of all that they have."

In Fernandina, in addition to things already seen, they first saw the hammock; "their beds and coverings looked like cotton nets," which they called *hamacas*.

No one who has seen Long Island, can doubt that it was the third one visited by Columbus, for the reasons above stated; in addition, his description of Clarence Harbor, "the very marvelous port with narrow entrance," is entirely confirmatory.

After cruising two or three days up and down the coast, detained and baffled by adverse winds, the Spaniards finally set sail for the southeast, and in three hours saw an island to the east, reaching its northern extremity before midday. Here the vessels anchored at a little islet, which, without doubt, was Bird Rock, at the northwest extremity of Crooked Island. There is a light on it now, and it is the point of departure for Watling's, Rum Cay, and Long Island, on the course from Crooked and Fortune.

As already intimated, I have been over the course, and have cruised along the shores of both Fortune and Crooked. And I can understand the enthusiasm of the Admiral, writing in his journal, with the scene before him at Crooked Island as I have had it: "If the other islands are beautiful, this is still more so: it has many trees, very green and very large, gentle hills enhance with their contrasts the beauty of the plains, . . . and this cape where I have anchored I have called Cape Beautiful, because it is so. I anchored here because I saw this cape so green and beautiful, as are all the things and lands of these islands, so that I do not know to which to go first, nor do my eyes grow tired with looking at such beautiful verdure, so different from our own. . . . Here are some large lagoons, and around them are the trees, so that it is a marvel, and the grass is as green as in Andalusia in April. And the songs of the little birds are such that it seems as if a man could never leave here."

Ah, yes! I, too, like the great Admiral, have heard those "songs of little birds," and have felt it was a joy to listen to them.

Now, even as then, the mocking-bird pours out his melody for all to hear. The great forests are gone;

THE COAST OF WATLING'S ISLAND.

their human occupants have passed away, a different race dwells here; but the odorous thickets remain, from which "the odors came so good and sweet, from flowers and trees on land, that it was the sweetest thing in the world;" and the mocking-birds dwell herein, gladdening the heart of man with their music. I remember, one was my neighbor at Watling's, living in an orange-tree near the eastern window of my hut, and his notes began at dawn, even before, continuing at intervals all the day. At hottest noon, when everything else was hushed and lifeless, he would mount to the topmost twig of his tree, and pant forth a gush of liquid melody. Without them, else, these thickets are silent and without sign of life.

The fauna of a country changes little, even in the lapse of centuries, and probably the bird-life was similar to what it is to-day. There may have been some changes, but mainly wrought through the agency of man; for instance: bird-collectors have nearly exterminated the song-birds of some islands, merely for the small sums they receive for the skins. Not only are they collected for the adornment of women's hats and bonnets, but there are men whose sole ambition is to possess the largest collection of birds of any given locality; these send out hordes of boys, who murder for money the choicest feathered friends of man. Were the inhabitants of the islands more enlightened, they would send these collectors to jail as soon as they began their nefarious work.

The sailors killed an iguana here, which they called a serpent; they found aloes, loading the ships with a quantity; they filled the water-casks, at a spot now called "Frenchman's Wells," and in this same island of Fortune first heard of "an island which the natives call Cuba, but which I think must be Cipango." The twenty-fourth of October they sailed, leaving with regret this island that had so entranced them.

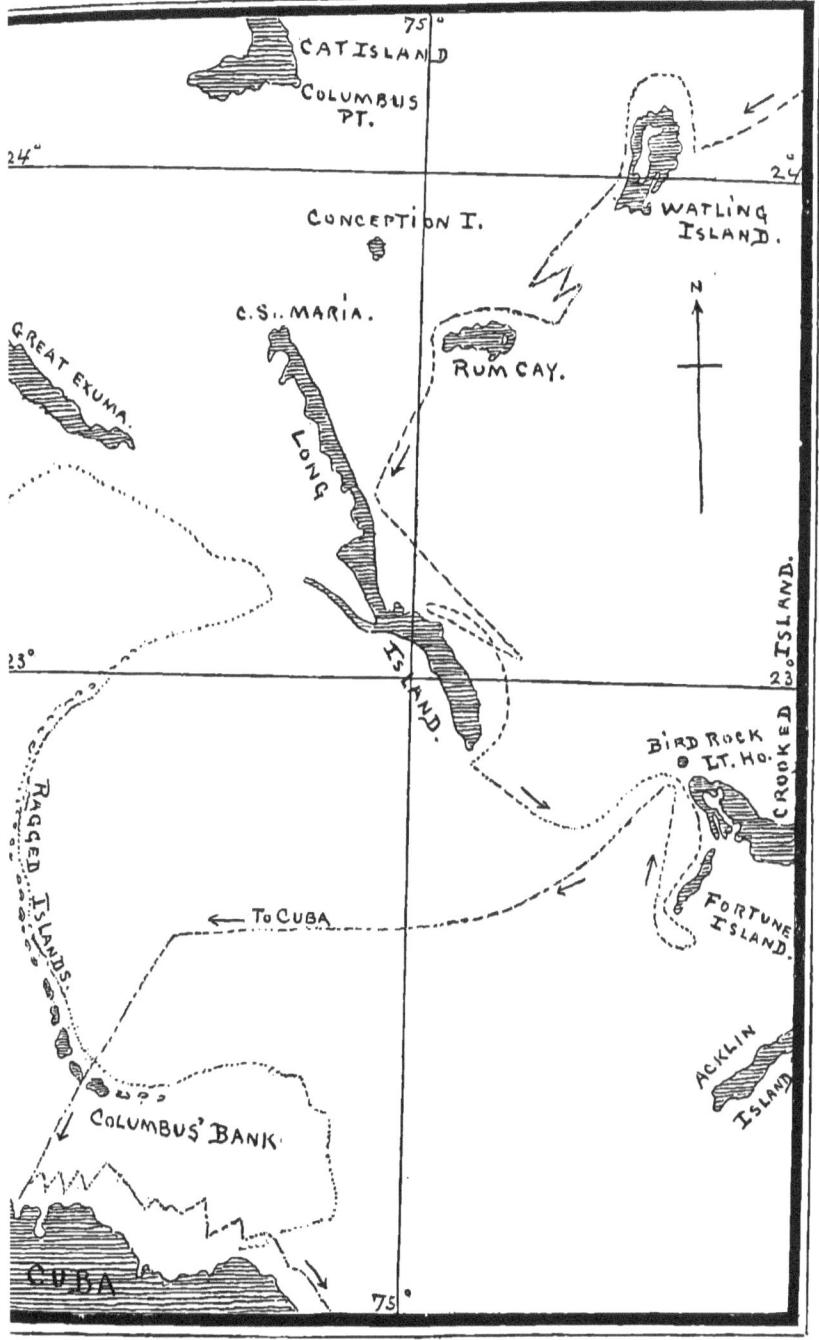

"At midnight I weighed anchor from the Island of Isabella and the cape of the Rocky Islet (Bird Rock), in order to go to the island of Cuba, which these people tell me is very large, with much trade, and yielding gold and spices; and by their signs I understand it to be the island of Cipango, of which marvelous things are related, and which, on the globes and maps I have seen, is in this region; and they told me I should sail to reach it west-southwest, as I now am sailing."

The next night, the southern cape of Fernandina bore northwest, and the next islands were sighted, called by the Admiral *las Islas de Arenas* (Sand Islands). Departing from these, leaving them on the north, at sunrise, two days later, October 28, he saw the island of Cuba.

With the discovery of Cuba, the voyage through the Bahamas terminates. After the first landing-place on the Cuban coast has been defined, the journal is less ambiguous, and we can follow the explorers step by step. Before we leave the subject, however, I desire one more word as to the latest conclusions regarding the landfall and the islands subsequently visited by Columbus. I have given a summary of opinions up to the time of my own investigation. But, since I was sent out specially commissioned by the Executives of the Columbian Exposition to ascertain the truth, if possible, and devoted much time and study to the question, it would only be fair to those gentlemen of the Exposition, as well as to myself, to present my own conclusions. They are fully borne out by the results of the expedition sent out in 1891 by the *Chicago Herald*, whose chief,

Mr. Wellman, made an able and exhaustive report at the time, and erected on or near the conjectural landing-place on Watling's Island, a handsome commemorative monument.

Our investigations were entirely independent, as I was in the Southern West Indies at the time of the *Herald* expedition and came up to Watling's from the island of Haiti, while Mr. Wellman went there from Nassau.

INDIAN CELT, FROM CAT ISLAND.

Our visits were exactly a year apart, but together we have surveyed the entire field of controversy, and the following emended table is given, as approximating a correct result:

| *San Salvador* *Guanahani* | *Santa Maria* | *Fernandina* | *Isabella* | *Islas de Arenas* | *Cuban* |
|---|---|---|---|---|---|
| Watling's | Rum Cay | Long Island | Crooked Fortune | Ragged, or Columbus Bank | Port Jibarra |

Crooked and Fortune are given as one island, for so they were regarded by Columbus, being separated only by a narrow sound, and doubtless they are the same that are figured on the earliest maps as the "Triangles," from their very obvious triangular shape, as taken together. In conclusion, to fix firmly the names bestowed by Columbus, we will quote from the letter written by him to Luis de Santangel, Chancellor of the Exechequer of Aragon, giving the first account of the first voyage:

"To the first island I found, I gave the name of San Salvador, in remembrance of His High Majesty, who hath marvelously brought all these things to pass; the Indians call it *Guanahani*. To the second, I gave the name of Santa Maria de la Concepcion; the third I called Fernadina, the fourth Isabella, the fifth Juana, (Cuba); and so to each I gave a new name, and when I reached Juana I followed its coast, and found it so large that I thought it must be the mainland — the province of Cathay."

INDIAN CHISEL FOUND IN THE ISLANDS.

He was undeceived as to the existence of a West Indian Cathay, but his surmise as to its insular character was not verified until after his death, when, in 1508, Cuba was first circumnavigated.

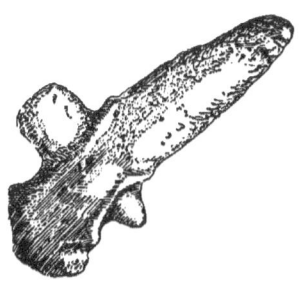

STONE AXE, TURK'S ISLAND.

## V.

### THROUGH THE BAHAMA ISLES.

WATLING'S Island is distant from New York, by the route the steamers take to Aspinwall, or Colon, just one thousand miles: a little more than halfway to the Isthmus of Panama. It is one hundred miles from Fortune Island, and one hundred and seventy-five miles from Nassau, the capital, on the island of New Providence. Its only connection with the outside world is by an infrequent sailing-vessel of small tonnage, and the mail-boat which runs irregularly between the capital and Inagua, touching at the "out-island," one way or the other.

Having dropped me at Riding-Rocks, the black man owning the turtler had performed his part of the charter, and he sailed away, leaving me dependent upon the arrival of the mail-boat. She might get here any time during the week, as her movements were erratic, and her master unreliable. I wanted to spend all the time possible at the north coast, in the vicinity of the light-house, so a strict watch was kept from the light-house tower for the first signs of her approach. Early on the morning of the fifth day, the mail-boat was signaled from the tower, and I tore myself away from the fascinating spot, regained our boat, which we had left lying in the mud of the lagoon, and hastened for the settlement at Cockburn Town.

Half-way down the lagoon we met a large boat filled with laborers going to their "farms," as they call the bare spaces of rock divested of all vegetation, which they try to cultivate. The boat was filled with women, for the men are nearly all engaged on the sea. When

NATIVES OF WATLING'S ISLAND.
(*Not found by Columbus.*)

they learned that the "mail" was coming, nearly all of them wished me to give them passage in my small boat to the town; for nearly all had friends or relatives on board. In my opinion, my craft had room for only one more, and I so told them; but in spite of my statement a woman and a baby got in, and then the mother declared her little boy must go, too. These accessions to my passenger list filled the boat to overflowing, so I sternly forbade any more entering the craft, and shoved away, leaving one young negress almost suspended in mid-air in her frantic endeavors to board us.

Arrived at the town, I found the master of the *Argosy*, as the mail vessel was named, fuming at the delay; but he waited until I got my effects together, and at noon we were sailing southwest to Rum Cay. It was hot, of course, at high noon, as in fact it is at any time between eight in the morning and five in the evening; but all among these islands the shores are bathed in the limpid waters described by Columbus, and the atmosphere is bland. At last, the white sands flashed a final farewell, the crimson bloom of the flame-trees became merged in the sky-line, turning the sunset clouds to pink, and Guanahani faded from my sight.

PUSHING THROUGH THE CANAL, WATLING'S ISLAND.

Coincident with its disappearance, Rum Cay rose, boldly outlined, and at dusk we anchored in behind the reefs. A sad little town sits here, by the white sand beach; its ruling people are blacks, its ambitions long since crushed, its future like the people — black.

After touching at Long Island, we reached Cat Island at dawn, and lay there all day, for no reason except that the captain did not want to reach the home port before Sunday. The sun poured down a fiery flood of torment all day long. I could get no other shelter than the shadow of the main-boom — which was barely enough to cover my hat — and to retain even this slight protection, I was compelled to dodge from side to side at every motion of the vessel. Under the circumstances, I did not consider a request for an awning, or the shelter of a sail, as unreasonable; but when I proffered it, he turned upon me with: "I'se got a yawning aboard, but I won't humbug wid it, to please nobody."

I expostulated, of course, for even a white man has feelings; but the only answer I got was, that others had lived through it, and he guessed I could. My every entreaty failed to move him. Fortunately, some men came aboard who knew of a cave in the cliffs on shore, and took me to it, where I found some human bones, relics of the Lucayos, who inhabited here at the time Columbus came. Some have claimed, as we have read, that Cat Island is the true Guanahani; but, as I have set forth in my chapter on the landfall, the proofs are wanting. In the Bahamas, the question of "the first land" is mostly a matter of local feeling. As the American Consul at Nassau once observed to me: "The generally accepted opinion here is in favor of Watling's, except at Cat, where the people are outraged that any place could be thought of except their own island."

Off the "Bight," the port at Cat Island at which we called, there was no sign of life ashore. One saw here, as in all the islands, blue water, glaring yellow sands, a narrow belt of far-extending reefs, very low hills without attractive vegetation, and a line of forlorn huts and houses near the beach. The chief production of the island is the pineapple, which is shipped in large quantities to Nassau and New York.

I met some charming people ashore: the clergyman, the resident magistrate, and their wives; they were

CAVE ON CAT ISLAND.

very kind during my brief stay, and, with one or two exceptions, were the first white people I had seen in two weeks. The white person, in truth, is a *rara avis* in the out-islands, being almost as scarce as the white blackbird is in nature. With the exception of the resident magistrate, and sometimes the collector, one finds none but the black man "on deck." The speech shows the trail of the African serpent, even in the mouths of preachers and teachers, who are nearly all black or colored. Aside from the amenities of the climate, and the delights of bathing, boating and hunting, there is little to tempt a person of sensibility and sympathetic nature to these islands; and to consign one here to fill out the measure of his existence, would be the crushing out of ambition and healthful zest in life.

A night's run brought us within sight of the island of New Providence, on which is the Bahama capital, Nassau. Here my disagreeable boat trip was to terminate, and here I should find the elegant steamers of the Ward Line, running to New York. The captain of the *Argosy*, whatever his failings as a man, was a good navigator; he had brought us safely through the intricate and shallow channels of Exuma Sound on a dark night, without a fault. We were all delighted to view the promised haven: my black companions, as well as the dogs, the pigs, the cows, and the hens, all of whom had enjoyed the run of the deck and the cabin equally with myself.

In the intense heat of noon, I made my way to a boarding-house, and sat down to await the arrival of the north-bound steamer. Meeting at Nassau many delightful people, the time passed pleasantly, although the regular season was long since over, it being then the last of July.

The Governor, Sir Ambrose Shea, was unfortunately absent from the island, having been called to Newfoundland by the disastrous fire which occurred there in July; otherwise I should have had the pleasure of meeting this distinguished gentleman, who has attempted so much toward improving the condition of the Bahamas. My mission to him, as the head of the Government, was

ON THE BEACH OF WATLING'S ISLAND.
(*Looking for the landing-place of Columbus.*)

to induce, if possible, the Bahamas to co-operate with us at the Exposition; in his absence I was referred to the Hon. H. M. Jackson, Colonial Secretary, and then acting Governor. This gentleman has had a wide experience in colonial affairs, and I am sure it was not due to his lack of ability that the Bahamas did not accept our invitation, and do themselves the honor of participating in the benefits of this great occasion.

It would seem that was Bahama's opportunity to emerge from a seclusion of centuries, and show to the world what she had worth the world's cognizance; but her rulers decided otherwise. Her Governor has spent a great deal of money, and dilated a great deal upon the future of these beautiful islands; he has made frantic efforts to induce investments of foreign capital, especially in the culture of hemp (the *agave*), and to call attention to the advantages offered as a winter resort. And now, to refuse the one opportunity of the century to make known all these desirable things, by sending to Chicago a representative exhibit of Bahama's resources, was, in my opinion (and with all respect due to one of His Excellency's age and exalted station), the depth of foolishness and absurdity. It reminded me, as I stated to the officials at the time, of a merchant who should stock his warehouses with a varied assortment of attractive goods, spending upon their accumulation the bulk of his capital, and then close his doors and shutters, and refuse to advertise. The Bahamas are dependent entirely upon the United States for their very life, and from mere contiguity, in common with all the West Indian islands, their future is bound up with ours.

The truth may as well be told now — for it is the truth, and will eventually "out:" all these islands are suffering from the dry-rot of foreign domination.

Whatever England may have been to her colonial possessions in the past — and it cannot be denied that she spent unrequited treasure, and shed unstinted the blood of her bravest men in acquiring and defending these possessions — she is no longer necessary to them now. More than that: she is a clog upon their progress, retarding their development, and draining their life-blood; first, owing to her inability to provide for them a lucrative commerce, through distance, and a meager market; second, through the immense army of officials saddled upon an unwilling people, in spite of their protests. Personally, I must confess to an admiration of the English in official station in the West Indies; I am well aware of their probity, and I know that they have operated to prevent many an island from lapsing into semi-barbarism; it will be a dark day on the page of civilization when England's cordon of soldiers is withdrawn again unto herself. But, in spite of herself, England's effect upon the West Indian is retardative, even retrogressive; if she had done nothing more than inflict upon an innocent people her archaic and monstrous monetary nomenclature and system, it would be sufficient. Locally, they have broken with their traditions on this score, and have substituted our own decimal system, to the great saving of time and friction of conscience; but, through the colonial banks, they still cling to pound-shilling-and-pence in their dealings with the "mother-country," and suffer their æsthetic sense to be violated through a circulation of bank-notes that would discredit even our provincial currency of a century ago.

To turn from this subject to one less likely to irritate my good friends in the Bahamas: I recall an incident of a previous trip, showing that the Bahama darkies do not discriminate against us on account of difference of silver, but accept with equal readiness English or American.

I was going about one day, with my camera, when I was hailed by a group of divers, huddled together on the wharf:

"Say, boss, don' you wan' t'row a nickel in de watah?"

"What for?"

"Wha' fo'? Why, fo' see um grab um, fo' he sink to de bottom."

"No; I've seen that too often, but I'll do better than that; I'll give you ten cents each, if you'll do as I tell you."

"Golly, boss; we'll do dat, you jes' bet. Now wha' yo' wan'?"

"Well, I want to take three photographs of you all: one on the wharf, one in the air, and another in the water. Now get ready."

"Yis, boss; wese all ready." They were, in fact, always ready, having nothing on but the airiest of clothing and an expansive grin.

"Very well; are you sure you're ready?"

"O, yis! wese a'ready an' waitin'; yo' jes' gib de word."

I gave the word: "One, two"— intending to start them at "three"; but they were so eager that all went into the air at "two,"—and the result was not exactly as intended.

But I got a snap-shot in mid-air, and afterward in

the water, where their heads bobbed about just like so many black Jack-o'-lanterns. They are jolly little fellows, these darky divers, and enliven the tedium of many a wait at the wharves.

One meets with these divers almost everywhere in the West Indies, but in Nassau and St. Thomas they are most numerous and proficient. When diving in

THE SILK-COTTON-TREE — NASSAU.

open water, they would seem to be in danger from sharks, but I never heard of an instance of disaster. In St. Thomas, I remember, one of these boys was seen to coolly kick a shark aside, that had come up close to a coin he was diving after, and the great fish swam off in apparent alarm.

In his journeyings in these out-islands one finds many strange people. Just before my arrival at Fortune Island, there had died a man with an idiosyncracy that made him locally noted. For many years he dressed as a woman, wearing the petticoats with all the grace attainable, and taking great pleasure in being addressed as "Miss Nancy." And as "Miss Nancy" he finally became known, no one thinking of calling him anything else.

He led a harmless, blameless life, always taking a great interest in the church, and at his death leaving quite a little property for its maintenance. He was everywhere respected, and although he wore a full beard, no one seemed to notice the incongruity.

The American Consul, Mr. McLain, who has resided in Nassau these many years, assisted me to the best of his ability, and made my stay agreeable.

The Vice-Consul, Mr. H. R. Saunders, was indefatigable in his efforts to inspire the business men with a sense of their responsibilities in the matter of exhibits, and addressed letters to all the out-islands requesting contributions to the ethnological collection I was endeavoring to form.

Everybody knows, of course, of the numerous attractions of Nassau: of its beautiful roads and drives, its delightful winter climate, the wonderful "sea-gardens" in the sound adjacent, the "Queen's Staircase" — which Her Majesty never saw — the magnificent silk-cotton in the court-house yard, and the Columbus statue. Regarded simply as a work of art, this statue in the Government grounds must be pronounced a failure; but there is a story told anent its landing, which may bear repeating, perhaps, as it illustrates the misapprehensions in the black man's mind regarding the great Navigator.

STATUE OF COLUMBUS — FRONT VIEW.

I remember the question of the old darky, who took me in his "turtler" over to Watling's Island, on learning that I was in search of information of Columbus:

"Say, boss, who is dis ole man Columbia? Ise been sailing hereabout dese forty year, an' Ise neber see him!"

But the story they relate of his colored brother in Nassau shows a better knowledge of historical events, and is as follows: Scene, court-room; lawyer for defense attempting to impeach veracity of a witness on side of plaintiff. "So you say you've lived here many years?"

"Yis, boss."

"Then I suppose you can remember when Columbus landed here."

"O, yis, boss! I 'members dat 'stinckly."

"You do?"

"Yis, sah."

"And you're sure you do?"

"Suttenly, boss."

"That will do. Your Honor, this witness's memory is evidently out of order, and I claim a verdict for the defense."

The judge was of his opinion also, when the plaintiff's lawyer rose to the occasion. "Wait a moment, gentlemen, perhaps the witness is not so far wrong. Now, Cuffie, when was it you saw Columbus land, and how did he come ashore?"

"Well, boss, I t'ink 'twas 'bout' 31, an' C'lumbus he come shore in de big boxes."

The lawyer for plaintiff claimed, and obtained, the verdict.

As I have intimated, travel in the Bahamas has not arrived at that point of perfection the visitor might desire, and before Nassau becomes the great and popular resort for winter tourists, steam communication must be established between the islands.

STATUE OF COLUMBUS — REAR VIEW.

The islands, rocks and cays of the Bahama chain aggregate some three thousand; they stretch from Florida to Haiti, and are uniformly level, the highest elevation not exceeding three hundred feet. Their formation is the same throughout: "calcareous rock of coral and shell hardened into limestone, honeycombed and perforated, with innumerable cavities, and without a trace of primitive rock. The soil, though thin, is astonishingly fertile, and vegetation grows luxuriantly." The population is from forty-five thousand to fifty thousand; about one third of the whole number being white. For many years after their discovery, the Bahamas were unvisited, the attention of the Spaniards being directed to the richer islands to the south, and to Mexico and Peru. They returned hither for slaves, but made no settlements. In 1512, Ponce de Leon threaded the chain in search of the Fountain of Youth — which, by the way, is said to be in the island of Bimini — but the first settlement was made by the English, in 1629. They were dispossessed, and the islands were a battle ground between the English and Spanish residents.

Then the buccaneers made them their rendezvous until after the Revolution; since that event Great Britain has held them undisturbed. The first inhabitants lived by buccaneering, piracy and smuggling, varying their pursuits, later on, by wrecking; this occupation, however, they have at length reluctantly abandoned; and there are many to-day who regard the light-houses with undisguised resentment, saying that they, by preventing wrecks, take the bread out of their mouths. But the good old times are gone, never to return, and the former wreckers now have to turn to sponging, turtling and conching, sometimes making great hauls. Among these islands, and only here, I believe, the famous pink pearl is found; it is highly prized, and sometimes brings enormous prices. About Crooked and Acklin Islands the conchs are found in great quantities, and

I procured a very pretty pearl from a fisherman at Watling's Island.

Not alone are the shells of the Bahamas beautiful, the tropical fish, as well, disport the brightest colors. These were particularly described by Columbus, who was attracted by them; and one should see them swimming amongst the coral branches, flashing silver-like

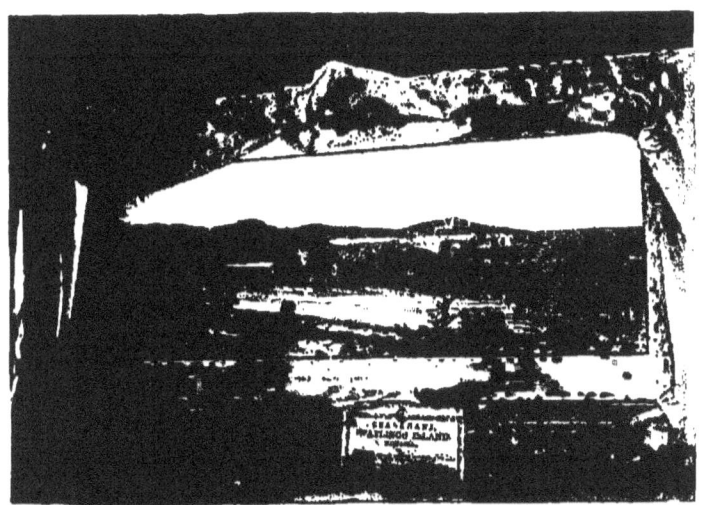

GUANAHANI, OR WATLING'S ISLAND — LADY BLAKE'S AQUARELLE.

gleams from their sides, and streaking the clear water with bright colors, to appreciate his enthusiasm. Aside from the sea-products, Nature has been prodigal with her gifts on land, for though the soil is scant, the wildflowers bloom in myriads. The talented wife of Sir Henry Blake, when residing in the Bahamas, made a series of drawings that embraced nearly all the wild flowers known to the islands, and exhibited at the

Jamaica exhibition above a hundred beautiful varieties. There are also many woods useful in the arts and *materia medica*, as well as all the fruits of the tropic zone. All this information is, I fear, more or less encyclopædic, and may be found in the guide-books; I would like my own work to be as free as possible from the commonplace; but if now and then I lapse into the statistical, it is only from a conscientious desire to be thorough.

The steamers of the Ward Line are perhaps the best known of any that ply between New York, the Bahamas, and Cuban ports; were it not for them these islands would, indeed, be badly off. I had sighted the *Santiago* of this line on her southward course, just off Rum Cay, passing almost within hail, but it was nearly two weeks before she returned to Nassau from the south ports of Cuba. I then embarked on her for New York. But although I returned to the States, and shortly after terminated my labors for the Exposition, my narrative does not conclude here, as I have taken my last adventures first, in order to have them in sequence with the route followed by Columbus.

## VI.

### THE COMMISSIONER'S MISSION TO CUBA.

TABLET BUST IN CATHEDRAL AT HAVANA, IN MEMORY OF COLUMBUS.

WHEN I received my commission as special representative of the World's Columbian Exposition, I was engaged in my profession of lecturing, and had "dates" in various parts of the country for the entire season. These I was obliged to cancel, of course, giving two months' notice, and my last lecture was delivered in Newton, Massachusetts, the last night of December, 1890. It was concluded at half-past nine; that night, at eleven, I was on board a train bound for Washington, which city I reached at three the next afternoon, received my instructions from the chief of the Latin-American Department, and at eight o'clock that evening took the train again for Chicago. There were nine of us, all newly-appointed Commissioners, each one assigned to a separate province of the West Indies, Central or South America, and all combined were to include the whole of that vast region lying between the United States and Patagonia: to cover the countries of America south of us, from the frozen North to the Land of Fire. Arrived at Chicago the following night, we were taken to the Palmer House, where quarters had been engaged for us, and the next day paid our respects to the Director-General of the Exposition, and to the officials comprising the executive department, by whom we were taken in charge and instructed as to our duties.

That afternoon we met the African explorer Stanley, at a reception at the rooms of the Union League Club, listened to one of his lectures in the evening, seated on the stage of the vast auditorium, and were entertained at a dinner given by one of the directors. Dinners and receptions followed swiftly after, and we had a taste of that hospitality for which the great Western city is celebrated; and if it was the intention of our friends to make us sensible of the joys we were soon to leave behind us, and extremely loath to turn our unwilling feet toward the fields of our labors, they succeeded admirably.

One day we were taken to the park, and shown the sites of the buildings that have since been erected; the next we had the pleasure of meeting the talented President of the Ladies' Board, and receiving from her information for our guidance in soliciting exhibits for the Women's Department; and we were impressed with the fact (since so conclusively confirmed) that her plans were wise, far-reaching, and well matured in advance. The ladies of the Women's Board were extremely anxious to reach and develop any latent resource of their sisters in Latin America, and we promised our active co-operation.

A week passed pleasantly, during which we became thoroughly imbued with the true Chicago spirit of energy and enterprise; then, having become acquainted with the aims, purposes and comprehensive projects of the executives of the great Exposition, we hastened away to our respective fields.

Within a month we were scattered all over the southern continent and adjacent islands; were preaching the Exposition gospel in half a dozen different languages, and expounding to a dozen different governments the greatness of the American nation, and the greatest of all its undertakings. We had been impressed with the ability and energy of our chiefs, and it was evident to us that they had a grasp of the situation that was perfectly amazing; guiding us, directing us, following every movement and anticipating every need, with an intelligent comprehension of our wants that was wonderful. Inspired, then, with the importance of our mission, in behalf of the greatest exhibition of the world's history, and supported by the sympathetic co-operation of our superiors in office, we could not but share in their enthusiasm. If any of us failed in our endeavors, it was not because of lack of support at Chicago, nor from any faults of our chiefs.

I was one of the first in the field, as my province lay contiguous, in a measure, to our own country. I was furnished with elaborate "instructions" for my guidance, of which the following is an abstract:

To FREDERICK A. OBER, ESQ.,
 *Commissioner to the West Indies.*

SIR: — You have been designed for duty under the Department of State, in connection with the World's Columbian Exposition, as a Commissioner to the West Indian Islands. The success of your mission will depend upon your own energy and discretion, but for your general guidance in the performance of your duties, I am directed by the Secretary of State to hand you the following instructions :

1. You will proceed at your earliest convenience to visit the several West Indian Islands, and upon your arrival at the principal cities thereof will report yourself to the Consuls of the United States, to whom you will be furnished letters of introduction and commendation. These officials will be directed to assist you, and promote the object of your mission in every possible way, and will present you to the Governor or Chief Magistrate of the colony in which they reside. . . .

2. Your first duty will be to explain fully to the proper officials of the islands you visit the plan and scope of the Exposition, express to them the desire of the Government and people of the United States that all of the islands shall be adequately represented, and ask their aid in securing the co-operation of commerical organizations and the public at large in obtaining as complete an exhibit as possible.

It will be necessary, also, to secure the publication, as widely as possible, under the official sanction, of the plan and classification of the Latin-American Department, the arrangements for transportation, care and custody of exhibits, and such other information as may be useful and interesting to possible exhibitors and the public generally. To this end it is essential that you place yourself at once in communication with the newspapers, and furnish them from time to time with such matter as they may be willing to publish. . . . It is of course desirable that every one of the islands should appoint Commissioners to the Exposition, furnish their own buildings, and make as large a display as possible

PALM AVENUE.

of their own resources, their industries and products. This matter should be brought to the attention of the several Governments as soon as possible, and cannot be too strongly urged; and in case such Commissioners are appointed, you will afford them all the information and assistance in your power. . . . If they cannot be induced to erect their own buildings, you are authorized to inform the proper officials and probable exhibitors that all the space they may need will be reserved for them, under the printed regulations furnished you by the Director-General. . . . You will inform yourself fully before starting upon your mission as to the customs regulations regarding the importation of goods intended for exhibition, so as to explain them intelligently to exhibitors, and will be furnished with printed forms prepared at the Treasury Department. . . . You will place yourself at once in communication with directors of museums, botanical gardens, scientific societies, etc., and secure from them such collections as they may be willing to furnish. . . . The local museums doubtless contain valuable archæological and historical collections, and it is desirable that whatever is interesting should be transported to Chicago, and you will take steps to induce the Governments to include them in their exhibits, as illustrative of the history of the islands. It is hardly necessary to speak of the desirability of securing exhibits illustrating the peculiar institutions, as well as the habits and customs of the people. You can furnish valuable assistance to the Government in securing, classifying and mounting these exhibits; and you may also be able to obtain their assistance in making archæological investigations to secure fresh collections. . . . You will be good enough to make as many photographs as possible of objects of interest noticed in your travels, as the educational value of a collection showing the homes, customs, and daily life of the people, cannot be overestimated. . . . While the details of routes of travel are left entirely to your discretion, it would seem advisable for you to visit the most unhealthy of the islands during the winter season; but you will kindly report your movements and plans to this office as regularly as practicable, and you will be furnished with a cable code, to be used in cases of emergency. . . . The West Indies are rich in fiber plants, and the same may be said of medicinal plants, barks, roots, seeds and flowers, which should in every case be labeled with care, and there should be full explanations in your note-books of the local methods of preparing and applying the same, as well as the diseases for which they are remedies. Superstitions and legends connected with such plants are always interesting, and often valuable."

Equally full and complete were my instructions regarding the woods of the West Indies, the minerals, mining operations, manufactures: in fact, every province of nature, art and science, was exhaustively presented, showing with what thoroughness my chief had prepared for the important work. Nor was the commercial world overlooked, as the following excerpt shows:

"As one of the important objects of the Exposition is to promote commercial intercourse, it is desirable to secure, for the information of the merchants and manufacturers of the United States, a complete display, showing the various classes of merchandise consumed and desired by the people of your province, the patterns and designs most preferred, the best methods of packing and preparing, practical illustrations of the obstacles in the way of extending our trade, and the advantages that are secured and enjoyed by European merchants in competition with those of our own country. The value of such an exhibit cannot be over-estimated."

And finally:

"Your attention is particularly called to that portion of the Classification which relates to a collection of the relics of Columbus. The field to which you are assigned must contain many things of great value and interest, and you will devote your energies to securing articles for this collection. It is understood that the ruins of the first city founded by Columbus (Isabella) are still extant, and exact information is particularly desired. You will be good enough to investigate this subject, and report to me at your earliest opportunity; and the results to be obtained from the investigation of any other similar ruins and relics will add greatly to the interest of the Columbian Department."

In order that I might be "instructed" fully, and not go astray from lack of good counsel, I was furnished with lengthy "instructions" from the Smithsonian Institution, the Fisheries Department, the Zoölogical, and Agricultural, and finally, the Secretary of State sent me letters to all the Consuls in my domain, one letter to each. They read as follows:

WASHINGTON, January, 1891.

*To —— —— Esq.,*
*Consul of the United States at ——*

MY DEAR SIR:—I take pleasure in introducing to you Mr. Frederick A. Ober, who, by the President's direction, has been designated as Special Commissioner for the purpose of interesting the Government and people of —— to participate with the United States in the commemoration of the Discovery of America by Columbus, by holding at the city of Chicago, in the State of Illinois, an Exposition of Arts, Sciences, Manufactures, and the products of the Mine, Soil and Sea. Mr. Ober will acquaint you with the general instructions he bears, and will consult with you as to the most convenient arrangement for successfully accomplishing his mission. You will, by your advice and counsel, and in every proper way, aid Mr. Ober in securing the appointment of Commissioners to represent the Government of —— at the proposed Exposition, and in interesting the people of that colony in presenting such a display as will fully and fitly illustrate its resources, industries, and progress in civilization. Confidently expecting your cordial co-operation in the furtherance of Mr. Ober's mission, I am, my dear sir,

Very truly yours,

*[signature: James G. Blaine]*

From the Director-General I had received, handsomely engraved on parchment, a "commission" for each of the Governments within my province, and as there were

CATHEDRAL STA. MARIA DE LA CONCEPION.—HAVANA, CUBA.

ten of these, all told, I was well provided. My chief occupation, on rainy days, was the reading of my "Instructions," and my chief concern was, how to get rid of my numerous "commissions," which, wherever permissible, I hung up on the walls of the different consulates.

My first field of operation was Cuba, which I reached by the new route via Florida, taking the Plant Line steamer at Tampa, and going direct to Havana. There I engaged rooms at the Hotel Inglaterra, but after a week of discomfort removed to a large boarding-house, or *Casa de huespedes*, on the Prado, near the Hotel Pasajé.

I lost no time in calling on our Consul-General, to whom I had two letters; one personal, the other official. He recognized the official letter, and one day took me to see the Captain-General, when I had an opportunity to initiate my work for Chicago. The Captain-General received me pleasantly (being a Spaniard he could not do otherwise), assured me that he appreciated the honor conveyed in the President's invitation, and also in the fact that the Commissioner had brought it to Cuba first of all the islands assigned him, and promised his hearty co-operation.

Some ten days passed by before he showed any signs of co-operating, and I was beginning to get impatient, although I had filled my time by writing articles for the newspapers, and had excited an interest in the Exposition which I did not allow to flag during my stay, but stimulated to the best of my ability. But when the announcement did come from His Excellency, the Captain-General, that he had appointed local Commissioners, the list he sent me showed that he had given the subject deep thought and consideration. It showed, also, that he had evidently intended to do the "right thing" by all the distinguished gentlemen of the island, and had included nearly everybody of importance on the list, as the grand total was twenty-nine. To this number he afterward added six provincial Commissioners, making thirty-five in all, including men from every rank and profession, but especially prominent were the ornamental members; for there were two *Marquesses*, and fourteen *Excellentissimos*.

It promised to be, I feared, rather "top-heavy" for active work; but that was now a matter beyond my control, and besides, at the head was a man of energy and fortune, Señor Don A. C. Telluria, a Biscayan by birth and a self-made man. Through his activity and enterprise he had gained control of the lumber trade of Havana, and he held high political position, being one of the leaders of the conservative party, and president of the provincial Deputation. One of the two titled members of the commission, the Marquis Duquesne, is a native of Cuba, a descendant of the French Admiral Duquesne, and one of the wealthiest planters in the island. He had latterly taken an active part in political affairs, and had recently been elected deputy from Cuba to the Spanish Cortes. The Marquis de Balboa was considered one of the leading politicians; a vice-president of the Conservative party, a Spaniard, bearing a distinguished name and controlling a large fortune; he was very popular.

Of the others, one was a poet, one an engineer, several were cigar-manufacturers, making those celebrated brands for which Cuba is famous, one was the rector of the university, one Alcalde Municipal, and there were four editors of as many influential papers of the city. Altogether, it was a commission to be proud of. And I

THE MORRO.

was proud; but I have never yet learned that they did anything except to meet and discuss what they were going to do — when they did begin to do anything.

But it pleased His Excellency to appoint these distinguished gentlemen, it pleased them to be appointed, and it pleased me to learn that they were appointed; and as for the newspapers, they went into raptures over the *personnel* of the commission, the wisdom displayed in their

LES CABANAS.

selection, and the great results likely to accrue to Cuba from this renewed evidence of the friendliness of the two countries, etc., etc. Although rather skeptical as to the great results, yet I went to work on these lines laid down for me by my chief, keeping the papers informed, and through them the people, of the vast enterprise going on in the States; and perhaps I even encouraged a little the grandiloquent style of the Exposition articles, as a better policy than to express one's own sentiments. At all events (strange as this may appear to a Chicagoan), I had first to tell the *Cubanos* where Chicago was situated before informing them what Chicago was doing; for the average Havanese knows little of the States, travel there being confined to the rich, and these only being acquainted with the city of New York and Saratoga. The fact of the Exposition being held at Chicago was a good thing in one respect: it made foreigners acquainted with portions of our country of which they would otherwise have remained in ignorance.

Havana, as every one knows, is delightful during a portion of the year, and disagreeable, not to say dangerous, to foreigners through the heated term of the summer months. It has been described so often, as well as the entire island, in fact, that I shall not waste the time of my readers in repetition. Even now, the Morro stands at the entrance to the harbor, the bastioned fortifications of the Cabañas frown above the bay, the Prado is the principal promenade, the streets of the older portion of the city are as dirty and as narrow as ever they were, the gardens of the Captain-General are as beautiful, and the alleys of palm-trees as majestic; while the people are as various as can be found anywhere throughout the islands; for they represent every part of Spain, and the mixtures resulting from intermingling with the American natives. Spanish speech and Spanish customs prevail, through the preponderance of Spaniards in the body politic, and the constant accessions to the population of soldiers and the crowds of fortune-seekers from the mother-country.

There are many fine old families here, but the bulk of the new arrivals are from the lower classes of Spain, hard-working and thrifty, but ignorant. Cuba, the only possession of value to Spain, of the many she once owned in America, is being stripped by the rapacious hordes that have flocked here, and is almost at the last gasp.

When I was there, a treaty of reciprocity was being negotiated between Spain and the United States, by which it was hoped exhausted Cuba would benefit; but it is doubtful if she will be accorded more than temporary relief, for Spain must raise her revenue somehow, and

MORRO CASTLE — HARBOR OF HAVANA.

she has but scant resources outside the Pearl of the Antilles, except in Puerto Rico, where likewise the people are groaning beneath their taxes. Before the treaty was negotiated, the tax on a barrel of flour was more than equal to the original cost in the States, and the millers in Spain even made immense profits by importing American wheat, grinding it, and exporting it to Cuba. Oppression had reached the point where even the Spaniards in Cuba, comprising the majority of the merchants and shop-keepers, protested against the exactions, and in the air were ominous mutterings of insurrections and rebellion. Little hope has Cuba of any successful uprising against the Spanish oppressor, who has all the forts filled with guns, and all the towns and cities filled with soldiers.

But even should the Cubans ever throw off the yoke that has so long been fastened upon them, they would

AT THE MARKET.

probably find worse enemies among themselves than in the ranks of the foreign foe. For the people are not fitted to govern; and there is no hope whatever of bettering their condition by a revolution.

The thing they hope for, yearn after, and desire above all things, is annexation to the United States; and in order to frighten old Spain at times, this bugaboo of annexation is elevated, by imaginative journalists, that they may have the pleasure of knocking it down.  The assumed "hostile attitude" of the Cuban Government toward the United States, is almost wholly the work of a few newspapers at Madrid; the intelligent editors of Cuban newspapers and the Government officials know that it means absolutely nothing.  As I frequently assured the *Cubanos;* the Government of the United States has no desire for the annexation of Cuba or Canada, Mexico or Patagonia.  The people of the United States are so self-absorbed, having yet a vast territory of their own undeveloped, and producing more than they themselves can consume, that they seldom cast a thought toward even contiguous countries, except, as in the instance of my visit, to invite their neighbors over to see them, and to participate in their prosperity.

But the Cubans themselves cannot understand the attitude of indifference maintained by "Uncle Sam" toward the attractions of their beautiful island; they see only the natural beauties of their possession; the thoughtful American sees farther; and it may not be amiss to mention that any student of history will understand the perils of the problem that might be presented for solution, were annexation to come about.  In truth, they don't understand the real nature of Uncle Sam.  He is such an easy-going, good-natured old gentleman, with a family increasing rapidly by immigration from the Old World, at the rate of half a million yearly, that he dreads the responsibility of adopting a "grown-up" family of children — and unruly children, at that —

suddenly bereft of maternal guidance so salutary as they now receive from the fair Queen Regent of Spain.

There is no question about the interests of Cuba being bound up with those of the United States, for, although politically united to Spain, she has nothing in common with that country, which is sucking out her life-blood and injecting a spurious serum in return. All the trade of Cuba belongs to the United States, and her very life depends upon our markets for her sugar and tobacco, while everything she produces could find sale here.

The United States does not wish for these islands; but they need the protecting arm of this strong and friendly nation around them, and the advanced thinkers of them all are looking toward this Government to save them from destruction.

Notwithstanding the great number of soldiers in the island, good order is by no means maintained throughout the country, and bandits of the worst kind keep portions of the interior in terror. Scarcely a week passes without accounts of their depredations, and notices in the papers of the pursuit, rarely the capture, of "*los bandoleros.*" When captured, they are shot, usually in attempting to "escape." Four bandits were shot in the very harbor of Havana, during my visit; they were lured thither by promise of amnesty, and had taken passage for Santo Domingo. Just before the time came for the steamer to leave, a boat load of policemen went off to arrest them; the bandits drew knives and pistols to resist, and all were shot. The police were badly cut up, but not a bandit lived to tell the tale. This event took place in the midst of the crowded shipping, and in open day, but the news did not make much stir in town.

The chief of the *bandoleros* was one Manuel Garcia, who signed himself "el Rey de los Campos," the King of the Country. He was exceedingly cunning; long escaping capture, though his wife was in jail, and many of his companions had been taken and shot. Their

ON THE PASEO.

field of operations was quite near Havana; generally between two towns called Güines and Aguacate, and their lairs were in the thick chaparral of the old fields and forests difficult for soldiers to penetrate.

News is rapidly gathered and disseminated in the island by the papers, which are numerous; in fact in excess of the number required by the population. Fifty periodicals of various kinds are published in Havana alone, including illustrated journals of the cheaper grade, and a great redundancy of the political stripe. The leading dailies are: the *Diario de la Marina*, founded in 1844; *El Pais, La Union Constitucional*, and *La Lucha*. A very bright and enterprising little sheet, devoted to fashion, art, literature, and especially to the

BELEM.

taking off of the follies of the day, is *El Figaro*, which has excellent illustrations.

Art and literature here have not the encouragement they deserve, in a land teeming with models of form and beauty, and rich in memories of great men and great deeds. The only library, the *Biblioteca*, is scantily supplied with books, and most of these were donated by private individuals; but there is a School of Arts, under the direction of Señor Melero, which, though in great need of money for the purchase of casts, etc., is in a flourishing condition. I visited it quite often, being charmed with the courtesy of the director, and entertained by the wit of his assistant. I was allowed to inspect the school, one day, and was surprised at the number of bright and alert young ladies, enthusiastically working at their tasks. I could not but notice, as I looked behind the easels, that they did not confine their efforts entirely to the adorning of their canvases, but that each one had a tiny box of powder at hand, which was brought into requisition whenever its fair owner thought her complexion needed a little touching up. But I am sure this is the only vanity those charming *Cubanas* have, for they are the sweetest most amiable, brightest and loveliest of girls. I recall one of the little artists, whom I was sometimes privileged to observe on a balcony, and who had a sweet and saucy face, lighted up by most wonderful black eyes, and the prettiest air imaginable.

In the convent school of Belem there is a fine collection of old books, as well as an attempt to get together a museum of the animals, minerals, shells, and other natural-history specimens. The church attached is over two hundred years old, and a beautiful structure, with magnificent palms in its court. The leading scientific society is the *Real Academia*, in Cuba Street, where are fine conchological and mineralogical collections. A few celts and implements of the Cuban aborigines are also shown, and two strange specimens of

Indian crania that were found in a cave, imbedded in lime rock. The society publishes a bulletin, which is eagerly sought as an exchange by the scientific societies of the world, and is under the guidance of learned and enthusiastic professors.

I had been anxious for many years to meet one of Cuba's famous men, of whom the whole scientific world

REAL ACADEMIA — HAVANA.

had been for nearly fifty years cognizant: Don Felipe Pocy. My intention was to seek him out at the first opportunity; but another visitor got ahead of me, and prevented. The very day of my arrival, seeing an imposing funeral procession pass the Inglaterra, I inquired who was so highly honored, and was told that it was the gentleman I was so desirous to meet. Another scientist, who has devoted fifty years to a study of the ornithology of Cuba, and whose work has made him famous, is Dr. Gundlach, whom I had long known by reputation, and whom I found in a room of the university, arranging his collections. Although over eighty years of age, fifty of which he had passed in the woods and fields, exposed to every hardship, yet he was alert and active, remembered me from my book on the Caribbees, which he at once produced, and discussed with great relish the joys and perils of camp-life in the Tropics. Like myself, he had enjoyed immunity from the stings and bites of poisonous reptiles and insects, never having been bitten by dangerous animals, nor even stung by a tarantula. Poey and Gundlach take one back to the days of Humboldt and Audubon; and one might do the world a favor, if he would write out their travels and reminiscences.

While I was in Havana, I was cheered by a flying visit from the chief of the department, under whom I was working, Mr. W. Eleroy Curtis, who held the important position of assistant to the Director-General of the Exposition, and was in close relations with the Department of State. He is a gentleman of great and varied attainments, formerly a journalist of reputation, and has won lasting credit in connection with the management of the "Bureau of the American Republics." He has visited nearly every portion of the West Indies and South America, has written an authoritative volume on the latter countries, and is thoroughly informed regarding their future and possibilities. A man of untiring energy and great executive ability, he infused into his subordinates the same spirit of hopeful labor with which he himself was animated. The department of which he was chief embraced Mexico, the West Indies, Central and South America, and was called, from the preponderance of people of Spanish origin, the Latin-American Department.

Owing to the fact that I was domiciled in a *huespedes*, he professed to have had great difficulty in finding me, and demanded why I was not flying my consular flag. I had been provided with a handsome flag at starting, and was supposed to keep it flying on the house I might happen to be in; but seeing no other flag in the air, on week-days, I had not, my chief thought, sufficiently asserted myself. So I ordered Manuel, my servant, to hoist the flag on the pole on the roof. The Cuban stared at me a moment, and then said respectfully, but in surprise:

"But, Señor, this is a week-day."

"No matter; up with the flag."

He took it down from between my rooms, where it had done duty as a portière, and went with it to the roof, while I hastened to the Hotel Pasajé, to point it out to my chief. We went out on the balcony, expecting to be refreshed with the sight of the glorious stars and stripes floating above a Spanish boarding-house; but casting our eyes in that direction, to our horror we saw it hung up Union down. I ran over and corrected that error, and all day long I saw the passers-by looking wonderingly at my flag, and little groups collect, evidently lost in admiration. But at nightfall I received a message from the Consul, saying that there had been an inquiry as to the meaning of the new Commissioner in flying his flag on a week-day. And it appears that no other flag was floating in the city, as the Spanish only fly their bunting on Sundays and holidays, when the Anglo-Saxons take theirs in.

A BIT OF OLD HAVANA.

# VII.

### NORTH COAST OF CUBA TO HAITI.

ROYAL PALMS.

PLACING myself in communication with the Commissioners appointed by the Captain-General, I had the great pleasure of daily intercourse with some of the most polished and highly-educated gentlemen of Havana, that city so noted for its talented and courteous citizens.

I found, as already stated, a large number of newspapers, employing the highest class of journalistic talent, and while I was in Havana the columns of these papers were always open for announcements regarding the Exposition.

Keeping ever in mind the purpose of my Government—to fully illustrate the history of the discovery, and so far as possible the growth and development of the West Indies, and secure everything valuable pertaining to the period of discovery and conquest — I was always on the lookout for things Columbian. Cuba, as we know, was not circumnavigated until after the death of Columbus, and the first settlement was not attempted until the year 1511, when a Spaniard, Velasquez, sailed from Santo Domingo, with four vessels and three hundred men, having as companions two who became more famous than he — Cortez and Las Casas — and landed on the south coast, at a port called Las Palmas, near the present Guantanamo. The year following, Baracoa was founded on the north, and, in 1515, Santiago de Cuba, whence, says the Cuban chronicler, Cortez sailed to his career in Yucatan and the conquest of Mexico. Between 1540 and 1550, there were six towns in Cuba: Santiago, Baracoa, Bayamo, Prince's Port, Espiritu Santo and Havana.

The capital of Cuba was founded in 1519, and the spot where the first mass was celebrated, beneath the wide-spreading branches of a silk-cotton-tree, is now indicated by a small structure called the *templeté*, in front of which is a bust of Columbus, and within three large paintings of great interest. It has been erroneously stated that Columbus landed here; but the first landing at Havana occurred thirteen years after his death. There are no authentic relics of him here, but there is a statue in the court of the palace, and a fine portrait in the hall-of-sessions of the city council. There is an inscription on it, stating that the original from which it was painted came from the island of Santo

Domingo, and that this one was sent by the Duke of Veragua, in 1796. In the same hall is an excellent painting of the landing of the Pilgrims, of Cortez burning his ships at Vera Cruz, with portraits of Alfonso XII.

SELLING PLANTS IN HAVANA.

and Fernando VII., while in the Captain-General's audience-room are portraits of all the captain-generals from the year 1777.

Most famous of all the relics claimed to be possessed by Havana are the alleged remains of Columbus, in the old cathedral. A full account of their removal hither will be found in a later chapter of this book, as well as a discussion of their authenticity. Pending the decision of competent judges, my chief thought it as well to have all the proofs in the case at hand when the Exposition should open; I therefore procured a cast of the tablet erected over the remains, and sent it to Washington. This tablet is affixed against the wall at the right of the altar, and has upon it a well-carved bust, and the following inscription:

> "*Oh! Restos e imagen del grande Colon!*
> *Mil siglos durad guardados en la urna,*
> *Y en la remembranza de nuestra nacion.*"

This may be freely paraphrased:

> "O, grand Columbus!
> In this urn enshrined
> A thousand centuries thy bones shall guard,
> A thousand ages keep thine image fresh,
> In token of a nation's gratitude."

The cast of the tablet was shipped to Washington, and a contract was made with a local sculptor to reproduce a remarkably fine statue of "Columbus in Chains," in the *Biblioteca*, sent there from Barcelona.

Thus, by bringing to the notice of the world the odd ends of historical productions, and half-forgotten facts of valuable history, and in calling attention to the scenes of occurrences that once enlisted the attention of all the civilized inhabitants of the globe, the directors of the Exposition have placed themselves upon a plane far removed from prejudice and local traditions.

Cuba played an important part in the conquest of

America, and cannot be ignored in the study of our history. In that subjugation there were four centers of conquest and colonization.

First: Haiti, from 1492 to about 1515, whence was explored the entire chain of the Antilles: Cuba, Puerto Rico, Darien, Florida and the Spanish Main. Within a generation the fortunes of Haiti (or Santo Domingo)

PLAZA DE ARMAS, HAVANA.

had sunk to the lowest point, and in the early years of the sixteenth century its colonists were eager to embark in any enterprise leading out to the discovery of other fields.

Second: Darien, in the year 1513, became another nucleus of adventurous spirits. From its mountains Vasco Nuñez de Balboa, first of all Europeans, saw the great

Southern Sea, and here began those explorations that eventually led to the discovery of Peru.

Third: Cuba, from 1513 to 1540, became the pivotal point of explorers. Remnants of the shattered forces of the various unfortunate adventurers in Darien and Panama straggled to Cuba, and from their reports resulted Yucatan, Mexico, and the further exploitation of Florida. A gallant hidalgo of Cuba, who had come over from Santo Domingo with Velasquez, Hernandez de Cordova, joined with him a troop of men from Haiti and Darien, and sailed on an expedition, disastrous to himself, but which led to the discovery of Yucatan. His pilot was the celebrated Alaminos, who as a boy was with Columbus, and he sailed in 1517. The next year a more successful expedition was sent out by Governor Velasquez, under command of one Grijalva, which went beyond the coast found by Cordova, and brought back treasures of gold.

Fourth: In this manner was ushered in the closing act of the great drama, the discovery of Mexico, by Hernando Cortez, in the year 1519. Governor Velasquez, instead of giving the command of this second and largest venture to Grijalva, who had shown himself fully competent to conduct it, "at length, after having seriously considered it, pitched upon the man who gave him cause to repent, and made his life weary," says the old historian. With the affairs of Cortez we have nothing further to do; we know the sequel: the conquest of Mexico and the further extension of the dominions of Spain. Fortunately, a hardier people and more warlike opposed the Spanish oppressors in Mexico than in the

West Indies; and to this is owing their preservation to this day. It was in July of the same year, 1519, that the first ship from New to Old Spain made the voyage through the Bahama Channel, to avoid falling into the hands of Velasquez, as it carried the rich and golden treasures sent by Montezuma to the king of Spain. The fourth center of conquest was, therefore, Mexico; whence New Mexico (by Coronado), Honduras, Guatemala, the Pacific Coast and Nicaragua.

But these adventures carry the field of action beyond our ken, for we have to do only with the first great voyages that opened the way for them.

We have followed the adventurous Spaniards on their first voyage to these shores, sailing with them through the Bahama chain, and finally reaching the north coast of Cuba. With my readers' permission, I will now return to our ghostly companions, whom in the fourth chapter we left on the eve of landing, and allow them to conduct us yet farther along the course of their voyagings.

Leaving Havana about the middle of March, I followed along the very route pursued by Columbus after he had landed on the shores of Cuba. It was difficult to tear myself away from the numerous attractions of the quaint old city and its fascinating people; but my mission had practically been accomplished, the Commissioners were actively at work, or about to begin, the press had already published an elaborate presentation of the plans of the Exposition, and my further stay could not result in any adequate reward. It was my intention to return; but the field assigned me was such

"MORNING MIST," YUMURI VALLEY FROM THE CUMBRES.

a vast one, with desultory and infrequent communication between the various islands, that I got entangled in the insular labyrinth far to the south, and never recovered my original route.

Although my official duties left me little time for recreation, or for excursions, yet I made several trips into the country; one to the celebrated Toledo sugar estate, where all the appliances of modern invention are in use for the extraction and crystallization of the cane juice, and another to the district of Matanzas. Near Matanzas is that most beautiful vale of Paradise, the Yumuri Valley, and the celebrated caves of Bella-Mar. No words can describe the beauty of Yumuri, as seen from the Cumbres, or from the chapel of Monserrate, with its stretches of level plain inclosed within steep hills, and its groves and groups of palms. On the way thither, one sees the graceful and stately royal palm, in ranks and single groups, but to know what beauty there really is in this child of the Tropics, one should gaze upon the glorious creations of Yumuri. They stand out on the ridges; white and ivory-stemmed they rise before you as the foreground of a vista transcendently lovely; they linger in memory like the ghosts of departed saints.

At Matanzas you find the best volantes; and so rough is the road that only by means of these lumbering and antiquated vehicles can you reach the Cumbres. Continuing the volante ride, the caves are reached; their fine galleries, rock forms and stalactites will well repay the exertion of a descent. Another journey should be taken to the Vuelta-Abajo district, if one be interested in tobacco culture, and afterward visit the great factories in the capital.

But all these things are in the guide-books; our time must be employed in exploiting the rarer beauties of islands farther on.

As we have already noted, the coast of Cuba was reached by Columbus the twenty-eighth of October, 1492. On landing he found a people, still uncivilized,

YUMURI VALLEY, FROM HILL OF GUADELOUPE.

yet in some ways in advance of the natives of the Bahamas; they had huts of palm-leaves in the shape of pavilions, and were discovered smoking tobacco, which plant had been first seen in the possession of an old Indian near San Salvador. "At that time it was thought Cuba was the end of the Asiatic continent, and then the islands were first called the West Indies, and the region the New World."

The first landing-place in Cuba is a matter of dispute,

like the first Landfall, but the weight of evidence seems in favor of the port of Jibara, or Gibara (pronounced Heebára), on the north coast. The best presentation of the subject is in a little book by a Cuban engineer, Sr. H. C. Leyva, called "*El Primer Viaje de Colon*," the "First Voyage of Columbus" — and the evidence there given shows conclusively that Jibara was the spot.

I left Havana one night of storm, when the whole sky was weeping, as if in evidence of my own sorrow at leaving behind so many pleasant acquaintances. The Spanish steamer in which I had passage, the *Manuela*, was stanch, but fearfully dirty; the cabins being filled with half-sick men and women, and the decks covered with cattle. In fact, the cattle and mules, comprising the deck-loads, were penned so far aft that their noses almost touched us as we sat at the tables, which were spread on deck; and not all the polite attentions of the courteous officers could divert our attention from our four-footed shipmates.

After thirty-six hours steaming we sighted the "Faro de Colon," a tall white shaft, with a light, standing out from an apparently wild and desolate shore. Entering the mouth of a wide river, an hour's slow steaming took us to a very broad bay, with two blue mountains distant in the southwest. Lying against the gentle slope of a low hill are perhaps a hundred stone buildings, comprising the sad-looking town of Nuevitas, the port of the inland city, Puerto Principe. The streets are merely water-worn tracks up the hillside, and the general air of the town is that of desolation and decay.

The second day took us into Jibara, at daylight. This

port the later historians have accepted as the true Cuban landing-place of Columbus. The approach to it is most picturesque, with numerous detached mountains rising above green forests and hills. The bay is open, yet somewhat sheltered, and its relative position to the islands of the mid-Bahamas is such that it would be very likely to receive the boats of Columbus as he was coming

MOUNTAINS OF JIBARA.

down from the northeast. The waves that break upon the coast outside are white-crested and dangerous; but inside there is shelter and a cheerful prospect.

At present, the town of Jibara is in that half-ruined state presented by so many of the settlements of Cuba, harassed by the revolutionists of recent years. A high wall extends around the inland portion, with very pretty towers here and there, built as a defense against the insurrectionists. There is little soil, the rock is calcareous, the vegetation is tropical, and the general aspect forlorn. There is a little square, a small church, an excellent casino and theater, but no private houses of importance. Off the harbor lie four great hills, or mountains, known as the Silla de Jibara, Cerro Colorado, Loma del Puñal, and Cerro Yabazon. These are conspicuous landmarks, and attracted the attention of Columbus on his approach, as stated in his journal.

Here the steamer took on another load of cattle, and I had my first view of the method of loading. A lighter comes alongside, makes fast, and then a rope is thrown down from the steamer's deck. One end of this rope is attached to the steam hoisting winch; at the other is a running noose. The noose is thrown over the horns of an unfortunate ox or bull, the winch is started to tighten the noose, and then goes ahead at full speed, hoisting the unhappy animal into the air. Sometimes there are two animals in the same noose, and the tortures they undergo cannot be imagined, as the rope draws around their horns, tightens into the hides, and the terrible strain of their weight comes upon the heads. Hoisted to a height sufficient, they are swung in midair over the deck and dropped heavily upon the planks, where they lie stunned for a while, or gather themselves up with an air of stupefaction. Altogether, the process is horrible and cruel in the extreme; but the Cubans think nothing of it, and have loaded cattle in this way for many years.

Here, as everywhere in Cuba, Spanish misrule is ruining the people, and Spanish soldiers are devastating the land like a curse of grasshoppers and locusts. The last revolution brought the people to poverty, and they cannot recover; there is not a plantation within range of the eye, except dry fields of Henequen, or Sisal hemp.

Away down to the southeast, lies the port of Baracoa, which we reached one morning, entering its beautiful harbor at daylight. This port was specially commended by Columbus, who found it as he coasted the Cuban shores, and whose vessels were the first to enter it; and it was owing to his glowing reports that it subsequently became the site of a city. It is situated, says the historian, near the eastern extremity of the island, "the surroundings presenting an extensive plain gradually sloping from the mountains down to the shore, intersected by valleys and richly wooded, from which streams of water fall into the sea, affording, with all the beauties of tropical vegetation, a picture of enchantment." This is true to-day; no lovelier view is afforded the traveler in any part of the world, than that of Baracoa as seen from the sea, or from the high hills that rise behind it. Palms, majestic and graceful, adorn all the slopes, and grand mountain forms rise through the sea of forest that seems to retain all its virgin freshness and primeval majesty.

The most conspicuous feature here, and one dwelt upon particularly by Columbus in the journal of his voyagings, is the great table-topped mountain that rises behind the town, and can be seen far out at sea. It is still called by its aboriginal name, *Yunque*, and traditions cluster thickly around it, the natives averring that sometimes, in the morning, the face and figure of an

Indian cacique can be traced against its rugged and almost perpendicular sides.

It was either here or at Jibara (but more probably at the latter port), that Columbus, thinking he had at last arrived at the border-land of the province of the "Grand Khan," dispatched an embassy to the fancied potentate, with presents and conciliatory messages, which wofully miscarried, for there was not any Grand Khan, nor any

NORTH COAST OF CUBA.

city of grand proportions, such as Marco Polo had described, and the Admiral was looking for. But he met some Indians different from those hitherto seen, one of whom gave him some advice, which it would have been well if he had taken to heart, and he saw some new things of interest. Among others, a strange animal, now extinct, called afterward by the Spaniards the "dumb dog," and which was highly prized by the aborigines.

"Ye Dumme Dogge," says Petrus Martyr, in his

history, first published in English in 1555, "is found in the islands lately discovered, and whose inhabitants go naked; and for scarceness of children sacrifice dogges, which they nourish as well for that purpose as we do connies. These dogges are dumme and cannot barke, having snoutes like unto foxes."

This "dumb dog" was, Dr. Gundlach thinks, a raccoon, but I am inclined to believe it a species of animal now extinct. The aborigines had domesticated another mammal, called the *Hutia*, and this, with three others, now comprises the four indigenous mammals of Cuba. There are two species of the *Hutia:* the *Hutia Pocyii* (named after Señor Pocy), and the *H. Forrier;* besides a small animal called the *Almiqui* — the *Solanum Cubanus* — and the *Javalli*, or native wild peccary; also, two species of Guinea pig, which have run wild.

Nearly twenty years elapsed between the discovery of Cuba and the founding of the first settlement, but the chief cacique of Cuba, Hatuey, had secretly informed himself of the movements of the Spaniards and their barbarous treatment of the Indians, and warned his people against them. Once he called them together, and told them that the Spaniards did all their cruel deeds for the sake of a great lord they were serving, and whom he would show them. Taking some gold from a basket, he said, "This is the lord whom they serve, and him they follow; they are coming here only to seek this lord; therefore, let us make a festival and dance before him, to the end that when they come he may order them to do us no harm." After they were spent with singing and dancing, the chief told them not to keep this god anywhere about them, for even though he were inside of them, yet would the Spaniards find him, and therefore they should cast him into the river; and this they did.

And it all came about as the poor old chieftain predicted, for the Spaniards hounded him and his followers through the thickest forests, until all were captured or slain, and Hatuey himself was burned at the stake. The cruelties of Haiti were enacted over again, and but a few years had passed before these harmless children of Cuba were exterminated. In order to get rid of the miseries of the mines, whole troops of Indians hanged themselves in the forests, and the suicidal mania was only checked when one of the overseers went among his miners with ropes, and threatened to hang himself, also, and thus accompany them into the next world, where he would continue the torments he had begun in this.

Nothing remains now of the native population, and the only reminders of them are the rude implements of warfare and agriculture sometimes discovered. Near Cape Maysi, at the eastern end of Cuba, is an immense cavern, formerly a dwelling-place of the natives, and here have been found some crania apparently petrified.

Our Consul and Vice-Consul received us with open arms at Baracoa, and treated us to a dinner cooked and served in the old Cuban style. The port was full of "fruiters" loading with bananas for the States; the banana trade to-day is enormous and increasing. At sunset we were rounding historic Maysi, the cape discovered and named by Columbus, and following in the very track he took when he left Baracoa and sought out the land of Bohio, where the natives told him he would find in abundance the gold he desired so much. He had reached the Cuban coast the twenty-eighth of October, and had lingered along its shores five weeks, taking his final departure the fourth of December. Off

BARACOA.

the cape he sighted high, cloud-like mountains, and for them he steered, crossing the channel between Cuba and Haiti. On the seventh of December, 1492, he reached the latter island at Point St. Nicholas, near which is the celebrated Mole which was recently the subject of controversy between the United States and Haiti.

Instead of following directly in the route of Columbus, our steamer turned to the westward, entering the picturesque port of Santiago de Cuba, where our Consul, Mr. Otto Reimer, who has held office during two administrations, entertained us delightfully, until we, too, essayed to cross the channel, seeking the Haitian shores. Twenty-four hours later we dropped anchor in the harbor of Port au Prince, after a very rough passage across, and having coasted the fine island of Gonaive, which lies off the harbor, covered with dense tropical vegetation, and which, though surpassingly rich, is almost uninhabited.

There was a long delay in securing permission to land, and it was afternoon when the quay was finally reached, there being few boats at hand, and the owners of these few lazy and insolent. The boatmen charged three dollars for myself and trunks; the porters demanded a dollar for taking the luggage to the custom-house, and another dollar for carrying it to the hotel. Thanks to the intercession of Mr. Bassett, the American minister's secretary, my luggage was passed without examination; the colored customs officials were courteous and attentive, and, my special passport being found all right, I was at last free to go where I pleased.

Securing quarters at the Hotel Bellevue, just outside the city and on the Champs de Mars, I hoisted the American flag, and devoted the two days left me before the sailing of the steamer for Jamaica, to important business with the Government. They were busy days, but I filled them, and enjoyed my stay exceedingly. Going on to Jamaica, I returned seven weeks later, and then accomplished the negotiations which the absence of the President had prevented on the first visit.

My first call, of course, after being settled at the hotel, was on the American Minister, the Hon. Frederick Douglas, to whom I presented my letters from the Secretary of State, and my credentials as attaché of the Haitian Legation. I was introduced by Mr. Bassett, his secretary, who was formerly minister here during most troublous times. I also met another ex-minister, Mr. Thompson, who had preceded Mr. Douglas. He was just leaving, having remained behind to improve the opportunities afforded one to make money in this rich island. Minister Douglas had a very nice country residence back of the hotel, but the office of the Legation was near the business center of the town.

There is a small American colony here, and in the evening I dined with Mr. Crain, an enterprising American who introduced the first (and last) street railway into the island. As an illustration of the fate of modern enterprise, when brought into contact with the Haitian barbarism, let this contractor's experience prove a warning to all who would seek investments in this republic. Mr. Crain secured a contract, put down his rails, imported improved cars and mules, and ran his street-cars regularly from the Mole to the Champs de Mars, and back. At first, the novelty of the thing "took" with the Haitians and all their spare cash, as well as all they could borrow — not to speak of their enterprise in defrauding conductors — was invested in rides over the rails. After a few weeks, however, the novelty had worn off, and the street-cars palled upon them; and when a thing palls upon a Haitian, he is not at all slow in showing it. It was shown in this instance by ripping up the rails and obstructing the track, and the first revolution next succeeding, aided by the summer floods, completed the work of devastation, so that there now remains of this great American enterprise only the road-bed and disconnected rails.

The streets of Port au Prince were as bad as they could be before the advent of the street-cars; but now

IN THE VOLANTE, CUBA.

they are simply exasperating, for the broken rails stand high out of the roads, and twist off the wheels of all vehicles with which they come in contact. As though the loss of his concession were not enough, it was seriously proposed, by the Haitian legislators, to force Mr.

Crain to take up the fragments of the rails, and restore the streets to their original condition. But the irony of it all is, that Mr. Crain owns a livery stable, and probably loses more wheels from his carriages than all the others combined.

Crain's was the rallying-place of the American contingent in times of peace, as well as their retreat in revolutions, and the holes made by flying musket-balls were numerous in the walls. At dinner, that evening, the frequent revolutions were alluded to, and my friends humorously described their various and numerous escapes. Mr. Crain related his last adventure, when the chair he sat in was shot from under him, but said he was unable to describe his sensations, the situation was so complicated. Mr. Bassett mentioned casually that the last time he was shot at one bullet passed in front of him and another behind him, and a ludicrous feeling of uncertainty possessed him as to whether he had best go ahead, retreat, or fall flat on the ground. But all agreed that, whatever troubles the Haitians might have among themselves, they did not really intend any harm to the foreigner. The only danger lay in getting hit by a bullet intended for somebody else; but, again, as the Haitian soldiers never did hit what they aimed at, it was generally the ball intended for somebody else that did the execution.

Although the Haitians are always fighting among themselves, yet it is the universal opinion that the foreigner is fairly safe, whether in city or country; the foreign residents travel about unreservedly, taking the "revolutions" as a matter of course, and interfering with nobody. This sense of security in the intervals of peace was illustrated the first night I was in Haiti, by the departure of one of our number, about ten o'clock, for his country house in the mountains, some seven miles away. The night was very dark, the roads unutterably bad, and the route lay near a district in which resided some of the worst Voudou people in those parts; yet our friend went off unattended, as though merely going across the street, and reappeared next morning, to repeat the ride again that night. The British Consul, Mr. Arthur Tweedy, and his brother, resided for a long time in the hills above the capital, going and coming daily, but never experiencing any trouble except during the revolutions. They took me up to their charming retreat, one evening, and I enjoyed a cool night, a superb view of the city and harbor, and experienced the delights of an English hospitality with Haytian accessories.

By the Haitian constitution, no foreigner can own any realty in the island; and if he would acquire real estate, he must do it through a third party, resident here; in other words, a black or colored man. It is rather refreshing to find a country where the white man has no rights, and has to go down on his knees for favors from his colored brother. It may be in the nature of a merciful dispensation of Providence that the black man has made it so difficult that the white man may not desire to come here; for certainly no one could ask a worse punishment for an enemy than enforced residence in Haiti. Still, all the foreign trade is in the hands of foreigners — chiefly English, French and a few Americans; and the fortunes some of them roll up would be enormous — if they were permitted to get away with them. But it usually happens that just as the merchant has accumulated a snug little fortune, an incendiary fire sweeps his warehouses out of existence, or his goods are plundered by rival revolutionists, and he has to begin again the weary life-in-death existence here. The amenities of life are few, aside from a tropical, equable climate, and the pleasure found in beautiful scenery. The best citizens here have instituted a fine club, the Cercle, at which they can lunch, play billiards and drink West Indian decoctions. I was introduced there, and found delightful gentlemen, the president being the richest man in town.

Several papers are published in the capital, the liveliest being *Le Peuple*, the editor and proprietor of which speaks and writes English, and is the father of nineteen children. Journalism is not without its reward in Haiti, and the road to eminence is always open to young men of enterprise and ability.

## VIII.

### THE HAITIAN CIVILIZATION.

FREDERICK DOUGLAS.

THE Hon. Frederick Douglas, our Minister to Haiti, at the time of my visits, is a celebrity of more than national reputation. Born a slave, yet his great natural force and talents won for him a position that entitled him to the leadership of his race. It interested me greatly to hear his reminiscences of the exciting times of *antebellum* days, and of his intercourse with such famous men as Webster, Winthrop, and the leaders of the anti-slavery movement. Though seventy-four years old at the time I met him, yet his form was erect, his memory of events that had long since transpired was wonderful, and he contemplated writing out his recollections of the stirring scenes through which he had passed. He recalled with affection the memory of his friends in New Bedford, when he made his first "break" for freedom, and detailed his experiences, and his reception as an orator, moved by the wrongs done to his people. As he went with me to visit all the officials here, including those highest in power, not omitting the President, I had good opportunity for comparing this man who had risen to eminence through the force of innate ability and integrity, with those who represented the best products of the Haitian civilization.

Before my arrival, under date of March 2, Mr. Douglas had addressed a note to the President, introducing the subject of the Exposition, and preparing the way for my invitation. This note was responded to by the Minister of Foreign Affairs, reciprocating the sentiments of our Minister, and giving assurances that it was the desire of Haiti to participate, but intimating that, in the absence of the President, who was in the interior, nothing could be done before his return.

I called on the Minister of Foreign Affairs, M. Firmin, in company with Mr. Douglas, Mr. Bassett, and our Vice-Consul. M. Firmin was a black man of great ability, affable, intelligent, and conversant with four languages. I met also the son of the President, a young man of excellent address, of a blue-black complexion, like his father, and, later, was introduced to the daughter and granddaughter of Soulouque, a famous ex-President

## THE HAITIAN CIVILIZATION. 175

of Haiti, who were living quietly here. They, too, had the African features and woolly head, and the easy manners of those who had been in position.

M. Firmin reiterated his assurances of esteem, and his interest in the Exposition, promising to do all he could when the proper time should arrive; but it was decided that I had better go on to Jamaica, and return when the President should have arrived.

I returned to Port au Prince the middle of May, and, in accordance with the understanding with Minister Douglas, was presented to the President, who had arrived during my absence. The national palace is situated on the seaward side of the Champs de Mars; it is an unpretentious building of brick and wood, rambling and misshapen. Ragged soldiers, barefooted and dirty, make a pretense of guarding this abode of authority, and one is ushered through a lower hall, adorned with Gatling guns and statuary of ante-negro times, into an upper saloon with little furniture and of drear aspect, to await the coming of "His Excellency." After a while he appeared — the renowned Hyppolite, the present

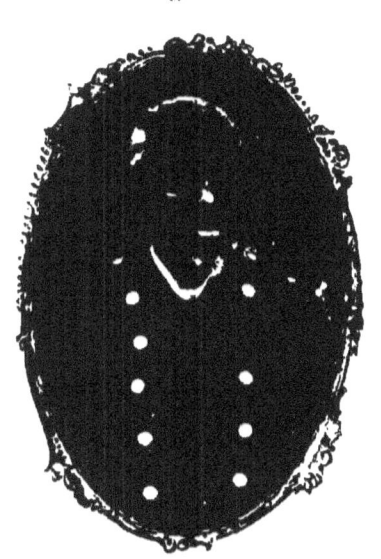

HYPPOLITE.

President of Haiti, the conqueror from the North and actual Dictator. I was presented in due form, my credentials and my mission were recited by the Minister's secretary, and I was then launched upon the long-expected interview.

As had been anticipated, "His Excellency" raised many objections to the proposed participation of Haiti in the forthcoming Exposition; and, in truth, it was not an auspicious moment for negotiation, owing to the very recent attempt at the acquisition of Mole St. Nicolas, and the bad odor of diplomatic failure attendant thereon, consequent upon bad faith on one side or the other. But, ignoring the fact that the President was nursing a feeling of irritation toward our Government, and would welcome an opportunity for the bestowal of a snub, I exerted myself to the utmost to win him over to my cause. It was but too evident, as the President observed and urged, that Haiti had nothing of consequence to send us, and she would run the risk of appearing ridiculous in comparison with other and greater Powers; but that was not the view of the question I chose to entertain. My mission was to get her to accept the invitation of our Government, whether she had an exhibit to send or not; and I determined to work to that end, keeping in mind the moral aspect of the matter, and allowing the subsequent details to settle themselves.

Consequently, when these objections of a purely negative character came up, and the Chief Magistrate arrayed them in order, presenting (as I had to confess to myself) a formidable appearance, I did not combat them; I merely soared above them. Pluming my wings

THE HAITIAN CIVILIZATION. 177

for a lofty flight into the empyrean (at the same time
feeling that the slightest mistake might precipitate a
lofty tumble), I looked His Excellency straight in the
eye, and raised him off his metaphorical feet. In a
word, I appealed to his patriotism, his *amor patriæ*, his
pride, his ambition; I reviewed the glorious history of
conquest, beginning with the immortal deeds of the

HYPPOLITE AND STAFF.

illustrious Toussaint L'Ouverture, and tracing the advance of liberty along the thorny paths of virtue, down
to the present day. I will confess to some misgivings
when I came to mention the doings of Toussaint's successors; but by that time I had really worked myself
into an oratorical frenzy. Magnanimously ignoring
their various misdeeds, I concluded with an impassioned

appeal to the sons of Haiti to remember the glorious triumphs of their ancestors, to recollect that their island was now the cynosure of all eyes, and that the world was watching, with bated breath, their treatment of the problem of self-government. In short, I urged them to send to Chicago an exhibit that should illustrate, not alone the vast natural wealth of Haiti, not alone her material resources, but above all these to hang out the banner of progress, and to show to the waiting world the advanced position she had taken in the galaxy of republics. With outward calm (though not without some inward trepidation) I awaited the President's response. It came, at last. Being a man of intelligence, who had sometimes aroused his own people to action in somewhat the same style, he was, perhaps, at first a little suspicious of my perfervid appeal; but a glance at my hopeful countenance reassured him. He acknowledged that my views were novel, and that he had not entertained them before; but that they were worthy of consideration, and he would submit them to his cabinet.

That was all I could do, and I retired, next day sailing for Santo Domingo; but soon after I had the satisfaction of hearing that his recommendation was adopted, and that the sum of twenty-five thousand dollars had been appropriated toward Haiti's participation in the Exposition. And, to show that it was not, as some of the enemies of the republic averred, an appropriation to be "appropriated" by the enterprise of some greedy politician, the following notice from a newspaper of Chicago, before this book went to press, is submitted:

## THE HAITIAN CIVILIZATION.

"CHICAGO, January 3, 1893. — Of all the foreign powers taking part in the World's Fair, the little republic of Haiti was first to complete its building, yesterday. It was the ninetieth anniversary of the independence of the island, the Haitian pavilion being dedicated in the presence of a small audience composed of Exposition officials and colored citizens of Chicago. Frederick Douglas, ex-minister of Haiti, delivered the principal address, at the request of President Hyppolite. Director-General Davis responded. The exercises were held in the main hall of the building."

Since I recommended the Haitians to make an exhibit illustrative of their advance on the road to civilization, perhaps I cannot do less than present herewith a statement of their actual status, as viewed by acknowledged authorities, and supplemented by my own observations.

The island of Haiti is one of the richest regions, in natural resources, on the face of the globe. God has endowed it with everything necessary for the maintenance of man, and in addition has bestowed upon it blessings, in the way of climate, scenery, and position, that render it an earthly paradise.

The greatest length of the island of Santo Domingo is some four hundred miles, its breadth over one hundred and thirty, and of this the portion known as Haiti occupies the western third. It is well-watered, with rich soil, beautiful scenery, tropical climate, and entirely in possession of the blacks.

The capital and largest city is Port au Prince. It is situated at the bottom of a deep and picturesque bay, facing west, and contains some twenty thousand inhabitants. Its natural advantages are many, but its social and intellectual advantages are conspicuous by their absence. Says a recent resident, one who was compelled to live for years in the city:

"It may bear away the palm of being the most foul-smelling, dirty, and consequently fever-stricken city, in the world. Every one throws his refuse before his door, so that heaps of manure and every species of rubbish encumber the way."

As to the streets, they do not seem to have been mended for the last hundred years. The Haitians have a saying, "*Bon Dieu gàte li ; bon Dieu paré li*"—God spoilt them, and God will mend them. As the "*bon Dieu*" only helps those who help themselves, and as the Haitians have no desire to help themselves in the way of making or repairing their roadways, their condition is frightful beyond description. "The gutters are open, pools of stagnant and fetid water obstruct the streets everywhere, and receive constant accessions from the inhabitants using them as cesspools and sewers. There are few good buildings in town, and none in the country, the torch of the incendiary being constantly applied, and no encouragement offered to rebuild, through protection of the Government or local enterprise. Buildings destroyed by earthquake or fire are never replaced, and the nearest approach to rebuilding is seen in the slab shanty leaning against the ruined walls of a large structure demolished." Fires are continually occurring, and are nearly always regarded as the precursors of outbreaks, or revolutions. During my brief stay several fires occurred, the premonitory symptoms of the great uprising that resulted in the terrible massacre of May, 1891. The town is more than half in ruins, but

## THE HAITIAN CIVILIZATION.

ABANDONED ESTATE — COAST OF HAITI.

the people residing here are a happy-go-lucky lot, good natured, self-sufficient, regarding Haiti as the center of the universe, and their capital as a second Paris.

During the French occupation, or until a hundred years ago, there were large estates on the island, and the planters derived immense wealth from an intelligent cultivation of the soil; but now there is not an estate under cultivation that produces more than enough sugar-cane to supply its miserable proprietors with rum. To the vast and numerous coffee plantations in the hills, the negro laid claim as conqueror, and these estates have been the chief source of Haitian revenue ever since. The negro peasantry in the mountains bring the produce of these plantations down to the cities, where it is taken in hand by the political workers who hold the customs and the bulk of the receipts appropriated. As the only revenue is derived from the customs at the ports, and as there are no other taxes, the most desirable offices in the gift of the Government, are those that enable the occupants to get their hands on the exports and imports. It is no crime to steal from the State, they say; indeed, it has passed into a proverb that passes current everywhere: *Prendre l'argent de l'état, ce n'est pas voler.*"

The office of collector of the port is regarded with highest favor, and if the incumbent does not collect enough for himself in a reasonably short time, he is removed, or "promoted," and another given a chance. This is their chief motive for the numerous revolutions: not the love of country, which they so frequently vaunt, but the desire to have a share in the spoliation of their island. Revolutions have occurred with rapidity and regularity for the past eighty years, and a narrative of the doings of the various black, yellow, or coffee-colored "Presidents" who have foisted themselves upon the people, and seized the spoils of their industry, would be as uninteresting as unprofitable. With here and there an exception, their only aim has been to enrich themselves; and it may be stated without fear of refutation, that there is not the shadowiest semblance of true patriotism in the island of Haiti; if there is, it does not appear in the acts of those in official life.

The present President, Hyppolite, has held office longer than many of his predecessors, having come down from the north of Haiti a few years ago and ousted Legitime, who was then the ruler, but who now languishes in Jamaica, awaiting an opportunity for reinstatement. Jamaica, in fact, is infested with ex-presidents and ex-cabinet officers, anxiously looking across the channel for some sign of disturbance that will enable them to return to their beloved country and more beloved positions of independence. Nearly all the "revolutions" that have appeared so frequently in the press, of late, have had their inception, as well as their scenes of action, in the neutral island of Jamaica. These ex-dignitaries and quasi-revolutionists are nearly all well supplied with funds, having taken care of themselves when in office and "skipped" at an opportune moment. It is only as they become impoverished and the necessity

D. F. LEGITIME.

for labor stares them in the face, that their patriotism asserts itself and they see in the present incumbent a vampire and a traitor to his country, who is waxing fat on the sweat and blood of his fellow-citizens. Then their indignation at these sufferings of the down-trodden and oppressed of Haiti knows no bounds, and they issue *pronunciamentos* calling upon their fellow countrymen to rise in their might and shake off the clutch of the oppressor. And if the down-trodden fellow-countrymen do rise, and in sufficient strength, these revolutionists charter a vessel and hasten to Haiti, hovering in the harbor until well assured their friends are likely to prove victorious, when they dash in boldly and valiantly, just in season to snatch the reward of the customs.

It was less than two weeks after my departure from Port au Prince, in May, 1891, that the bloodiest outbreak occurred in the annals of recent Haitian outrages. A body of men marched upon the prison and liberated the convicts; next they attacked the arsenal, possessed themselves of arms, and met the Government troops; but they were finally dispersed, retreating upon the smallpox cemetery, near the town. They were eventually driven to the woods, but many were captured and summarily shot, more executions occurring in cold blood than in the heat of conflict. The prisoners were shot without trial, so it is said, until over two hundred were executed, and the name of Hyppolite became a stench in the nostrils of the revolutionists. For this massacre of his subjects he was blamed without stint, by those not cognizant with the circumstances and the dangers surrounding him; but the simple truth of the matter is, that it was either Hyppolite or the rebels that must perish, and the President naturally preferred it should be the other party. He may have erred on the side of excessive severity; but at all events, there will not be so many revolutionists to rise in rebellion next time, and the Haitians in Jamaica have since been remarkably quiet.

To show how little attention the foreign residents paid to this massacre that was going on among them, I may quote from a letter written me at the time by a friend dwelling in Haiti, in which he alludes to it as a "disturbance," saying that many summary executions took place in the streets, but that, though many innocent lives were lost, he hoped peace would soon be restored.

Founded as it is upon force, with the strongest man at the head, nominally as president, but in reality a dictator, the Black Republic cannot endure another century as it is going now, without calling to it the attention of the world, and exciting its strongest reprobation. It is the desire of more than one Government that the United States should take this irresponsible Island republic in hand and administer to it a salutary lesson. Nothing short of extermination, some aver, could effect a reform in the Haitian body politic; but as this age does not tolerate the radical measures of the olden time it is not probable that the present generation will experience a reformation. Sir Spencer St. John, who was formerly the English Minister-Resident in Haiti, and who wrote an exhaustive account of the doings in the Black Republic, says of it, amongst other things not complimentary: "No country possesses greater capabilities, or a better geographical position, or more varied soil, climate, or production, with magnificent scenery of every description; and yet it is now the country to be avoided, ruined as it has been by a

A VIEW FROM THE RESIDENCE OF THE ENGLISH CONSUL — HAITI.

succession of self-seeking politicians, without honesty or patriotism." And he adds: "I know what the black man is, and I have no hesitation in declaring that he is incapable of the art of government; and to intrust him with framing and working the laws for our (English) islands is to condemn them to inevitable ruin. What the negro may become after centuries of civilized education, I cannot tell; but what I know is, that he is not fit to govern now. There are brilliant exceptions, doubtless, but as a race they are incapable."

He does not deny that the Haitian of the better class is well educated, as the wealthy class send their children to France, sparing no expense to secure them an education. But he declares that they do not benefit by these advantages as they should, and that the average Haitian is only an American negro with a French veneer.

So many hard things have been thrown at the Haitians, that I myself do not feel inclined to join in the attack; but truth compels one to admit that there is very little visible to the stranger, either in their private or public life, worthy of emulation. It would seem, then, that the Haitian civilization has not been a brilliant success: that, in fact, it has not been advanced any during the century that has passed since the expulsion of the French and the negro has had the privilege of governing himself; but, on the contrary, that it has retrogressed.

At the time of my visit, the city was practically under martial law; soldiers were camped in the streets, cannon and Gatling guns were at every corner, and all life in the streets was suspended after dark. No one could pass unchallenged; the cries of the sentinels were heard on every side throughout the night, with occasional reports of firearms by way of emphasis. The soldiers composing the Haitian army are the sorriest specimens of humanity that were ever put into uniform. They are generally barefooted, clad in rags, and many seek subsistence by begging through the streets. I have been approached many times by these poor beggars, asking alms with humble mien, and satisfied with the smallest coin. The pay of the rank and file, it is said, is only twelve dollars a year, and of even this small sum they are sometimes defrauded. The nominal strength of the army is some twenty thousand, composed of general, staff and regimental officers to the number of about fourteen thousand, and the remainder, privates, who do the fighting and have little chance of promotion. Their guns are rusty old rifles, and the principal weapon which nearly all carry is the "cocomacaque," a tough stick, with which terrible blows can be inflicted. Every man of prominence is called "general," and men of this rank are very numerous everywhere. The "generals" wear all sorts of uniforms, without reference to their rank, apparently; in one group, at Cape Haitian, I saw five brigadiers, each one with a coat of different cut and color from that of his fellows, but all with long plumes in their cocked hats.

In writing of Haiti, one cannot ignore the fact that the masses, especially in the mountains, are steeped in the superstition of the African Serpent-worship, or Voudism. I saw the objects used in the cannibal ceremonies in the museum of the Petit Seminaire, at the capital, which had been taken from convicted cannibals, who were executed for their crimes. These were: a Voudou drum, a *tambou*, collars of the *papa loi*, or high priests, etc.; and these visible reminders of cannibalism set me to inquiring as to its prevalence in the island.

We must not, however, confound the African Serpent-worship, called Voudou, with cannibalism, for the latter is an excrescence, or outgrowth of the former. The whole island is tainted with the Voudou, but comparatively few of its followers practice the grosser rites.

It is distinctively derived from Africa, and has been in practice ever since the first importation of African slaves, or for at least three hundred years. During the French occupation it was suppressed to a great extent, but at the massacres and after the extermination of the white people, it revived in all its original strength. It was then, perhaps, that the horrible practice was introduced of sacrificing white and colored children; and, like tigers that have had a taste of human blood, the cannibals still thirst for it with terrible intensity. They prowl around the settlements, seeking occasion to abduct young white and colored children, whom they carry to the mountains, fatten, keep until certain days appointed for their ceremonies, and then kill and devour. The constant and haunting fear overshadowing every white mother in Haiti is of these *Loup-garous*, or human wolves. Nurses are sometimes in league with them, and even the grave is made an instrument for their horrible designs.

It is well known that the negroes of the mountains are acquainted with the properties of plants as yet unknown to the *materia medica*, and with them work wonderful cures, as well as evil spells, even apparently bringing the dead back to life. So it happens that, when the cannibals are in want of victims for sacrifice, they find some means of administering a native narcotic, which soon produces coma, and apparent death, to some white or colored child, and after it is buried, disinter and resuscitate it for their horrid feasts.

The serpent is the deity of the Voudous, and he is represented by a high priest, called the *papa loi*, and a priestess, the *mama loi;* meaning the father and the mother king. Their commands are absolute, and no sectary dare disobey them. In this lies their menace to good government, and it is well known that even some of the rulers of Haiti have been dominated by them. The worship of the serpent is carried on as secretly as possible; the sectaries are bound by oaths of secrecy, and their incantations take place in the night. The serpent is consulted, through the priest or priestess, and the devotees then indulge in dancing and song, generally ending in the grossest forms of debauchery.

Thus far, except for the influence exercised by the *papa* and *mama loi* and the menace to the State of an oath-bound order of the most degenerate people, the Voudous are not particularly objectionable; but they are soon carried away by excess of frenzy, and demand a further excitement in the shape of a sacrifice.

Usually, this offering of propitiation to the serpent is in the form of a goat or a cock, always white and spotless. These offerings satisfy the milder members of the order, but there are others who will not be content without the sacrifice of a child. This human offering is called "the goat without horns," and when such a

## THE HAITIAN CIVILIZATION. 191

demand is made means are always found for furnishing a victim. Verified statements of the occurrences of such sacrifices and the subsequent cannibal feasts have been made to the authorities, and men and women have been shot for their indulgence in them. Within a few years an account was published in the leading paper of Port au Prince of the arrest of some men and women who had carried on a regular business of killing people and of selling their "meat" in open market. This was in 1885, and a year later the same paper makes mention of the arrest and conviction of several people who had killed and eaten others, and among the victims the sister-in-law of the chief.

But enough has been cited to show that cannibalism still flourishes in Haiti, and that it will take more vigorous action on the part of the authorities than has yet been exercised to extirpate this evil.

## IX.

### THE BUCCANEERS AND THE BLACK KING.

ADJACENT to the north coast of Haiti, less than five miles distant from the harbor of Port de Paix, lies the desolate island of Tortuga. It was at one time the pirates' rendezvous, the ancient haunt of the dreaded buccaneers.

This small island, called by the Spaniards Tortuga, from its resemblance to a sea-turtle, *tortuga de mar*, commands the great sea channel between Cuba and Haiti and the water highway to Jamaica. Early perceiving its importance from a strategic point of view, the pirates who had marked the commerce of Spanish America for their prey, took possession of and held it for many years.

It had no harbors large enough for the entrance of ships, but it abounded in numerous coves and shallow bays, while the interior was a vast and tangled forest; the situation was, therefore, all but impregnable. With their sentinels on the watch for the richly freighted galleons coming up from Panama and the Spanish Main, the pirates had the king of Spain's revenues at their mercy. Many a million in gold and silver have they carried to that wild retreat, and to many a bout and carousal have the now desolate crags reverberated. Orgies were the order of the night, and murders the business of the day, while Spanish wine supplied the stimulant, and Spanish gold procured the luxuries of the world.

The discovery of Tortuga was coincident with that of Haiti, for Columbus sought shelter from a storm in a

TORTUGA — THE PIRATES' PARADISE.

bay on its southern shore, one night in December, 1492. Thirty years later the French, who had been attracted to the Spanish acquisitions in America, drew stealthily into the Caribbean Sea, and the French corsairs became annoying.

In the year 1529, a French squadron was in the Caribbean, and an English vessel arrived at Santo Domingo. In 1538 (the same year that De Soto arrived at Havana), a protracted and bloody sea-fight occurred off that port between a Spanish and a French corsair, while in 1541, the year that Orellana sailed down the Amazon, the French and English did great injury to the Spanish trade; though the West Indies were then in decline, while Mexico and Peru were yielding stores of gold and silver.

In 1563, that prince of slave stealers, Sir John Hawkins, brought negroes from Africa to Spanish American ports, which he had obtained "partly by the sword and partly by other means," and sold them at immense profit. Nine years later, in 1572, there came into these seas, pillaging and burning, Sir Francis Drake — that knightly pirate, who, the year following, from a peak in Darien, first saw the great Pacific, the waters of which no English keel had ever cleft.

Succeeding the invasions of these pirates, came another class of voyagers; the adventurous colonists. Another noted name now rises against the widening horizon. For, in the year 1585, Sir Richard Grenville, with seven sail, cruised from Dominica to Puerto Rico, and thence to Virginia, where he left a colony of one hundred men upon the island of Roanoke. The year following, Drake, after attacking and capturing Santo Domingo and Cartagena, coasted Cuba and Florida, and finding the perishing colonists on Roanoke took them home to England. The next year came the expedition of Mariner White, who, with three vessels and one hundred and fifty men, sailed between Dominica and Guadeloupe and touched at Santa Cruz. Here the sailors were poisoned by the attractive manchineel apples lying on the sand, as the log-book quaintly says: "By eating a small fruit like green apples they were fearfully troubled with a sudden burning; also a child at the breast had its mouth set in such burning that it was strange to see how the infant was tormented for the time." On the fourth of July, 1587, they made Haiti; on the sixteenth, Virginia, and on the twenty-second landed at "Haterack," where the first child was born. And this first infant born to that ill-fated colony of Raleigh's, was Virginia Dare. Thus we note how inextricably interwoven are the threads of history in this New World, and the intimate connection between the sunny isles I am describing and our northern colonies.

Sir Walter Raleigh, who had long viewed this western continent from a distance, at last arrived at Trinidad and ascended the Orinoco, in 1596. Sir Francis Drake died the same year, and was buried at sea, off Porto Bello. The closing decade of the sixteenth century finds English ships everywhere ploughing West Indian waters, and, in 1607, three great names sail across our vision as we scan those southern seas. Sir Christopher Newport, in company with Captain John Smith and Bartholomew Gosnold, sighted Martinique, landed at Dominica, and in Guadeloupe found a wonderful hot spring. "Our admiral, Captain Newport, caused a piece of pork to be put in it, which boiled it so in the space of half an hour, as no fire could mend it." Thence, after three weeks among the Caribbees, they sailed by way of Nevis, to Virginia, founding the first permanent colony on the James. Ten years later, Raleigh again sailed for the Orinoco, in the ill-fated *Destiny*, from which expedition he returned to be beheaded in the Tower.

And now, after this roundabout digression, pursuing those historical personages who had invaded our chosen field of action, we return to the little island off the coast of Haiti; for it was shortly after Raleigh and his companions had done their work of colonizing that this island rose to prominence.

The English and French colonists were looked upon by the Spanish as intruders; they were ousted on every occasion, and, in 1630, a Spanish admiral, Don Frederic Toledo, drove them away from the island of St. Kitt's, where they were doing no harm, forcing them to seek another retreat. The most desperate of them settled on the island of Tortuga, joined with them some Dutch adventurers, styling themselves the "Brethren of the Sea," and began to prey upon the Spanish commerce. The Spaniards termed them ".Filibusteros," from the little boats they used called *filibotes;* hence our term, filibuster; but eventually they received the generic name of "Buccaneers," derived from the Carib word *boucan* — applied to the process of cooking meat on a spit over an open fire, in the Carib Indian fashion. They derived many words direct from the Carib; as, for example, *ajoupa*, a native hut, which is used to designate such a shelter to-day; I myself have many times slept in the woods beneath an *ajoupa*, my companions the descendants of the very Caribs from whom the buccaneers obtained their words and wigwams.

During the greater part of the seventeenth century

## THE BUCCANEERS AND THE BLACK KING. 197

these buccaneers ruled the seas adjacent to Tortuga, and even made plundering expeditions to Cuba and the Spanish Main. They divided themselves into groups, or bands, one for plunder on the high seas, one for hunting the wild cattle that swarmed in the island of Haiti, across the channel, and another for killing and salting the meat of the wild hogs. They were rarely defeated in an encounter, for they fought to the death, sinking or burning their boats when they boarded an enemy, and staking everything on their ventures.

Their first great leader was called Peter the Great, and his initial adventure as their captain signalized him as desperate enough for any deed of blood or daring, for he boarded the ship of a Spanish vice-admiral, seeking him out in his cabin, and taking the big ship through sheer pluck and bravado, having only a handful of men at his back.

The greatest name the buccaneers have handed down to history is that of Morgan, who, with twelve sail and seven hundred fighting men, took and sacked many cities on the Spanish Main. In 1671, he captured the city of Panama. Then, with the immense plunder in his possession, he retired to Jamaica, where he lived in honored retirement, and was knighted by the British crown. Another famous buccaneer was Van Horne, who robbed Vera Cruz of over six million dollars, and escaped with his boats in the sight of a Spanish squadron.

Now and then the buccaneers turned their attention to the sunken galleons that storm or battle had sent to the bottom of the sea, recovering great treasure therefrom; but the largest "haul" of sunken silver was made by a man of different pursuits in life, under the very noses of the buccaneers, and at the time they were in the heydey of their career. This man was Sir William Phipps, the New England baronet, and at one time governor of Massachusetts. He raised a wrecked galleon off the coast of Haiti, and took from her thirty-two tons of silver, and pearls and jewels to the amount of one million five hundred thousand dollars.

But the trade gradually became too precarious for even the hardy settlers of Tortuga, and at last the merchant vessels were freed from their depredations, except for desultory attacks. Attracted by the fertile fields of Haiti, across the channel, many of the buccaneers turned planters, bought or stole slaves for the cultivation of their estates, and settled down to earn an honest livelihood. This departure may have taken place about the beginning of the eighteenth century; at all events, the best portions of the larger islands were eventually appropriated, and those vast sugar and coffee estates were begun that at one time supplied France with much that she obtained from abroad.

From men who had trodden the quarter-decks of pirate ships, and from their descendants, what could be expected but cruelty and oppression in their attitude toward their slaves? The French planters had the reputation of being more cruel than any others. In the year 1768, it was estimated that one hundred and four thousand slaves were bought on the coast of Africa —fifty-three thousand by British merchants alone; the consumption of negroes at that time was some sixty thousand annually, and the total number up to that time brought into America estimated at above nine million. During the first decade of the nineteenth century, it is said that negroes were so abundant in the West Indies that slaves were "cheaper to buy than bread." It was

OLD BUCCANEER WATCH-TOWER — COAST OF HAITI.

in 1789 that Wilberforce, in the House of Commons, made his famous plea for the abolition of the slave trade; the annual shipment from Africa to the West Indies, at that time, being thirty-eight thousand, of which a great number perished on the voyages.

The French colonies received their share of the imported slaves, and it was admitted that Africans were brought to the island of Haiti even during the revolution. Regarding this great uprising, by which the richest colonial possession of France was completely lost to her, we have but little space for details. Briefly stated in the words of another writer: "The summoning of the States-General in France created much enthusiasm in Haiti; but all classes were disappointed: the planters, the low-class whites, the free blacks, and the colored; while the slaves, although discontented, were only formidable from their numbers. The firebrand that lit the combustibles was the utterance in the Assembly, 'Perish the colonies rather than a principle,' on the fifteenth of May, 1791. . . . The negroes of the North rose in insurrection, put to death every white that fell into their hands, and then rushed *en masse* to pillage Cape Haitien; but the French troops drove them back to the mountains."

The ferocity of the negro nature then had full swing; and all the prisoners were put to death with terrible tortures. Several leaders assumed to command. Eventually there rose to view preëminent among his fellows, that Haitian whom history and poetry have made known to fame as Toussaint L'Ouverture. He was born a slave, on an estate called La Breda, in the north of Haiti, near the city of the Cape. There he remained until above fifty years of age, when the exigencies of the revolution called him to the front. Tradition says that he was indirectly descended from an African prince, but when I made inquiries at the Cape, in 1892, this story was laughed at by the Government representative. In 1796, Toussaint had gained complete ascendancy in the North, Cape Haitien being the capital and center of operations, and by the year 1800 the whole of Haiti was under him.

The island was finally united and on the road to promised prosperity, for Toussaint's rule was enlightened and wise, and he showed signs of being anxious for the highest welfare of his people. He prepared a liberal constitution, which he submitted to Bonaparte, but the latter unwisely replied by sending soldiers instead of encouragement, in the person of General Le Clerc with thirty thousand men. The French general tried to surprise the Cape, but the negro general, Christophe, then in command, set fire to the city (applying the torch first to his own house) and retired to the mountains. Toussaint gave orders to his other generals to follow this example; but finally, influenced through the defection of some of his officers, he submitted to Le Clerc; he was later arrested, sent on board a French ship, and taken to France, dying a captive in exile. Not long after, a fearful epidemic fell upon the French soldiers. What the natives could not accomplish the fever did, as it carried off some forty thousand victims in the two years of 1802 and 1803, among them being the commanding officer and twenty of his generals.

Freed from the French, whose evacuation of the island took place on the twenty-eighth of November, 1803, the Haitians had only themselves to contend against. Dessalines a negro, was chosen general-in-chief, and on the first of January, 1804, an Act of Independence, signed by all the generals, was promulgated.

In this they swore to posterity, to the whole universe, in fact, "to renounce France forever, and to die rather than live under her dominion;" an oath they and their descendants have nobly kept.

Dessalines was a monster of cruelty, whose name has long been held in detestation, and his accession was signalized by the massacre of all the whites who had hitherto escaped the fury of the blacks. But his reign was short, as he was killed by his own troops, in 1806.

Two rival chiefs then fell to fighting for the succession, and the country was deluged with blood; but finally, in March, 1811, an act was passed establishing a Haitian royalty, and General Christophe was declared king, under the title of Henry I.

Christophe, the first black king in America, was a negro from the English island of Grenada, and spoke both French and English, though pretending not to understand the latter when it might serve his purpose to remain in ignorance.

The Haitian burlesque of royalty was most complete, and the world has never witnessed a more delightful piece of buffoonery than the establishment of the "royal court," the elevation of ignorant black men to the ranks of the "nobility," and even the creation of an order of knighthood. The "Knights of St. Henry" have long since disappeared; the royal court held its last audience many years ago; but the titles of nobility (though conveying no meaning) still survive; the Count of Lemonade, the Duke of Marmalade, etc., are frequently heard of, and an "Almanach Royal" was published so late as 1820, giving the list of the nobility, the officers of State, the privy council, and the knights of the order of St. Henry.

I myself recall a meeting with a descendant of one of these *ci-devant* nobles on the saline back of Cape Haitien, where I was photographing some natives. As I was picking my way through the mud, two horsemen cantered by, one of them in the faded and tattered uniform of an officer of the guard, with a cocked hat on his woolly head and enormous spurs on his naked heels. Inquiring the name of this imposing individual, I was informed that it was no less a personage than General Limonade, who resided on the ancestral estates near Petit Anse, and who did the best he could to maintain the prestige of his noble grandfather. The grandiloquent dispatches of the Count de Lemonade are part and portion of Haiti's history, and his fulsome eulogies of Saint Henry may be found in a volume entitled "Relation des Glorieux Evenements" of the great king.

It was as a despot that Christophe ruled in the North, plundering his subjects, who held their lives at his pleasure, and building his throne upon the murdered minions who prostrated themselves before him.

He was a savage, with a desire for the advancement of his people to the rank of those who had long enjoyed the benefits of civilization, and, too, he tried to force them. He invited scientific and learned men from abroad; he encouraged commerce and protected foreigners; he established schools, and promoted a feverish activity that subsided at his death. But his passions, and not his intellect, drove him on, and if balked in any of his plans he wrecked revenge upon the nearest victim, with most ferocious cruelty. He massacred a great number of colored women, at the Cape, on the strength of a rumor that they had prayed for his defeat in battle, and no domestic circle was safe from his invasion. An English minister, writing in 1830, states that he saw, at the Cape, a ruffian-like negro who at one time was chief executioner to the king, but was then acting as a common porter. He was a savage of massive build, and it was told of him that he had acquired such dexterity, from long and frequent practice, that he could, with his saber, decapitate a man at one blow, without staining his collar with blood.

The character of Christophe has been accurately analyzed by Minister Mackenzie, who visited the scenes of his cruelties and achievements only six years after Christophe's death, and upon whom I have relied for my data in this description. "As an ignorant, untaught man, he may be considered one of those phenomena that occasionally excite attention, but leave scarcely any beneficial trace behind. He seems to have had a rare degree of native acuteness, activity, intrepidity, and the art of commanding the respect of those around him. These qualities, however, united with his absolute ignorance, were disadvantageous, as, while they made him master of one view of a subject, he was blind to every other; and thus, knowing nothing of the almost imperceptible degrees by which alone civilization can be rendered permanent, he attempted to carry his object by storm, and succeeded, until bodily infirmity convinced his barbarian subjects that he was mortal. With all his strength of mind he could not resist the temptation of encouraging a belief that he was protected by a tutelary demon, who would have instantly avenged any insult offered to him. It is also said that he had great

SANS SOUCI — THE BLACK KING'S PALACE.

faith in the sorcery of Obeah. With all his atrocities, he was an affectionate father, and endeavored to place his children above him in mental culture."

His efforts to improve the condition of his subjects were futile, and of his great enterprises not one has conveyed a lasting benefit. But the black king has left behind him at least two monuments to his genius that are unique and unapproachable. These are his royal palace and his mighty castle. As has been mentioned, he invited scientists and architects to Haiti, and the structures erected during his reign show that the latter possessed talent of the highest order. This is shown in the palace of Sans Souci, and the great fortress of La Ferriere. The palace was built at the head of a beautiful valley, two hours' ride from the Cape; the castle

SANS SOUCI — RUINS OF THE BLACK KING'S PALACE.

was erected in the mountains the same distance farther on. I visited both, of course, and was lost in wonder and admiration, alike at the genius that could conceive, and the will that could execute such stupendous works. It is necessary to ride thither on horseback; but good beasts are difficult to procure at Cape Haitien, and had it not been for the kindness of Mr. Frank Dutton, son of the agent of the Clyde steamers and a merchant of repute at the Cape, I should have had to take the journey on foot. Mounted on the gallant roan Mr. Dutton had loaned me, and with two intelligent friends acquainted with all the points of interest along the route, I cantered gayly over the road to Millot, the town nearest the palace, and reached it at dusk after two hours in the saddle.

The first view of Millot and the palace is obtained through an avenue of tall trees, nearly a mile in length, its yellow walls shining over the greensward and against a furrowed mass of wooded hills. It is beautiful beyond description, and the air of desolation hanging over the scene enhances the soft beauty of the landscape, giving the charm of romance to one of Nature's loveliest creations. Notice of our arrival had been sent ahead, and we were domiciled in the hut of the schoolmaster of the village of Millot, which settlement was once dependent upon the palace and court for subsistence, and now lingers in the memory of happier days departed. Our host was a black man of good presence, who placed all he had at our disposal, and gave us assistance without asking anything for his trouble. I had been provided with letters to the commandant of the station here — for without permission from General Alexis, commanding in the North, no one can visit this spot — and in the morning several soldiers were placed at my orders, and we explored the palace. It is now in ruins, as earthquakes have rent its walls and shaken its foundations; but even in its decay it gives evidence of magnificence beyond anything ever attempted elsewhere in the West Indies. In truth, it may be called, taken in connection with the fortress, the wonder of the islands. Situated in a most commanding position at the base of high hills covered with tropical trees, and pouring down sparkling streams of purest water, with a view of the vale of Millot spread at its feet like a bit of earthly Paradise, dotted with cocoa palms, and with the palm-covered huts of simple cottagers peeping out here and there; with a climate soft and provocative of luxuriant tropic growths, this palace of Sans Souci must have offered a retreat from the cares of the world such as few spots on earth can afford.

As you ascend the hill, at the left is a circular ruin, once the chapel of the king; beyond this a long flight of steps leads to the esplanade; above it are the terraces and the stairs leading to the palace itself. It is roofless, with great trees (the *ficus indica*) growing out of crevices and fringing the walls, while vines of many kinds creep in and out the windows and doorways. In a court outside stands a great star-apple-tree, beneath which King Henry held audience with his officers, and behind the palace are the remains of extensive gardens, irrigated with water from the hills. There are numerous apartments in the palace, and the room is still shown (though inaccessible now from the falling of the stairway) where Christophe killed himself. This event occurred in the year 1820, at the news that some of his generals had revolted, and were marching upon Millot. The king

THE BLACK KING'S CASTLE.

was then suffering from partial paralysis, but with terrible energy he called for a bath of stimulating herbs, mounted his horse, and tried to take the field. But the disease had too strong a hold upon him, and he was compelled to retire to his room. There, realizing that his end was near, he shot himself with a silver bullet, and in the morning was found dead.

His remains were taken to the castle, two hours farther in the hills, and there his tomb may be seen to-day, surrounded with high and frowning walls.

One bright morning we climbed the steep trail that led from the palace to the castle. The trail so rough that I feared for the footing of my brave steed. It led along the bases and brinks of precipices, and all the way through wild coffee groves and banana gardens, with such glorious views of land and distant sea that I was filled with delight and thanksgiving. At last we reached the fortress, built upon a high hill in the bosom of the mountains, far distant from all human life, and so solitary that it pained one to contemplate it. A work that would command the attention and admiration of man in any country, that would have taxed the genius and resources of any people, even with the aids of modern civilization close at hand. Yet this great fortress was built by a semi-savage; all its material had to be drawn from the wild mountains, all its defensive equipment imported from other lands, whence, also, came its architects and its skilled workmen.

An old negro appeared out of the surrounding wilds, announcing that he held the key of the castle; and gradually a retinue of barbaric boys and savage-looking men surrounded and followed us up to the grim entrance of the tower and into the gloomy apartments. A heavy door protects the only entrance; and this once gained you find yourself in a dark keep, climbing out into a covered way, and at last crossing a deep fosse over a narrow plank that now takes the place of the ancient drawbridge. Thence we groped our way into the low galleries filled with cannon — long rows of grim monsters of the last century — some captured from the king of Spain, some purchased from France, and some of England. There were three hundred of them, the guide told me — and I believe it, from the number lying in the galleries, and scattered about the fortress. And every cannon was hauled up here by toiling, suffering men, urged to incredible labors by the tyrant's brutal overseers. Some of these guns must have weighed four or five tons each, being those old pieces as long as a Columbiad, heavy and unwieldy. No one knows to-day how they were taken here, except that it was solely by the unaided labor of men, and through long years of toil.

My guide related an instance of Christophe's cruelty and the torments he inflicted on his men. One day, seeing a party of some forty men toiling vainly at the removal of a heavy gun from low to higher ground, he inquired the reason of delay. The overseer told him they could not start the cannon. "Take away twenty of those fools, and haul it up with what are left," thundered the tyrant; and it was done. It is not strange that the trail was full of dead and dying laborers, and that the walls of La Ferriere are built upon the bones of a thousand victims of the cruel king.

The castle walls tower above one, standing at the entrance, to a height of nearly a hundred feet; they are rent and toppling from earthquake shocks but are still strong and massive. Within this vast fortification Christophe built chambers for storing grain, powder and ammunition, it being his intention to make this his last

OLD MORTARS IN THE BLACK KING'S CASTLE.

retreat. For he ever feared the return of the French, and it was his intention to retire to this fortress, as his forlorn hope, and here immure himself, in this place which Nature and man had combined to make impregnable. To this end he accumulated here vast stores, and I have seen thousands of flints and balls, in the chamber devoted to the ammunition. It is said that at the time of his death he had hidden here more than thirty millions of dollars. I have penetrated the inmost recesses of the treasure-vaults, have seen there several old iron chests, clamped and bound about with hoops, their locks

BROKEN ARCH — THE BLACK KING'S CASTLE.

broken and their lids wrenched off, just as they were left by the plundering soldiers after the death of the tyrant. We wandered about the fortress for hours, coming upon some new thing at every turn, and I was forced to render tribute to the misguided genius of this great and fierce nature warring with the forces of his environment.

His character is well illustrated in a story the guide

told me of the time when Christophe lived here. One day a fearful thunder-storm swept over the fortress. The savage nature of the king responded to this warring of the elements, and he awoke to the implied challenge of the bolts that struck his castle. "Aha!" he cried, his eyes gleaming and dilating, "the Almighty thinks he can frighten Christophe, does he? *Sacre — Tonnerre!* we will show him that we can make as much noise as he can. Ho, there, gunners! stand by all the guns. Load them to the muzzle. Fire! all at a time. Again, again, all! give the Almighty good as he sends! I, the king, will show him what it is to thunder!"

The great guns roared their salutes, drowning the din of the elements, filling the galleries with sulphurous smoke, amidst which the sable gunners appeared like demons; and the heart of the savage was filled with a fierce joy, having had a tilt with forces elemental, and silencing with a counterblast the voice of Heaven's artillery.

In the center of the fortress stands the tomb in which were placed the remains of Christophe, in 1820. But it is vacant, having been rifled of its contents by vandal tourists and revolutionists. The bones are said to have been large, and to have belonged to a man of immense frame. His bones are scattered and no one knows their resting-place; his works are crumbling, but still attest the indomitable will, the striving after greatness, the blind groping for power, of this great savage, who has the honor of having been the first black king in America. His castle is in ruins, his palace an abode for owls and bats, while the people he strove to elevate are as deep as ever in the mire of ignorance, and apparently lapsing into savagism.

Down at Millot I found a relic of his times, in a beautiful bust of Melpomene, stuck up in the dirt in front of the barracks. Carved from pure white marble, the classic face and shapely shoulders showing those perfect curves, yet the Muse of Tragedy was degraded to this. I revenged this outrage to my æsthetic sense, by placing a dirty soldier on one side of the Muse, and another on the other, and photographing them thus: a type of Haiti.

BEAUTY AND THE BEASTS — FOUND AT MILLOT.

## X.

### THE FIRST AMERICAN CHRISTMAS.

AS we have digressed, in the last three chapters, from the course pursued by Columbus, we will now return to gather up again the threads of history temporarily dropped. Taking his departure from the eastern point of Cuba, at Cape Maysi, the Admiral sailed easterly until he finally saw before him the towering mountains of a magnificent island which, while yet more beautiful than Cuba, was strikingly different in the sweep of its hills and the contours of its shores.

The fleet of Columbus, consisting of the *Niña*, the *Pinta* and the *Santa Maria*, had held together during all the tedious voyaging across the ocean and through the Bahamas; but, on the coast of Cuba, Captain Pinzon had sailed off on his own account, so that but two vessels and less than one hundred men arrived off this unknown island, on the sixth of December, 1492.

The native name was *Bohio*, and the Cubans had called it *Babeque*, describing it as a region where the Spaniards would obtain in abundance the precious metal for which they were continually inquiring and seeking. The Indians resident here called it Haiti:

"Ai," high, "Ti," land, or the Island of Mountains, and by this native appellation the western portion is still known. To the eastern half the aborigines applied the term Quisqueya, or "Mother of the Earth," now called Santo Domingo.

The western portion was also known as Bohio, the "Great Country," the word itself being still used in

A RELIGIOUS PROCESSION AT CAPE HAITIEN.

the interior, to designate the huts of straw or cane built and occupied by the poorer people.

The port of Bohio first entered by Columbus, he called Saint Nicolas, in honor of the saint's day on which it was discovered. It is the same Mole San Nicolas over which the governments of the United States and Haiti almost had a quarrel, a year or two ago. Sending the little *Niña* ahead for soundings, the

Admiral followed in the *Santa Maria*, and dropped anchor in the spacious harbor to which the smaller craft piloted. Desirous to unfold the beauties of the coast beyond, Columbus and his crew did not tarry long, but sailed on again, a storm accelerating their progress until they found refuge under the lee of Tortuga. Beyond, again, they opened up a delightful valley with a fine river flowing through it, and withal so beautiful that the Admiral mamed it *Val de Paraiso*, or the Vale of Paradise. Leaving its harbor at midnight, their next anchorage was off a sandy beach near which was a large native village, since known as Port de Paix. Here the Spaniards saw a great many Indians, whose king, or Cacique, told them that the Land of Gold, Babeque, lay two days' sail to the eastward. Pursuing the direction indicated, they next anchored in the great bay of Acul, of which Columbus writes in his first letter: "I have now been at sea twenty-three years, with scarcely any intermission, and have seen the East and the West; but in all those parts I have never witnessed so much of perfection in harbors as in this."

It was in this beautiful bay that they first heard of the Indian king, Guacanagari, so famous subsequently, and so unfortunate, and who assisted them to pass their first Christmas in comfort. Here, also, for the first time they heard of the heart of the gold country — the Cibao. This Columbus, in his eagerness to arrive at the regions of the Grand Khan, felt sure must mean the Cipango described by Marco Polo in his most wonderful book. Cacique Guacanagari cordially invited the strangers to visit him, and accompanied the invitation with a rich present: a cotton girdle, attached to which was a mask with ears, tongue and nose, all of beaten gold. This golden present seemed such an earnest of

THE SANTA MARIA, THE FLAG-SHIP OF COLUMBUS.
(*Wrecked Christmas eve, 1492.*)

the rich gold mines beyond, that Columbus lost no time in following after the returning messenger, and one morning at sunrise the ship and the caravel spread their sails to the breeze, and sailed again along their eastern course. The day was bright and beautiful, and nothing presaged the dire disaster that was so soon to overtake them. The breeze was light and baffling, but the sea was smooth as glass, and unseen currents drifted them along. For three months the sailors had been apprehensive of accident, and on the lookout for some calamity; they had feared the trade-wind would always blow from the east, and that they could never return to Spain; that if they sailed so far down the watery hill they could never sail back again; they feared the serpents and the mermaids, the submarine monsters and the terrene bipeds, but they never dreamed, now that their fears had been allayed, that the evil spirits of the sea were even then hurrying their vessels to destruction. Yet so it was. The two vessels drifted over the glassy sea till near midnight, when the Admiral, worn out with constant watching, retired to his cabin to sleep. Following the example of their commander, although they had been cautioned by him to maintain a careful watch, the seamen then on deck also seized the occasion to sleep, leaving the helm in the sole care of a boy.

I always felt pity for that boy; the only mention of him at all is the brief statement that the helm was left in his charge. But, although he goes unmentioned thereafter, I am sure he got kicked and cuffed by the sailors for their own negligence! Poor little chap! I can imagine his terror when the accident happens, and his big black eyes filling with tears at the reproaches of the men. The winds were light and the sea was calm; but there was an unseen force at work tugging at the vessel's keel, that the mariners had not reckoned on; a strong and treacherous current that forced the *Santa Maria* upon a sand-bank, and the first intimation the boy at the helm had of anything amiss was through the beating of the waves against the side of the ship. The rudder became immovable, and the young sailor, greatly alarmed, cried out to the men who, with the Admiral, acted with great promptitude, lightened the vessel, cut away the masts, and carried an anchor out to windward; but all to no avail, for the ship was too firmly fixed in the sands.

She was a total wreck, and the crew were finally transferred to the *Niña*, which came as near to the reefs as was deemed prudent, and lay by till morning. This, in brief, is an account of the first accident of moment that befell Columbus on his first voyage to America.

He was then, as we have seen, on his way to visit Guaçanagari. When the vessel struck the reef, he was only four or five miles away from the Indian village of Guarico. Columbus lost no time in sending news of the disaster to the chieftain and imploring his assistance, which was at once afforded, the Cacique sending a fleet of canoes to the reefs, in which all the wreckage was taken to the shore and stored in huts assigned by Guacanagari for that purpose near his own residence.

It was on Monday, the twenty-fourth of December, on the eve of our Lord's nativity, that the little fleet sailed from the bay of Acul, arriving at the scene of disaster about midnight. The first hours of the morning succeeding were passed in rescuing the wreckage, and in conveying it all to Guarico. At dawn this had been accomplished, and at daylight the shipwrecked mariners were sharing the hospitality of the noble Guacanagari. Not a man was injured, not an ounce of

THE FIRST AMERICAN CHRISTMAS.   223

THE WRECKED CARAVEL.

provisions lost, not a spar nor a nail detachable that was not safely landed with them; yet in the words of Robinson Crusoe, "what an awful deliverance" was theirs! The rising sun of that Christmas morning shone with tropic fervor, the dewy thickets of precious woods exhaled delicious odors, the birds caroled their welcomes to the morn; yet these men noticed not the signs of awakening life around them, so plunged were they in deep despondency.

And this was Christmas morning. This was the first recognition of the birth of the Christ-child in this New World then just brought to light. And how did they pass the day? At first, deep gloom enwrapped them all — these hundred men, two thousand miles from home, and with but one frail caravel to take them back. But the Cacique was unwearied in his attentions; his grief at the disaster was so manifest, and his attempts to divert them from their trouble so delicately proffered, that finally hope returned to cheer them, and they thought upon their blessings.

The little *Niña* lay anchored off the village of Guarico, and at sunrise of the day after Christmas, the Cacique paid a visit of state to the Admiral, when Columbus was so pleased with his frank and manly bearing that he repeats his encomiums, declaring him preëminent in virtue. While the king was on board, his Indian subjects swarmed in canoes around the caravel, holding out pieces of gold, and crying out, "Chug, chug!" intimating that they wished to barter the nuggets for hawksbells, over which they went wild with joy. Seeing that such trifles brought in exchange great pieces of gold, Columbus was delighted, and at the sight of the pleasure expressed in his countenance, Guacanagari, quick to note the change, assured him that if gold was the object of his desires, he would direct him to a region where the very stones were golden, and where it was in such abundance that the people dwelling there held it in light esteem. This region he called Cibao, which Columbus construed to mean Cipango, so long the goal before him in his voyagings. He found it later, on his second voyage, and thence drew millions of treasure.

After breakfasting, the Cacique took the Admiral ashore, and spread a banquet, at which several sub-chiefs were present, probably coming from the interior, each one wearing a coronet of gold. Two of them presented their coronets to Columbus, and confirmed the story of the abundance of the precious metal in the mountains of the Cibao.

Guacanagari also wore a golden crown, but nothing else save a shirt and a pair of gloves, given him by Columbus, and of which he seemed prouder than of his coronet. The repast consisted of *ajes*, or nutritive roots, shrimp, and native bread called *cassavi*, which is in use there to-day. After it was over, he rubbed his hands with fragrant herbs and washed them carefully. More than a thousand Indians are said to have been present, and the Admiral, wishing to impress them with his strength, sent for a Moorish bowman, who astonished the natives with his skill. Afterward a lombard was fired, the report of which so frightened the Indians that they all fell flat on the ground.

From the wreckage of the *Santa Maria*, from its strong timbers and planks, a fort was constructed near the village of Guarico, and in it a garrison was left; for the remaining vessel was not large enough to carry them all, and many of them desired to stay. Work on the fort proceeded so rapidly that it was completed within ten days. It was in the form of a tower, protected on every side by a broad and deep ditch. Thus was founded the Fortress of Navidad, the first structure raised by Europeans in America. Small cannon, called lombards, were mounted on its walls, the garrison of forty men were supplied with biscuit for a year, as well as wine, besides all the merchandise that remained, that they might exchange it for gold. And Columbus, in his letter apprising his sovereigns of what had been done, wrote that he trusted in Providence that he should return here from Castile and find at least a ton of gold collected, as well as spices in great quantity.

Then he sailed away, leaving here this handful of men in a land of savages, not one of whom would he ever again behold alive.

Where did the flag-ship founder, and where was the first fort built? These have been vexed questions with the historians, ever since Columbus became an interesting subject of study; it was to attempt to unravel the mystery surrounding those important events, that the writer was dispatched to Haiti, in 1891 and 1892.

And it was my good fortune to unearth a chain of evidence that brought to light many important facts, and placed in the possession of our own Columbian Exposition an invaluable relic of the *Santa Maria*.

In brief: the reef on which the flag-ship grounded lies off the city of Cape Haitien, an important port in the island of Haiti; a mile or so distant is Point Picolet, called by Columbus, Punta Santa. Rounding Point Picolet, that memorable Christmas Eve, the *Santa Maria* was forced by the current upon the first of a line of reefs that stretches in front of Cape Haitien, from three to five miles distant, and a little farther from the Indian village. This Indian settlement of Guarico has been located at the present bourg of Petit Anse, two miles from Cape Haitien; it is now partly in ruins, and occupied by fisher-folk. There is a small chapel here

IN PETIT ANSE.

rudely furnished, and a few small huts and houses, while beyond and around are extensive salines, or salt-flats, and the coast in every direction is low, and bordered with mangrove swamps.

We know that everything pertaining to the wrecked vessel was brought here, and that the fort was built near Guacanagari's village for mutual protection; hence we must look for its site not far away. This site I have found on the summit of a small hill, called San Michel, isolate in the saline and near the beach, with slopes so nearly perpendicular as to appear artificial. I found no relic there; but its position, so near the ancient Guarico, the only elevation within two miles or more, and its strategic advantages over every other situation, marks it, without much doubt, as the spot where Navidad was founded.

Passing over the subsequent events of the first voyage of Columbus, let us have recourse to the journal of the second, and learn at once the fate of Navidad. The *Niña* had sailed for Spain, leaving the little garrison alone in the fort. Eleven months later the Admiral returned, as he had promised he would, with a large fleet, to receive the ton or two of gold he confidently expected. They arrived in front of the fort, but it was night, and as a vessel had been lost here the year before on these same reefs, no communication was established with the shore, but the ships lay to till morning. Two cannon were fired, but there was no response from the shore, which lay enwrapped in darkness, without sign of light or life.

Great uneasiness prevailed throughout the night, and in the morning early a boat was sent to land, when the fort was found dismantled, not one of the garrison being encountered alive. It was learned finally that a few of the garrison had died of disease, a dozen had been killed in an expedition into the mountain region, and all the rest had been massacred by the fierce Caonabo, the Cacique of the Golden Mountains, who had secretly marched upon the fortress in the night. He had also killed many of the subjects of the friendly Guacanagari, who was found by the Spaniards reclining in a cotton hammock, suffering from a wound received in personal encounter with Caonabo himself.

We cannot believe that the Cacique had any part in the massacre, except in defense of the garrison, and even the suspicions of Columbus were allayed at sight of his wounds and his tearful protestations.

Columbus had come here with the intention of establishing a settlement, but, although Guacanagari would have welcomed him, notwithstanding his village had been burned, and his people ruined by the coming of the Spaniards, yet the Admiral was too much oppressed by what had occurred to entertain the thought of founding a city upon the ruins of Navidad. The situation was excellent, the scenery magnificent; but a pall of gloom now overshadowed this fair land, which he had discovered only a few months previously rejoicing in plenty and peace. So he sent a caravel along the coast to search for a site.

The founding of Navidad is the most interesting incident of the first voyage of Columbus, after the first discovery of land. Hence, anything throwing light upon that exciting episode should be welcomed by the world as an important contribution to the stores of history. Such contribution I have made, and its authenticity established beyond a doubt. Arrived at Haiti, I landed in the port of Cape Haitien, on the northern coast of the island. I had an important clew to a most valuable "find," and at once sought out our Consul, who because of my official position as Commissioner of the Columbian Exposition, put me in communication with the head of the Government. This gentleman was General Nord Alexis. He was the actual president in the North, having rendered invaluable aid to President Hyppolite in his struggle for power.

It so happened that the brother-in-law of the general owned the estate upon which was the article I sought, and he took me out to view it. This relic was nothing more nor less than an anchor of the *Santa Maria*. A learned friend in Santo Domingo had told me of it, and I was most anxious to obtain a view of it, and, if it

SOLDIERS OF THE GUARD AT REST.

proved a genuine relic of the past, to purchase it. My friend had investigated the subject, and had determined that it could be regarded as authentic. It is a very natural question: How can you prove the genuineness of an anchor lost four hundred years ago, and trace it back to the very ship from which it was taken? This would seem difficult, on its face, but if I had the space I could give all the links in the chain of circumstantial evidence which leads directly back to the time and

THE ANCHOR OF COLUMBUS — FOUND AT PETIT ANSE.

scene of the wreck. However, I think I can make out a case without wearying my readers.

Following the main features of the historical narrative, we recall: that the fortress was entirely destroyed; that all the men were killed; that some of the plunder was found scattered about in the huts of the natives, and amongst these articles recovered, "an anchor of the caravel which had been wrecked." We know that the spot at which the wreckage was deposited was Guarico, now Petit Anse; that near this point a fort was built, and stocked with everything necessary, and that on the return of Columbus in the latter part of the year 1493, everything was destroyed or dispersed. Following out the clews afforded him by unvarying traditions and the historical evidence, my friend then discovered two ancient anchors, one about two, and the other three miles from Guarico, and bearing every evidence of extreme antiquity. Each is of forged and hammered iron, about nine feet in length, and with a great ring over a foot in diameter. Sketches and photographs have been sent to Paris and Madrid, and these have been pronounced types of the anchors in use at the end of the fifteenth century.

ST. JOHN AND THE AGNUS DEI.
(*Carving at Petit Anse.*)

At the time he re-discovered these anchors, my friend was living at the Cape, and from the proprietor of the estate on which one of them was found he received it as a present. But he did not take it away, and when I met him in Santo Domingo, he very kindly gave me permission to take it for exhibition at the Columbian Exposition at Chicago.

Armed, as I have already stated, with a letter of introduction to the proprietor, I went in quest of the relic. General Nord's brother-in-law was also a "general," but, unlike the legion of black gentlemen at the Cape who bear this title without a distinction, he had seen actual service. Together we rode over the salines, and then through scattered gardens and the remains of ruined estates, to the ruins of the old "great house," about three miles distant from the city. The estate is one of the many wrecked plantations left abandoned at the time of the massacre of the French, a hundred years ago. The general, my companion, is descended from one of the black liberators, to whom, as a portion of his share of the spoil, fell this once beautiful estate, now in a condition of abandonment. We rode through the remains of a great avenue of tall trees, and hitched our mules at the corner post of a dilapidated dwelling.

A few yards distant stood the anchor, leaning against the stone pillars of an old well-curb, across which it had once been placed as an attachment for a rope and pulley. A single glance convinced me of its genuineness, and that, if not the veritable anchor of Columbus, it belonged to the times in which he lived. If it should be asked how came it so far from the shore, and a mile away from its conjectural landing-place, at Guariao? I should say, first, that it may have been brought here for the very purpose which it so evidently served. Again, it may have been carried a distance inland by the Indians, after the attack on Navidad.

Either the mountain chieftain, Caonabo, undertook to transport it to his interior province, and, finding it a burden, dropped it on the way, or else, in their ignorance, reasoning blindly that the anchor was an engine of destruction, or essential to the working of the caravels on the sea, the simple savages had intended removing it as far as possible from the coast. No mention is made of any plunder of importance carried away by Columbus on his second visit, and not only the anchors may have been left, but also the lombards of the fort; which, likewise, may have been taken by the Indians to a distance, or to their strongholds in the mountains. But there it was before me at last, and I lost no time in negotiating for this precious relic, with the result that next day it was on board the Clyde steamer, the *Ozama*, and on its way to Chicago, via New York and Washington.

## XI.

#### ROUND ABOUT ISABELLA.

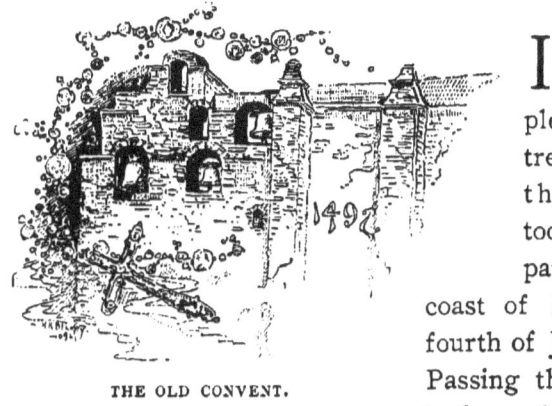

THE OLD CONVENT.

IT was after having completed the fortress of Navidad that Columbus took his final departure from the coast of Haiti, on the fourth of January, 1493. Passing the reefs that had wrecked the *Santa Maria*, their largest vessel, the Spaniards sailed toward the east, and anchored at the base of a high, tent-shaped mountain, which Columbus called Monte-Cristi, a name it bears to-day.

About a league distant from Monte-Cristi they watered their boats at a river, the sands of which glistened with particles of gold. Many of these precious particles clung to the hoops of the water-casks, and, for this reason, Columbus gave the stream the name of *Rio del Oro*, or the River of Gold. He did not, however, stop to explore its sands, but left that for the garrison at Navidad to do, as they were but eight leagues distant. Here, also, the Admiral saw those wonderful mermaids, three in number, standing high out of the water, and which have since been shown to be manatees, abundant in this River Yaqui, the name by which the *Rio del Oro* is known to-day. Columbus avers that he had seen

HUCKSTER'S SHANTY, ON THE RIVER YAQUI.

such mermaids before, in Guinea and on the Pepper coast; but he says these American mermaids, though they had the faces of human beings, did not appear so handsome as represented. Any one who has seen the only American mermaid — the manatee, I mean — will agree with the Admiral that its face is not attractive.

A little more than a year later, Columbus sought out the source of those golden sands, and I, who followed in his wake four hundred years after, have a half-ounce nugget, from the head-waters of the River of Gold. I did not see the mermaids he describes, but I have seen the great gray sharks that infest the harbor of Monte-Cristi, the shooting of which from the steamers' decks, is about the only diversion afforded a passenger on the coast-line vessels.

It was at Monte-Cristi that they met with the derelict *Pinta*, their companion across the Atlantic. The *Pinta* had run away from them when off the coast of Cuba, and had made an independent voyage to the eastward. Martin Alonzo Pinzon was her captain, and his brother, Vicente, was master of the *Niña*, so that Columbus, being in a measure at their mercy, could not reprimand Don Martin Alonzo as he wished. That he nursed his wrath, however, and took revenge when once back in Spain, is a matter of history. But the two little vessels were now together again, and they remained in company till a storm separated them off the coast of Spain.

Setting sail from Monte-Cristi at midnight, on the ninth of January, they cruised in company along the coast of what the Indians had told them was Babeque, or the Land of Gold. Its shores, eastwardly from their port of departure, were very attractive, and Columbus went into raptures over "the country beyond them; level and beautiful, with tall mountains in the interior reminding me of the Sierras of Cordova, and the whole abounding in streams, and offering views of such variety, that the thousandth part cannot be described."

And in truth, as I myself can testify, there was no exaggeration in this enthusiastic language, for the north coast of Santo Domingo presents the grandest combinations of natural attractions the voyager could desire. The discoverers were then coasting off the locality in which, one year later, the initiatory attempt was made at a settlement, and to which Columbus returned on his second voyage.

Abundance of sea-turtle were found along the shoals, many of them as "big as a buckler," and the second day they sighted a most magnificent mountain, with its feet in the sea and its head in the clouds. This mountain Columbus named *Monte de Plata*, or the Silver Mountain, because its crest is usually cloud-capped and wears a silver turban. Hence the name, and that of the town subsequently founded here, called Puerto Plata, to-day the most enterprising and the prettiest settlement on the coast of Santo Domingo. An excellent harbor was noted here, with a depth of fourteen fathoms at the mouth; and with the knowledge of its many advantages, it is a matter of wonder that Columbus did not return here, instead of passing it by to found the city subsequently started a year later at Isabella.

Once having left the coast of Santo Domingo (or Española, as Columbus named it), the Spaniards sail beyond the bounds of this volume. We know, however, that the home-voyage was tempestuous; that Columbus believing the vessels would sink, prepared a statement of his discoveries, inclosed it in a cake of wax, and cast it into the sea; that they made first land at the Azores, and were driven by a storm to the mouth of the Tagus; that they gave an account of the voyage to the king of Portugal, and that the *Niña* finally anchored in the harbor of Palos, on the fifteenth of March, 1493, after an absence of seven months and a half.

The court was then at Barcelona, and going from Palos to Seville, Columbus made thence a triumphal journey across the entire peninsula of Spain. Of his enthusiastic reception, of the honors heaped upon him, when he was dignified with the title of "Don" and confirmed in his claim to be styled the "Admiral of the Ocean Sea," we can make no mention here, merely noting that which concerns the land we are describing. But it was at the court at Barcelona, as shown in Balaca's spirited painting which has been selected as the fitting frontispiece for this volume, that were first displayed the Indians, the parrots, the golden ornaments, the rare plants supposed to possess medicinal virtues, and many another thing the Spanish sovereigns wondered at and admired.

Soon after the Admiral's arrival at court, royal orders went forth for the preparation of a fleet of seventeen vessels, to be well manned with most experienced seamen and pilots, and also to carry miners, carpenters, husbandmen and mechanics — such persons, in fact, as would be of the greatest service in colonizing.

Besides the crews and mechanics, great numbers of adventurers desired to embark, including in their number many hidalgos of high rank, lured by the stories of gold and silver to be had for the seeking in that far-off land.

These "gentlemen of Spain" proved the most worthless of all recruits for colonizing; they mainly committed the murders; they brought disaster to Columbus. They were brave; many had fought in the Moorish wars, and carrying out their schemes of plunder they carried fire and the sword amongst a peaceful people who had never lifted their hands against another except in self-defense. At last the fleet of carracks and caravels — seventeen sail in all — left the harbor of Cadiz, on the twenty-fifth of September, 1493.

On the third of November, land was sighted, in the Caribbees, or Southern West Indies, but it was not till the twenty-fifth of that month, after leisurely sailing through that golden chain of islands, that Columbus arrived at the site of Navidad. As we know, he found the fortress destroyed and the garrison massacred; and, whatever may have been his original intention as to fixing here the settlement he had been commissioned to found in the New World, the circumstances attendant upon his return thither prevented, if he had ever contemplated, the consummation of such a scheme.

The aspect of brightness worn by the country less than a year ago, was now changed to one of gloom. Confidence in the Indians was impaired, suspicion and distrust had taken its place. The occupants of the vessels were anxious to disembark, even suffering for a change of environment; but no settlers could be induced to fix their abode here, with the fate of their predecessors ever in mind.

The fleet weighed anchor, and stood eastward from Monte-Cristi, and Fate, in the shape of an adverse wind, threw in their way what they had been so anpiously seeking — a secure harbor, with an advantageous site for settlement. It was not far from a cape seen and named by Columbus on the previous voyage, in January.

Within a line of frothing coral reefs is a deep basin, spacious enough for many ships the size of those in use in the time of which we write, and a great breastwork of coral rock, with a beautiful beach on one side and a river on the other, gave promise of an excellent site for the city that was to be. The ships were brought within the line of reefs, and the weary passengers, together with the live-stock and provisions, were landed on a little beach.

It was on the seventh of December, 1493, that they arrived here, and they went to work with such diligence that soon houses were built, and at least four buildings erected of stone, the remains of which have endured till the present time. Two months from the day of landing, a church was dedicated, and the new city, which Columbus had named "Isabella," presented a very creditable appearance. But it was not long occupied. Because of the insalubrity of the climate and the recklessness of the settlers, many deaths occurred, and in a few years it was abandoned. Ever since, or from the beginning of the fifteenth century, it has lain in desolation, no one living in it, and as it lies out of the track of travel, its very site was forgotten, and re-discovered only recently. For nearly four hundred years it remained buried in obscurity, and almost forgotten until the year 1891, when it became my duty to search it out.

The nearest port is Puerto Plata, about sixty miles away, and at this place I disembarked, one day in May, 1891. Two days after my arrival, I found a small coasting vessel, called a *golcta*, the captain of which promised to drop me at Isabella, as he passed on his way to the mahogany district. The American Consul secured me letters of introduction to residents in the country, and

THE BAJO-BONICO.
(*The River on which Isabella was founded.*)

the manager of an estate situated near Isabella gave me orders on his *mayor-domo* for shelter and assistance.

From Puerto Plata down the coast the scenery is extremely picturesque; near Cape Isabella great gray cliffs of limestone stand boldly out, like battlements of vast fortifications, with a sea of verdure behind and crescentic beaches of snow-white sand intervening. The ancient city itself was situated on a plain which terminates in a bluff of coral conglomerate twenty to thirty feet high, facing the west and the ocean. A line of foaming breakers seems to forbid approach, but beyond them is a shallow harbor, off the mouth of a river which is known as the Bajo-Bonico.

The *goleta* was called the *Olivia*, a pretty name for a very filthy vessel, and she was manned by four black men. The blackest of whom was the "captain." The heavy seas and the nauseous odors made me very ill, and I had to endure six hours of condensed misery before the breakers off Isabella were weathered and the little harbor gained. As we anchored half a mile from shore, the rain came down in torrents, and for an hour we were huddled together in the sweltering hole they called the "cabin." After a while the rain ceased, my effects were loaded into the small boat, and we made for the river. We could see no entrance, but we finally ran the breakers, and after bumping on the sands several times were well inside. We then found ourselves in the dreariest river I had seen for many a month. It was a swift-flowing stream of yellow water between banks of mangroves, the only sign of life some blue-and-white herons, plovers, and black-neck stilts. Our boys pulled hard against a four-mile current, and half a mile up landed us opposite a collection of small houses on a bluff. We were met at the landing by a young man who had once lived in Florida; and, though we were in a Spanish-speaking country, all the men then in our employ spoke English, the sailors having come from Grand Turk, in the Bahamas. The young man, Washington Banks, had been recommended by our Consul, so he was at once installed as factotum and general purveyor. He took us to the house on the bank, which we found to be a very

ON THE BLUFF AT ISABELLA.

comfortable dwelling; here we swung our hammocks, and we were well housed against the rain, which fell the whole night through.

At daybreak, next morning, the mocking-birds awoke us, and crawling out from under our *mosquiteros*, we shook the fleas from our blankets and were assailed by myriads of mosquitoes and sand-flies. At six o'clock or so, after the morning coffee, Washington or "Wash," as he was called, guided us along the steep river bank and through a dense forest growth in the direction of the lost city.

The morning was cool and fresh, the bushes wet with rain, the trees above filled with birds — cooing doves, moaning pigeons, chattering parrots, with now and then a darting humming-bird, crossing our path like a sunbeam. Beyond the woods we passed through a mangrove swamp, with the river on one side and steep coral rocks on the other, reaching after that a bluff headland, covered with densest vegetation of cactus and almost impenetrable thickets of spiny plants.

This bluff faces the west, and is composed of coral conglomerate, evidently upheaved, containing branches and sections of coral, beautiful in shape and infinite in variety of form. This is the plain upon which unvarying tradition, as well as ancient ruins and environment, locate the city founded by Columbus and called by him Isabella, after the Queen of Spain. It is not large, containing perhaps two acres. It slopes gradually upward toward steep and densely-wooded hills, on either side a half-submerged basin covered with mangroves. The soil, in no places deep, becomes thinner and thinner toward the hills, where there is none at all except in holes in the white coral rocks; and yet, these rocks are covered with a dense growth of such hard woods as lignum-vitæ, and such a mass of thorny bushes and vines as to be well-nigh impenetrable. The bluff faces the ocean, west; the forest-covered hills lie to the east, while north and south are the mangrove swamps. The northern one is sometimes filled with water and looks like a lagoon, and when the water comes down from the hills, as it does in the rainy season, through a picturesque *cañada*, and as it did when Columbus landed here, it must appear like the "lake," as he called it.

It was around this lake that the first settlement was located, and directly in front of it is a beautiful beach of yellow sand, where, without doubt, Columbus landed, as a channel admitting small vessels through the reefs comes directly up to the sands. This beach is two hundred and seventy-five feet in length, with a coral bluff at either end, and a border of sea-grapes behind and between it and the mangroves of the lagoon. Here, four hundred years ago, the caravels and carracks disembarked their living freight of sea-worn sailors and Spanish cavaliers, the horses the cattle and the sheep. Here were accumulated the munitions of war, the provisions, plants, articles for trade and barter, and the little beach piled high with the freightage of the ships. Even to-day the sands sometimes disclose most interesting relics of that far-away time when first the products of Europe were landed on American soil. I have had in my hands a fragment of chain armor and a stone ball, which were found here, and I possess pieces of the tiles that covered the houses erected by the Spaniards, and of the crucibles in which the first gold was smelted.

The morning sun lay aslant the beautiful beach, and cool shadows lurked in the hollows of the rocks, tempting us to strip and plunge into the limpid waves that lazily lapped the sands. "Wash" was dubious about this experiment, because the water inside the reefs is sometimes alive with barracudas, more dreaded by the natives than the sharks; but we paddled about in great glee, and emerged refreshed and unharmed. After that, and during the week that we were there, a bath on the beach in the cool of early morning was our regular "refresher." I used to take a big stick in with me, plant it firmly in the sand beneath the water, and with the stick always within reach swim about to my heart's content. And so gentle was the movement of the water that the stick would sometimes remain where I had placed it till our return, next morning. Many a tropic bath have I enjoyed, in river and sea, but the sea-baths are the best, and taken at early morning are delightful preparatives for the labors of the heated day. The morning is always cool, no matter what the day may be, and it is a luxury merely to lie on the beach listening to the songs of the birds. No less delightful was the exhilaration of the plunge, the freedom of a vigorous swim, and the abandonment of floating listlessly on the breast of the wave, looking up skyward into the fleecy clouds.

Lying on my back, and watching the clouds as they floated over, I tried to bring back those departed days when this solitary beach was populous with soldiery, and I imagined the men-at-arms coming here to bathe. The clang of metal as they divested themselves of their heavy armor, the sigh of relief as they at last stood free from the galling steel, and the pleasure that possessed them as their brawny arms parted the waves. Yes; even the "Great Admiral" must have bathed here, and have found at least temporary relief from the thousand cares that harassed him, as the waters closed around him. His serious nature could not find pleasure in the bath as a diversion — but history would record fewer sins against him to-day, if his taciturnity had been penetrated by these simple delights, and he had allowed himself to become as a little child, at one with Nature. Nature's children, the Indians, would have suffered less at his hands, and letters of gold might to-day record his deeds, instead of letters of blood.

Overlooking the beach, at its southern point, once stood, according to tradition and the evidence of visitors of fifty years ago, a pillar of masonry, or a monument, which formed a conspicuous landmark, visible some distance at sea. Local tradition states that this pillar was destroyed about fifteen years ago, and the marble tablet it bore carried away. It is supposed that it was erected by Columbus, to indicate the site of the city to passing vessels, and its destruction is attributed to treasure-seekers, who blew up its foundations hoping to find it covered hidden gold.* It was seen by Mr. Gibbs, of Grand Turk Island, in the Bahamas, who, some fifty years ago, came here for the purpose of comparing it with two similar ones that then existed in the Bahamas, at Grand Turk and at Sand Key. He thought that these monuments were built to commemorate some great and similar event, extrinsically connected with the places themselves. Be that as it may, the only indication of the Isabella monument now, is a hollow in the earth surrounded by heaps of loose stones.

---

* Paper read before the New York Historical Society, sixth of October, 1846, by the Hon. George Gibbs, in support of Turk's Island as the Landfall of Columbus.

Fifty years ago, much of the original city was visible, and in the midst of the forest the traveler saw all the remains of the structures erected by Columbus: the pillars of the church; remains of the king's storehouse; part of the residence of Columbus; the small fortress, and a circular battlemented tower. When Mr. Gibbs

SITE OF ISABELLA.
(*The first city of the New World.*)

was here he saw the ruins of the church, fifty feet wide by one hundred feet long; now nothing can be seen but the faintest outline. Nothing remains here as a structure, or of great importance as a ruin: shapeless heaps, only, or *montones*, of stone and brick, with here and there a hewn rock, occasional shards of pottery and fragments of tiles. From the northern point of the bluff, where the pillar stood, following along the shore, there is a semi-lunar-shaped heap of débris about a hundred feet long. A little farther on, at about the center, a quadrilateral depression in the soil, where the church once stood, and near there are some traces of what may have been a fortified wall, and scattered stones. At the southern bluff, overlooking the river, and perhaps five hundred feet from the pillar-site, is the most conspicuous *monton*, or heap of stones, mixed together with tiles. This is conjectured to have been the "king's house" or the smelting works, where the gold was assayed that the explorers brought from the mountains. I found several hewn stones here, as well as heaps of tiles, and what we think were the fragments of crucibles. This is the most commanding point of the bluff, and it appears possible that the river, though now some distance away, once laved the base of the cliff. Not far away, buried in the woods, is another large heap of stones and bricks near a hole some ten feet deep. This is supposed to have been the powder-magazine, and has often been searched for treasure.

The week previous to my visit, a party of naval officers, from the United States steamer *Enterprise*, made a hasty examination of the plateau, and their excellent report substantially verifies my own. They concur with me that the place was well intended for defense, locally advantageous as the site for a small settlement, but illy-adapted to the requirements of a large and permanent population. The entire plateau is now covered with dense thickets of thorny and spiny plants, chiefly cacti, very difficult to penetrate, but presenting strange and beautiful shapes, and through them most entrancing glimpses of the bay, the river, and the sea. It is a beautiful site for a camp, and notwithstanding the difficulties of penetrating the undergrowth, I wandered about in great delight, visiting the bluff at sunrise, at sunset, and at heated noon.

The beauty of the place was not the motive that induced Columbus to settle here, but probably its contiguity to the gold region of the Cibao; for, by passing up the Bajo Bonico, and then crossing the plain beyond, the mountain-pass could be reached that gave entrance into this region. It is difficult to account for the total disappearance of all the buildings in the comparatively short space of four hundred years, unless the stories are true that many of the best buildings of Puerto Plata are built out of the rocks taken from Isabella. Time alone would not cause this marvelously rapid disappearance, and the hand of the vandal has been more destructive than the tooth of time.

Founded as Isabella was, in order to give access to the interior mines, as soon as the line of forts was established, in 1494 and 1495, the tide turned thence, and toward Santo Domingo City in 1496, and it was soon after abandoned. We know that after the men and cargoes were landed and the settlement well begun, Columbus cast about for means of communication with the gold-country, and selecting a small body of adventurous men, he sent them out to explore. They broke through the mountain wall beyond the plain and followed an Indian trail through its defiles to the beautiful valley beyond. Before them then lay the valley of the Yaqui, and along its banks they marched far into the interior region of the Cibao, where they discovered a great deal of gold, in nuggets and grains, the sands of the rivers glistening with it. This was the first Spanish expedition into the interior, and the gold brought

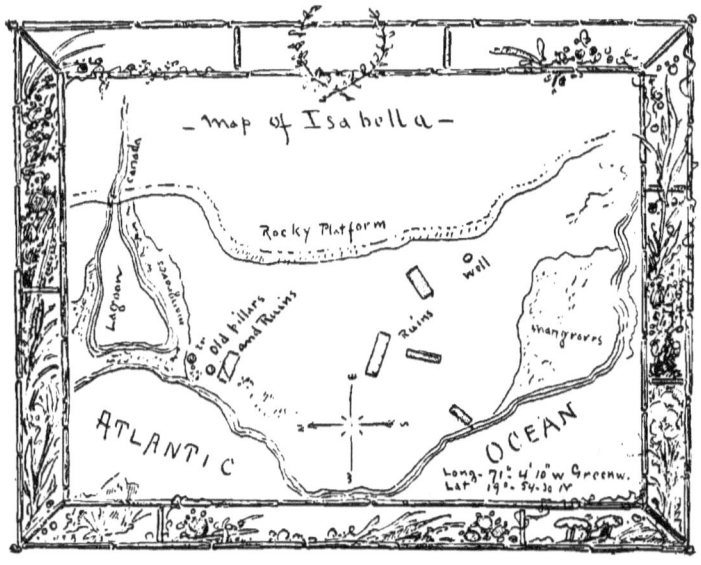

MAP OF ISABELLA.

out was sent to Spain in the fleet that returned in February, 1494.

It did not take long to ascertain the little that remained of Isabella — a day or two did that — but the remainder of a week was consumed in proving what was not there. This is always the task of the explorer. He must investigate and search out, not alone the actualities, but the fallacies and distorted statements. What

I refer to is this: there was a tradition current that the original church built by Columbus was not at the bluff, but deep in the forest. Furthermore, it was said that it remained even now, only partially in ruins and retaining much of its ornamentation. This, of course, fired my imagination and stimulated my desire for research, and I at once made careful inquiry. "Wash" Banks declared that he himself had seen it; but when I had dispatched him on an exploring expedition all by himself, the result was that there was no result, though he declared the ruins existed nine years ago, and that he believed they had been removed bodily, possibly by the spirits, which, as everybody knew, haunted the site of dead Isabella. He then bethought himself of a native who had seen it within a year, while out in the woods hunting wild hogs. This man was a mahogany-cutter, who was drifting some mahogany logs down the river, and wouldn't reach us until the next day. When he arrived, he was not very prepossessing; he was stark naked and the color of the mahogany logs he had brought along; for he had been two days wading and swimming the river, pushing the logs ahead of him. He rolled the timbers upon the bank and left them there, in just the place where another lot had been left, which had been carried out to sea and lost, the last time the river came down in a freshet.

This mahogany-cutter had been working several days to earn a dollar and twenty-five cents, which he did not get after he had earned it. He received only an order on a merchant at Puerto Plata for that amount, and for this he would have to travel one hundred miles. Even then, he would find that one dollar and twenty-five cents cash was a euphemism for "goods," to the value of perhaps sixty cents. It was hard for the poor fellow; but I had little sympathy for him, because, when asked what he would take to guide us to the ruins, he replied very

THE CACTUS-COVERED RUINS OF ISABELLA.

promptly, "Twenty-five dollars." He claimed to possess an exclusive right in the ruins and meant to make me pay for it; but as I made a point of "no ruins no pay," we did not conclude a negotiation.

It so happened that an old woman in the kitchen had overheard the man describe the place to a friend, as he stepped in to light his pipe, and when he had gone she offered to guide us. So one morning we started out —

or at least we essayed a start, for it always takes these people a long while to be about to begin. Arrived at the bluff, I separated my party, placing them within hail of each other, and covering the entire plateau as well as the hillside.

We worked carefully, traversing the woods in every direction, but without result. We crawled through thickets and briers, sweltering in the terrible heat, pestered with mosquitoes and sand-flies, but meeting with no noxious insects. The bushes were thickly hung with spider-webs, occupied by bad-looking owners; but we did not encounter, fortunately, the very poisonous ground spider, whose sting is death, though it is abundant there. After some hours, we all met, by appointment, in the *cañada* at the head of the lagoon, and after refreshing ourselves started again, probing the woods in every direction, but without any reward.

The old lady had worked as hard as any of the party, and seemed as little fatigued. They called her *La Vieja*, or the old woman. When *La Vieja* saw that we had exhausted our endeavors, she came to the rescue with a proposition to invoke the powers that hide in darkness, with which she professed to be familiar. In order to humor her, I assented, and she led us back to the fort at the bluff, and then to the *pozo*, or the well, in the woods. Here she halted at the foot of a tree. Producing from her ragged garments a candle made by her own hands, of the brown wax of native bees, she lighted it, and commanded us all to keep silence. Then, carefully protecting the flames from the wind, she mumbled something over it, watching anxiously the direction of the smoke, and then said, pointing east, "Go there; that way is the *capilla.*" So I started my men off east, *La Vieja* with them, ranging toward the hillside. But they soon came back exhausted, every one, and cast themselves down upon the sands beneath the sea-grapes where I was awaiting them. *La Vieja* was not at all downcast at the failure of her incantation, but was exceedingly chipper, and walked home with us through the terrible heat without showing the least fatigue. And so our hunt for the ruin ended.

In the Smithsonian Museum, at Washington, are two idols of carved wood, from the island of Santo Domingo, grotesque in appearance and of unknown antiquity. No one knew where they were found, or their history, until I stumbled upon the information here at Isabella. "Wash" brought an old negro, with bushy brows, and mounted on a jackass all too small, to the door, one day, and explained that he was the man who had found them, and that he would conduct me to the cave in which they were taken. We walked an hour through the woods on the hill, over the narrow trails made by the wood-cutters, to a slope where, half-hidden in the thickets, was the yawning mouth of the cavern.

Old "Coco," the bushy-browed negro, showed me the shelf of rock upon which the idols were sitting when he discovered them. He came upon them suddenly, as he was cutting lignum-vitæ, some fifteen years ago, having had no previous warning of the cave's existence. He was so frightened that he was completely paralyzed, and dropped on a rock, unable to move his eyes from those hideous and grotesque beings which grinned at him from the cave's mouth. He, of course, thought them alive; but as they did not offer to get down, he recovered confidence, and advanced to examine them. Then he saw their character, took them down, and carried them home with him. Poor old idols! they had been sitting there, probably, for nearly or quite four hundred years, waiting patiently for some enchanter to come along and remove the spell that held them there. They had been placed there, in all probability, by the last of the Indians who once resided here, either to save them from falling into the hands of the Spaniards, or to be worshiped in secret, guarded by their priests. "Coco" thought they were there as guardians of treasure buried in the cave, though he found no other articles at the time of the discovery. We penetrated the cavern

COCO'S IDOL.
(*Now in the Smithsonian Institution.*)

perhaps sixty feet, and then could get no farther, owing to the masses of rock in the way, probably dislodged by an earthquake. No living thing was observed there except small crabs and numerous cockroaches.

Having investigated everything that had been the object of the journey, after a week's residence here I concluded it was time to go. But I was loath to leave this pleasant place, and at night strolled up the hill and into the woods to a point that must have been a favorite outlook with the early settlers — those poor unfortunates who perished here so far from home and friends. Little wonder that Columbus was execrated, but great wonder that he was not killed, by these dupes of his ambition. They died so rapidly that consternation seized them, and sickly Isabella was abandoned as soon as the interior was opened to adventure.

They were fine hidalgos, these victims of Isabella, whose ghosts yet retain the traditions of departed greatness and high-bred courtesy, for they yet haunt these same woods, it is said, lingering in the ruins. They can be distinguished from ordinary and common spirits by their invariable politeness to a stranger; for some of them, it is declared, have been encountered here, and, though wrapped in gloomy meditation, they courteously returned the salutes, which indicates innate refinement in ghosts that have been running wild in the woods four hundred years.

I waited late, hoping to get a glimpse of one, and much regretted that there was no moon; but the sun descended, the shadows grew to shades, and the woods became black long before I left them; and I cannot say that I saw an Isabella ghost. The night before our departure, the horses were sent over by Don Ricardo; their fodder of Guinea-grass was piled before them, and they themselves were tethered to the fence. There they remained through the night, and we took an early departure for Puerto Plata on the morrow.

## XII.

#### WHERE THE FIRST GOLD WAS FOUND.

IN what spot and at what time was found the first American gold?

We know that the yellow metal was first seen by Columbus in possession of the natives of Guanahani, in the Bahamas, but only rarely and in minute particles. As the Spaniards progressed through the islands, and reached the coast of Cuba, evidences of a golden country to the south grew stronger; but it was not until the coast of Haiti was reached that indubitable proof was obtained that the region of riches was not far away.

Just before the shipwreck of the *Santa Maria*, golden ornaments were brought them by the natives, in such quantity that even the most skeptical were convinced. The Indian chieftain, Guacanagari, gave Columbus some gold and told him of Cibao, in the mountains, which Columbus was certain must be the Oriental Cipango, or Japan, so long and vainly sought.

It is to this veritable Cibao, which yet retains its Indian name, the similarity of which to Cipango deceived Columbus, and which yet yields nuggets of purest gold, that I shall conduct my readers in this foray into fields historic. The first voyage accomplished and the first settlement effected, Columbus next turned his attention to the development of the interior of the island, and the discovery of the gold region.

Isabella, the first city founded in the New World, was an unfortunate selection as the site for a settlement. Its immediate environment of mangrove swamps was inimical to health; its harbor was not a secure one for large ships; its soil was scant and poor, and added to these it was so crowded upon by the rocky hills, and hemmed in by river and lagoon, as not to permit of expansion. In fact, it was a fairly good situation for a camp or a village, but not ample enough for a city. It had been planted by Columbus solely with a view to its contiguity to the gold region, and unless gold in abundance could be found in the hills and mountains within reach of the sea, the enemies of the Admiral could prove that he had committed a blunder in his initial settlement, which would surely injure his cause at the court of Spain.

A preliminary expedition had brought back sufficient gold to warrant the belief that it existed in quantity, and could be found in abundance by systematic exploration. This gold was sent home by the return fleet to Spain, together with a most flattering account of the country. Then, anxious to bring to light the hidden treasure in the mountains, and at the same time to pacify the

## WHERE THE FIRST GOLD WAS FOUND. 261

haughty spirits of his insubordinate cavaliers, Columbus organized a second expedition into the Cibao region, and assumed personal command. The previous one had been merely a reconnoissance; this one was to have for its object the founding of a fort. It was also intended that the warlike equipment and display should be such that the Indians would be impressed with the strength and resources of the strangers, and perceive the futility of subsequent attack upon the isolated outpost then projected.

The total population of Isabella at this time was about one thousand men, and of this number Columbus selected four hundred of the choicest spirits to accompany him on this expedition. They marched up the main river bank, rejoicing to escape their irksome confinement on the plain between the mangrove swamps. Flags were flying, drums beating, and trumpets sending forth their inspiring sounds, while in the semi-obscurity of the forest glittered helm and corselet, lance and arquebuse.

The first day's march took them across the plain between the sea and mountain range, at the foot of which the weary soldiers encamped for the night. Next day they began the ascent of the range; and as the tortuous Indian trail would not suffice for the passage of this body of men, with cavalry and munitions of war, it was necessary to open a road. Then it was that the galliard young cavaliers volunteered their services, burning with an enthusiasm hitherto repressed amid the dismal surroundings of Isabella. By their energy and example a road was opened through the mountain gorge. It is the only trail to-day at this point, and it still bears the name given to it — *El Puerto de los Caballeros*, the "Hidalgos' Pass," in token of their achievement.

Among the many photographs that I have taken of the scenes identified with the voyages of Columbus, none has the peculiar interest attaching to it possessed

VIEW ON THE BAJO-BONICO NEAR THE HIDALGOS' PASS.

by one I secured when at Isabella from the right bank of its river, the Bajo-Bonico, showing the trail of the cavaliers across the plain, and the Monte-Cristi mountains with the Puerto de los Hidalgos. The scene is almost as wild of aspect as at that time, now four hundred years past, when the forest stirred with martial life. Life here is more listless than at that time, also, for the wheels of the chariot have sped by it never to return, and the few people here are inert and dead to passing events.

The Spaniards who marched through the defile cleared by the cavaliers, saw before them the magnificent valley of the Yaqui, where verdant plain and luxuriant forest alternated, strung upon a noble river's silver chain. They did not know it then, but it was the same river seen by Columbus just a year before, in January, 1493, and named by him the *Rio del Oro*, or the River of Gold, from the particles of gold that clung to the hoops of the water-casks, and which gave promise of a rich country in the interior. This hope they were now about to realize, and with elastic step they marched forward, up the valley and into the mountains.

For two days they continued their march, meeting everywhere with the most hospitable treatment from the natives, who dwelt here in idyllic ease and contentment. The Indians were at first afraid of the horses, and of the men clad in shining armor; but, when once their confidence was won, they were only too anxious to serve the invading strangers, and place before them all their little wealth. This was, in all probability, the first expedition in which horses were used in the New World. On the evening of the second day, the Spaniards came to a different country, where the mountains not only reached down into the valley, but rose before, impeding progress. Beyond this point, next day, the army entered upon the veritable Cibao — the stony region, rugged and mountainous — the streams of which indeed ran over sands glistening with gold.

Convinced that he was now at the portal to the hills of gold, Columbus concluded to penetrate no farther, but to erect here a fortress to serve as an outpost, and

THE AMERICAN FERRY ACROSS THE YAQUI.

leave a garrison to guard this region, conjecturally so rich in the precious ore and sands. He chose a headland, half-surrounded by a crystal river, in the bed of which jasper, porphyry and golden grains were found. On this spot he caused to be erected a wooden tower, protected on the land side by a ditch, and with the clear-running stream in front. This fortress was soon completed, and as it was built on the bank of the river Yanique, it was given the name by which it is still known — *Santo Tomas de Yanico*.

Fifty years ago the site was seen by an English gentleman, who found the ditch in good condition, as well

IN THE VALLEY OF THE YAQUI.

as the entrance and covert ways for descending to the river. This was the first outpost established away from the coast, and, if we include Navidad, the third attempt at planting a settlement; it took place about the middle of January, 1494. While the fortress was being built, active exploration of the country adjacent was going on, and glowing reports brought in of its richness. When the Indians residing along the banks of the river learned of the desire of the strangers to obtain gold, they ran to the streams and sifted the sands in their primitive way, one of them bringing a nugget of virgin gold of an ounce in weight, and which he gladly exchanged for a paltry hawk's bell. To-day, as at the time of the Indians, the inhabitants here gather a golden harvest from the streams. When they need a little money they go to the streams and wash it out of the sands. I secured for the Exposition one of their primitive washers, it is merely a shallow dish whittled out of a slab, but with it the owner had washed large sums out of the earth and sand of the stream flowing past her door.

The Spaniards found much gold in the sands and in pockets, nearly all surface indications, but they never touched the real treasure-vault. That lies deep-buried in the all-but inaccessible hills, and, as the great Humboldt has declared, what the Spaniards got was the surface accumulation of centuries, and the first Europeans gathered it all in a comparatively short time. But the real source of supply has never been touched; and whereas what has been found is like the scattered flakes of snow before a storm, what remains may be compared to the boreal snow fields that have never lost their stores.

Santo Tomas lies about six hours' distant, by horse, from Santiago de los Caballeros, one of the oldest towns in the island. Santiago itself is difficult to reach, being only accessible from the coast by a trail horrible in its pitfalls and mudholes, requiring a day and a night to traverse. From Santiago my companion was Señor Don Juan J. Hungria, editor of the leading paper of Santiago, the *Eco del Pueblo*, and he took along a friend from the country, who rode the most magnificent gray stallion I have seen in the island. We left Santiago on a beautiful day in May, 1892, well-mounted, and with a peon riding atop a small mountain of provender, carried by a stout mule. Riding down to the river Yaqui, which is here a broad and swift-flowing stream, muddy and turbulent, we crossed its raging flood in a ferryboat of unique construction, owned and operated by the only American in this region. He had drifted here in search of gold, but had met with the customary fortune of gold seekers in general, and had finally

"THEY BUILT A WOODEN TOWER."

settled down to a legitimate and profitable occupation as ferryman.

Leaving the river, and turning our backs upon the beautiful city, we entered upon the country trail with good heart and in high spirits. The scenery was grand but solitary, there being but few houses or huts along the trail, and the woods were silent and sad.

After an hour or so, we crossed a small stream, with which we were destined to become well acquainted before the journey was over, as we crossed it, my friends said, above one hundred times. It was the same stream the first Spaniards had found and followed in their search for gold, so many years before, and I viewed its every feature with exceeding attention. I am sure my readers will appreciate my interest in this region, which had such a share in the beginnings of American history, and will understand my enthusiasm.

Climbing some steep hills, we finally sighted the little hamlet of Santo Tomas, lying in a hollow. Arrived at the *fortaleza*, we at first saw nothing to indicate ruins, or even remains; but a peon living here guided us through the fields to a bluff headland, covered with low trees, and there we saw that of which we had come in search — the outlines of an earthwork and a deep ditch, all that remained of the fortress of Santo Tomas, erected by Columbus four hundred years ago.

Excavations were then being made to obtain articles for the Centenary at Madrid, and for our own Exposition. But where was the river — the Yanico, with its golden sands, which was the reason for the building of the fort? A low murmur of running water fell upon our ears, and following the sound we came to that veritable stream, deep hidden between steep banks, and purling over rounded pebbles. It was inclosed between walls of rose-apple-trees, then in blossom, and was of itself

VIEW OF SANTIAGO, ACROSS THE YAQUI.

so attractive that it needed not the tradition of gold to enhance its attractiveness. Here was the spot where the first military post was established, away from the coast, and isolated from all human intercourse. When it was completed, this fortress was placed in charge of one of the bravest soldiers in the service of Columbus: Pedro Margarite, a noble Catalonian, and Knight of the Order of Santiago, in command of fifty-six men.

This done, Columbus returned leisurely to Isabella, lingering at the Indian villages and cultivating friendly relations with the aborigines. The hospitality of the latter was excessive, and their kindness to the strangers greatly in excess of the deserts of these cruel invaders, who were overwhelmed with everything these simple people possessed. Leaving these happy dwellers in this vale of indolence and plenty, Columbus at last withdrew his troops through the pass of the Hidalgos.

But no sooner had Columbus reached Isabella, than a messenger from Margarite was at his heels, with the startling news that the Indians were manifesting unfriendly feelings and withdrawing from the vicinity of the fort. The fate of Navidad, it seems, whose garrison was massacred the year previous, by Caonabo, must have been forgotten, for the soldiers of Santo Tomas gave themselves over to the same passions that wrought the destruction of their compatriots. Columbus sent back a re-enforcement of fifty men, and this served temporarily to check the advance of the mountain Indians under Caonabo; but the fire kindled by Spanish atrocities was smoldering, and the fierce cacique was massing his warriors for a descent upon the fort. He had preserved an ominous silence since the massacre at Navidad, even holding aloof when his territory was invaded; but the Spaniards were to hear from him — they were to learn that not all the caciques were like Guacanagari, and that one at least had the spirit to resent their dastardly affronts.

In order to relieve the congested condition of Isabella, and give scope for the enterprise of his chafing cavaliers, Columbus decided to dispose the bulk of his troops in the interior, where they could obtain needed exercise, live on the country without charge, and make a protracted search for gold. He sent Alonzo de Ojeda to relieve Margarite at Santo Tomas, and the latter took charge of the main army of some five hundred men and explored the Cibao. Having thus dispatched the main body of the army into the interior, Columbus placed the affairs of Isabella in the hands of a *junta*, presided over by his brother, Don Diego Columbus, and set out upon another voyage of discovery along the south coast of Cuba.

Before his return great changes were wrought in the condition of affairs; the storm burst upon the garrison of Santo Tomas, and the commander was kept penned within the fort a long while before he could sally out and disperse the Indians.

This denuded piece of ground, surrounded now with the forest, and without a trace of the structure erected here by the Spaniards, is all there is to remind us of those stirring times and those valorous deeds. It was a place to dream in a while; but we had no time to lose, and after photographing the salient features of fort and river, and obtaining from the family residing here some relics of the Indian times, we set out to depart.

We were among the pines, and in fact Santo Tomas is in the region of pines, where the air is delicious and pure. We rode over the hills and through deep gulches till it became so dark that we could not see before us; then appeared signs of the village of San José de las Matas.

No one expected us there, for visitors rarely troubled the place, but Don Juan knew the parish priest and felt sure of a welcome. A welcome we did get and a hearty one; but the poor *padre* had neither provender for us nor the wherewithal to buy it. We were dripping with

THE SITE OF THE TOWER OF SANTO TOMAS.

water, for it had rained upon us as the village was reached, and our poor beasts were shivering with cold. Shelter was at once forthcoming, and some of the people were aroused to open the only shop, where I bought some eggs, ham and drinkables, returning with them to the priest's house, where we soon feasted merrily.

The *padre* was thin and emaciated, but though an ascetic he was hearty withal, and loved good cheer with the rest of us. He had a little garden behind his house with a papaw in it, some sparse shrubbery, and various things that indicated a liking for the grotesque—such as a little man of bronze perched on a pillar, and weather-vanes of queer shapes. He gave us hammocks to sleep in, and in the morning took me to the church and the goldsmith's shop, where I found specimens of gold from the nearest rivers. The goldsmith lived in a hut with a mud floor and a roof of thatch, his shop being merely a corner with a bench in it.

His instruments and tools were of the simplest kind, and to try the gold that was brought him he rubbed it upon a curious black stone; this I found to be an Indian celt, and after much bargaining bought it of him. This celt is beautifully polished and of perfect shape, of a dark-green color, and may have been used by the Indians as a chisel or knife.

I bought also some dust and flakes of gold, which I still have, and some more gold-dust of the neighbors. For this is the center of the operations carried on by the first gold-seekers after Santo Tomas was founded. But still, although gold has been found here for so long a time, and is still found, all the dwellers here are very poor. They are extremely lazy and improvident; and when they need anything they merely run over to one of the streams and wash out enough gold to last them a while, and then live on it so long as it will last, repeating this operation next time their necessities get oppressive. Thus they live, from hand to mouth, and so their ancestors lived before them.

In the church the *padre* had a small bell which, he

told me, had been taken out of the ruins of the first city founded in this region — the old Jacagua, near Santiago. He offered it to mê, and I accepted it for the Exposition, promising in exchange a new one. I had done the same for the church of Santo Cerro, not far away, the year before, and even then they were calling the people

THE BED OF THE RIVER YANICO.
(" *The River of the Golden Sands.*")

to worship with the bell I had sent them. The church at San José is very old and massive, and has stood at least three hundred years.

After the *padre* had performed the functions at morning mass, he went with us about the town, and when we left accompanied us a good bit on our journey. The ride back was delightful, most of the way through forests of tropical trees, in the branches of which the pigeons and doves cooed contentedly, and parrots innumerable chattered noisily. We were loaded down with our plunderings, and our little mule groaned desperately at the load the peon put upon her, for the bell the *padre* had given us weighed well, and there were cutlasses and swords of the time of the *conquistadores*, pottery, iron spurs, and similar "finds" of times most ancient.

Through the fragrant woods, that were as dense, as delicious, and as new as at the time Columbus saw them, we rode happily, the hoof-beats of our horses beating rhythmic time upon the stony ground, and the bell of the *padre* ever and anon sending its metallic note out into the woods that it had traversed centuries before.

And should you come across an ancient bell from Santo Domingo, at our great Exposition, labeled from "Jacagua, Ancient Santiago," you will know that is our old relic of the woods of Santo Tomas, and is the same one that, probably, called religious men together years and years before our country had a name.

## XIII.

#### THE PORT OF THE SILVER MOUNTAIN.

A DIFFERENT coast character greeted me as I went on deck the morning after leaving Cape Haitien. It was more open and less gloomy, yet not so rankly luxuriant. This, too, is the difference between the people of the respective republics of Haiti and Santo Domingo: in the one they are lapsing into the tropical savagery of their own rank forests; in the other, while yet buried in the gloom of their sad heritage of woe, they are still struggling toward the light. They are open and frank, yet suspicious of the motives of strangers; but, at least on the surface, are hospitably inclined and disposed to grant to every one his face value.

The town of Puerto Plata, lying at the foot of its silver-capped mountain, is brighter, more cleanly, and in general appearance more progressive, than the coast towns of Haiti, about which hangs ever an air of desolation and decay. This town has the most attractive situation of any I have seen in Santo Domingo, with its small, land-locked bay, its green slopes covered with tropical gardens, and the adjacent valleys filled with sugar-cane. The most conspicuous object is the old fort on the point that makes the harbor. Two or three great guns are mounted here; and they point toward the town — not out at sea — as the island's only enemies are of her own people.

The customs officials who came off to meet us, seemed to partake of the general neatness and thrift, for they were well-dressed, courteous and alert. With an air of honesty and good intent, the boatman with whom I bargained for passage to the shore, "took me in and did for me," and caused the milk of human kindness that had surged around my heart, to curdle at his perfidy.

After many encounters with boatmen and hackmen the world over, this is my advice: treat with them as if arranging terms with an enemy; stand up squarely and tell them that you know their rates are exorbitant, no matter what their rates may be, and do not relax your rigidity till well out of their reach. If you meet them afterward, give them whatever you like, but purely as a gratuity; then they will respect you as a man of sense, for the grit that is in you, and not for your money.

But I was taken at a disadvantage. My feeling of gratitude at my escape from Haiti, and the softening influences of the beautiful landscape, rendered me an easy victim to the wiles of the boatman. I made what I thought was a very good bargain for the transportation of myself and effects to the shore; but I paid the rascal in advance, and there is where the trouble came in. Under the plea that the boat was overloaded, he pushed off with my luggage, promising to return shortly for me. When he got about half-way to shore, I saw, to my horror, an ox-cart draw up alongside the boat, and all my effects transferred to the hands of a stranger whom I had never seen, and might never see again. Then I knew I was in the hands of the Philistines, for I had not even the semblance of a "capitulation" with that ox-cart man, and he had my goods.

Of what avail to stamp upon the deck; to vow that you would have the life and blood of that boatman, that

LOADING A BULL CART.

you would not have your luggage go by that route; and that the authorities should hear of this outrage, when the man was out of ear-shot, and the luggage already in possession of a villain with murderous visage and a knife in his belt? What, indeed? It seemed a long half-hour before the pirate returned, but when he did, he had the most energetic Castilian that my acquaintance with the Spanish language permitted me to express. It did not matter, as I knew it would not; but I had the happiness of restoring, in a measure, my outraged equilibrium, and of causing a temporary flutter in the morning calm. And the worst of it was that, as I was rowed ashore, I met the consular barge, pulled by six oars and with the American flag at the stern, coming out to convey me to the shore. It all came of arriving too early in the morning, for if it had been later, the Consul would have been on hand to receive me.

Arrived at the customs, I found the grinning villain of the ox-cart awaiting me — for all luggage must be examined before entry — and I then expected another "row" with these officials. But, whatever the character of the boatmen, I knew the officials were gentlemen — and there was no trouble about the effects.

In truth, I have never allowed the customs officials of any island to examine my luggage, for, traveling as the accredited representative of my Government, I always held it to be an insult to that Government to permit the effects of its agent to be disturbed. If I were not worthy of trust, I should not have held the position; holding that position, I merely demanded the recognition due me, not as an individual, but as the representative of a powerful and friendly government. To their credit be it said, the insular customs always recognized the justice of my position, and I am sure were only too glad to extend a courtesy that cost them nothing.

The cartman did not wait to hear my opinion on diplomatic amenities, but hastened off, and was out of sight before the officials and myself had half-performed the ceremony of assuring each other of the love borne and the respect entertained for our mutual and respective governments. After that, a cigarette or two, a formal and then an effusive shaking of hands, a ceremonious lifting of hats, a parting salutation and renewed expressions of mutual good-will, esteem, admiration even, and I tore myself away, followed by the adieus of my new friends.

And I found the cartman awaiting my coming. He had stowed away the trunks in a room assigned me at the hotel, and was only waiting to present his little bill, that was all! It was not the bill that concerned me; it was the attitude of the man — his evident intention to take me by the throat and cram that bill into my system. So, with inward trepidation, though I flatter myself outwardly calm, I demanded his price.

"Four dollars."

"*Cuanto?*" I thundered.

Firmly, but respectfully, the man replied, "*Cuatro.*"

I drew forth two dollars and extended it to him. He spurned it with a glance of scorn that I couldn't have duplicated for the life of me. He also toyed quietly with the huge knife and revolver in his belt. Then, though, I will confess, with a creeping sensation along my spine, I turned my back upon him, and shut the door in his face. I busied myself with opening my trunks, at the same time wondering at which point the door would be perforated by the bad man's bullets. A little later, hearing the ox-cart move off, I peeped out and saw him going away. But he came back, and he kept coming, during two days. Our conversation at these interviews consisted of:

"*Cuanto?*"

"*Cuatro pesos.*"

"And you won't take two?"

"Señor, I'll perish first."

"Then perish."

Exit cartman. I might have complained to the police and had him arrested; but the farce was rather amusing, and I liked to keep it up.

Finally, he came up with a broad grin on his dirty face, and said he would take two dollars. And as soon as it was safely in his possession, he asked me humbly if I would give him one dollar (the regular price, by the way), to take the same things back to the boat. His change of demeanor had been brought about by a lecture he and his *confrères* had received from the alcalde, who, hearing of the affair, had assembled them all, and assured them that at the first intimation of another attempt at fraud, he would revoke their licenses, and send the whole lot to the calaboose.

The Hotel Cibao is the best in the place, and the landlady made me as comfortable as possible, though the mosquitoes of Puerto Plata are the most active and utterly depraved of any I have ever encountered. The servants at the "Cibao" smoked at all times, even while waiting on the table and making up the beds. And they smoked such rank, evil-looking and foul-smelling cigars that my feelings almost overcome me at the reminiscence.

Although depraved in their tastes, yet they were

assiduous in their efforts to please, while our talented landlady could converse in any one of the four leading languages of the world, or all at once — depending upon whether she was discoursing with a boarder, or rating a servant for disobedience to orders.

I found that the generally bright and active appearance of the town was due to the residence here of some very intelligent foreigners, mainly Americans, who had initiated enterprises of public benefit and utility. I met the best of these, and they exerted themselves to forward the aims of my mission, and make my stay socially agreeable. Our Consul, an American long resident here, introduced me at the *Club del Comercio*, and to the dignitaries of the place, who gave me letters of introduction to other influential men in the country, which were especially available in the exploration of Isabella, already described, and my acquaintance with the President of the republic.

After my return from Isabella, having a week to wait for the next coast steamer, I settled down to the business of the Exposition, the British Consul kindly giving me the use of the consulate as an office. Over the door was the customary shield, with the coat of arms of Great Britain.

One day, as I was within, busily writing, I noticed a small boy at the door, evidently lost in rapt admiration of the numerous and ferocious lions that adorned the shield. They evidently struck his fancy, for he began to count them; and it was fortunate for that boy that the occupant of the office did not happen to be a "Britisher," for this is what he said. Regarding the lions aforementioned very intently, he counted them slowly as follows: "*Dos perros, tres perros, cuatro perros grandes — y cinco perritos.*" "Two dogs, three dogs — four big dogs, and five pups!"

I dashed out to chastise the little wretch; but he looked so innocent and happy that I refrained, and to this day that insult to the British crown goes unavenged.

VIEW OF THE PLAZA AND CHURCH AT PUERTO PLATA.

The greatest curiosity here is the *Sereno*, the night-watchman, of the real Spanish type, who wears a long cape, carries a pike, and swings a lantern. Every half-hour through the night he cries out the time, first blowing a shrill whistle, and ending up with the state of the weather. First you hear a click, then a whistle, and then he lets loose his lungs, at concert pitch. "*Las nueve*" (or whatever the hour) "*tiempo sereno. Noo-oo-oo-oo-ay-ay-ay-vay-vay, tee-ee-ee-em-emm-po-oo say-ay-ay-ray-ay-ay-no-o-o.*" It always frightens the strangers, and is an excellent thing for the evil-doers, because they can always locate the police.

It happened that the President of Santo Domingo arrived at Puerto Plata during my stay, and I soon had the pleasure of an introduction, and an opportunity to informally present my papers. He expressed himself as desirous to "assist" at our Exposition, but said he would have to consult with his cabinet at Santo Domingo City, before replying officially to the invitation of my Government. He was a very able and intelligent man, of medium height, slight build, dark mahogany complexion and close-curled hair, quiet in manner, and not given to dress. He spoke English imperfectly, but French and Spanish with facility.

At the time of our meeting he was on his way to "pacificate" the Cibao country, this being done by the distribution of money to those whom he considered worth placating, and the imprisonment of those not having that importance. With him was his Secretary of War, whose attachment to his person and elevation to office illustrates the sagacity of this pacificator of Santo Domingo. This secretary formerly held the position of collector of the port at the capital; but the President found he was collecting too much for himself and too little for the country, so he pondered a while, and then promoted him. Nanita, the collector, had aspirations for the presidency, and a strong following, so it would not be politic to antagonize his friends, hence the "promotion" to the portfolio of war.

At the time of our visit there were a good many Dutch and French engineers engaged in locating the line of the railroad from Puerto Plata to Santiago. This is an enterprise which, if ever completed, will be a disastrous speculation for its promoters, or at least its stockholders, as it (the line) connects only the two towns of Puerto Plata and Santiago, and has a very rough and mountainous country to traverse.

This port has long been the outlet of the tobacco country in the interior, of which Santiago is the center, and in the season thousands of horses and mules come groaning down the horrible roads, each with a load of two hundred and fifty pounds on its back. Their backs are raw and bleeding, their tails caked and draggled with clay, their legs masses of mud, and their whole aspect woe-begone. They travel in droves, without rope or bridle, are trained to push on and over all obstacles, and have only scant fodder of grass to eat at the end of the long and dangerous journey. All the tobacco raised here is sent to Germany, as it is too poor for the American market, and all business is controlled by two or three firms. This monopoly of affairs extends even to the sale of postage and revenue stamps, which can be obtained of but one firm. The same system prevails all over the country, making a few big concerns very rich, and keeping the bulk of the population very poor.

It is in Puerto Plata that one sees the bullocks and cows pressed into the service of transportation; not only harnessed into carts and drays, but ridden with saddles.

No more interesting objects present themselves than these beasts of burden, with huge *aparejos* on their backs, sometimes covered all over with stalks of sugar-cane, and again with bales of tobacco. Boys and girls ride them in from the country, leading or guiding each beast by means of a great ring through the nose, to

GIRL ON BULLOCK-BACK. — PUERTO PLATA.

which a rope is attached. These rings remain in the noses permanently, and sometimes have caused the breaking away of the cartilage and have been inserted afresh — giving the noses of the patient animals a ragged appearance.

The Dominicans have inherited all the cruel traits of the Spanish character, including the barbarous treatment of the lower animals, and have them all under subjection. At first glance it seems very cruel, and one's sympathies go out to the dumb beasts; but as the Dominicans look at it, if they think of it at all, the choice lies between an unruly beast and danger to human life, and a tractable animal in complete subjection, and to be

THE TYPICAL BEAST OF BURDEN.

handled without harm. Indeed I can hardly recall in my years of travel amongst Spanish and Spanish-American peoples, a dangerous dog in the streets, a refractory horse, a kicking mule, or badly-balking donkey.

After my return from Isabella, I wrote a short article for the local paper, the *Porvenir*, about my visit, and an interest was excited that bore fruit the following year in an expedition to the ruins, by some of the best people of the place. They discovered several relics of the early times, including a fragment of a coat of mail, which they kindly loaned me for the Exposition, and also defined the exact site of the first church erected here.

Following upon their discoveries and my reports to the Department at Washington, an association of gentlemen was organized in Massachusetts, having for its object the erection at Isabella of a monument to commemorate the event of the founding of this church, at the head of which were the Rev. Father O'Brien, of Cambridge, Massachusetts, and Capt. Nathan Appleton of Boston.

Their plans were subsequently changed, the monument erected in Boston, and the original scheme enlarged to include a church, or chapel, on the site of the first Catholic church in America. The necessary permission was obtained from the Dominican Government, and a large tract of land most generously donated by the owner of Isabella, Mr. Passailaigue, to whom I myself was indebted for favors during my visit. The American Consul secured the clearing of a space sufficient for the purpose, and at the time of my last call at Puerto Plata — in the midsummer of 1892 — all was in readiness for the foundations to be laid.

For the cultivation of a spirit of research, and the keeping alive of an interest in history and tradition, the people of Santo Domingo are indebted to a resident of Puerto Plata, Doctor A. Llenas, who has written much, and published in the local papers valuable articles upon the aborigines, the antiquities, and the first settlements.

It was to him that I was indebted for the information that led to the recovery of the long-lost anchor of

WASHERWOMEN OF HAITI.

Columbus's caravel, in Haiti, and from him I was promised the loan of a small but valuable collection of antiquities for the Exposition. Would that the island held more of his type, and less of the paltry politicians; for men like him keep alive the spark of civilization, and bring the country in touch with the thought and progress of the world.

I left him, and all my good friends of Puerto Plata,

with regret, as the Clyde steamer bore me away toward Samana, late one evening.

The same cartman who had charged me four dollars for the transportation of my effects, took them back willingly for a dollar, and I had my revenge in photographing his bull-team — the cart piled high with the Commissioner's luggage — as it stood by the boat, half-submerged in the sea.

## XIV.

### SAMANA AND THE BAY OF ARROWS.

A NIGHT'S run from Puerto Plata, on the slow-going, but comfortable Clyde steamer, took me to Samana Bay. At daylight we rounded Balandra Head, the great commanding headland of the bay.

This grand promontory is the fore-foot of Morne Diablo, the mountain rising behind it, and rests at the water's edge like a New World Sphinx. With its great granite face looking seaward, and draped in a flowing garb of tropic tapestry, Balandra Head guards the most magnificent bay, or gulf, in America. I rarely deal in superlatives, but in this case, even superlatives cannot adequately express one's admiration. From this headland, with its terraced coast line, and its upward sweep of forest-growth backward into the clouds, there is a constant succession of alternate beach and bluff. Beaches are palm-bordered, bluffs are forest-crowned, white sand glistens in crescentic spaces, deep hollows lie amongst the hills, which themselves are cultivable, and frequently cultivated, to their very tops.

The only entrance to the great bay lies well in toward the black cliffs, and the steamer glides past the beautiful beaches, almost within hail of the cabins behind them, and the black men fishing on the shore. Half a dozen times since my first acquaintance with Samana, I have looked upon this range of hills rising above the blue-and-silver shore, and every time my enjoyment of the glorious scene has been intense. I have seen many other fair places in the world, and do not lack the mate-

COALING STATION. — SAMANA BAY.

rial for comparison; but this is indeed beyond compare, and unique in its own aboriginal beauty.

Interwoven with its picturesqueness of superficial aspect is its fascinating thread of history, leading us back to that very first voyage to the New World, when Columbus came here. Coasting easterly from Puerto

Plata, on the twelfth of January, 1493, he passed several capes, the loftiest and boldest of which, round, and all of rock, reminded him of Cape St. Vincent in Portugal, the same that is now called Balandra Head. Behind this promontory, he found a large bay of at least three leagues' breadth, with little islets near the middle. Landing in a sheltered bay, he remained some time, and discovered here a naked Indian, differing from the others in the West, and probably a Carib, who gave him much information regarding the unknown islands in the East.

Later, at another little cove in the woods behind it, the Spaniards ran across "a body of fifty Indians, all naked, with coarse hair as long as the women wear it in Castile, the backs of their heads adorned with parrots' feathers, and in their hands big bows and arrows."

At first appearing friendly, these Indians suddenly changed front, assumed a hostile attitude, and attacked the Spaniards. This, at least, is the story of the Spaniards themselves; the other side has not yet been published.

The Indians were of course repulsed, and fled, leaving several wounded, and their bows and arrows scattered on the ground. This was the first encounter in the New World between the Indians and Europeans, and here the first blood of the voyage was shed.

From this encounter, and from the numerous arrows picked up after it was over, Columbus named the body of water the *Golfo de las Flechas*, or the Bay of Arrows. He remained here several days, eventually treating with the cacique of the Samana tribe, from whom he received a golden crown; and hence he virtually took his departure, from this same Bay of Samana, for Spain and the triumphs that awaited him at the Spanish court.

Taking on board a few of the Indians as guides, he sailed in search of the Isles of Madanino, where the alleged Amazons were said to dwell. It may be remarked in passing, that the Admiral held these Ama-

SCENE OF THE FIRST ENCOUNTER WITH THE INDIANS.
(*Bay of Las Flechas.*)

zons in mind all through his second voyage, and thought he identified their island, Madanino, with Montserrate, in the Caribbee chain. But after sailing about rather aimlessly for a while, he gave up the search for the Amazons and the Caribs, and headed the vessels homeward for Spain. Thus, as we have seen, he took his last land view at the Bay of Samana, and from the headland at its mouth commenced the home voyage that eventually brought him to Lisbon and to Palos.

I took, one day, a boat trip to the veritable Las Flechas, which is now, as in the days of Columbus, lonely and unvisited. Two or three huts occupy the lands adjacent, and a few negroes find an easy existence on its shore. The beach is of firm white sand, o'ertopped by cocoa palms, and a small islet breaks the force of the waves from the sea.

The real harbor of Samana lies some five or six miles within the gulf, and is called, from the town there, Santa Barbara. It is a perfect *cul-de-sac*, with deep water close up to the cays that lie opposite, and a most desirable place of anchorage for even the largest vessels. It is protected by a line of reefs and connected islets that render it almost landlocked, with a narrow entrance open to the east. The hills on the land side are rather steep, but are cultivated to their tops, and offer fine sites for houses; the valleys are fertile for tropical products; the beaches, with their beautiful fringes of palms, are delightful for bathing; the bay for boating, and the reefs for fishing.

The entrance to the Bay of Samana, and the harbor of Santa Barbara in particular, has long been in the eyes of different nations as the best of all points for a West Indian coaling station. Its advantages are so numerous and patent that no doubt at all exists as to its desirability; but for various reasons, fortune has thus far passed it by. The name will recall to the reader the great "annexation scheme" of President Grant, and the commission of experts and scientists sent down, during his administration, to spy out and report upon the resources of the island. Samana at that time narrowly escaped the great good fortune of being brought under the folds of the American flag, the benefits of which would have been lasting and undoubted. As to the advantages likely to accrue to us from such an acquisition, there exists a greater doubt, for we have not yet arrived at the point of national growth that will warrant us in acquiring and holding extraneous possessions. The "holding of it" would be the difficult matter, for the Dominicans are born to strife; they are all ambitious and brave, and every man in the peninsula would feel that he, and he alone, should be elected to the presidency. Our little army, that now suffices to awe the Indians on the border, would be totally inadequate to keep in subjection these residents of Santo Domingo with the presidential "bees" in their bonnets.

A TYPICAL WASHERWOMAN OF SAMANA.

Below the town, in the direction of the head of the

gulf, the vegetation on the hills is very varied, from the bright cocoa palms along the shore, with their gray stems and golden crowns, to the somber forest leaves, and all intermixed with black rocks and red spaces of earth, giving variety of color. Some ten miles down, there is a large plantation owned by a Boston company, devoted to the culture of bananas; but owing to lack of transportation facilities it has not as yet yielded much.

Two hours' steaming takes us to Sanchez, at the bottom of the bay, with the same beautiful hills on the right as greeted us at the entrance. Sanchez itself is merely a gray streak of buildings against dark hills, all covered with woods. There are few bright beaches, but there are many palms and fine headlands, with attractive retreats snuggled in amongst the hills, but with a general aspect of depression. This is not owing to the lack of business — for it is the busiest town on the north coast — but to its situation. So shallow is the bay at this point, that the steamer anchors some two miles from shore, a landing being effected in a little tug belonging to the railroad company.

This railroad is the only one in active operation in the island, and is under the management of Mr. Thomas McLelland, a Scotch gentleman of tried discretion and ability, who has resided here many years. The first concession for a road into the interior of Santo Domingo was granted to an American, about 1882. It was to connect the Bay of Samana with the city of Santiago, and open the rich and vast valley lying between the two mountain ranges that traverse this part of the island. This valley, or rather succession of valleys, has a varying width of thirty to fifty miles, running in a northwesterly direction from the Bay of Samana at Sanchez, to Manzanillo Bay on the extreme north coast, near the Haitian boundary; the distance in a straight line is about one hundred and twenty miles. Scattered along the course are several populous towns: as Moca, Macoris, La Vega, and Santiago. The concession passed into the hands of a Scotchman, Mr. Alexander Baird, in 1883, who, alone and unaided, pushed the work to the town of La Vega, the present terminus. Formidable difficulties were encountered at the outset, the first being a nine-mile swamp, with a depth of filling necessary, at times, of fifteen to twenty feet. A port had to be created, and this was done at Las Canitas, since christened Sanchez; big buildings were erected, and tugs and lighters provided for the steamers that came here for cargo. An inducement held out by the Dominican Government toward construction, was the offer of every alternate section of land along the line; but upon investigation, after the work had been well begun, it was found that the Government did not own any land at all; and not alone this, but all the settlers in the valley put in heavy claims for damages and right of way. All obstacles were finally overcome, and, in 1887, the line was opened to La Vega, sixty-two miles inland. The hitherto unknown Canitas soon became an important point; where before were only palm-tree and guava bush, a thriving town sprang up, with regular steamers calling there, and Sanchez is now a place of about one thousand inhabitants.

The railroad, owing to the enormous expense of

location and the scarcity of skilled labor, has cost about two and a half millions of dollars; but it is owned and operated by one man, and no one but himself has been a sufferer. It has never paid, as an investment, and it may be some years before it will; but it is carefully, intelligently and economically managed, and if there is any chance whatever for its development and extension, the present manager, Mr. McLelland, will avail

THE APPROACH TO SANCHEZ.

himself of it. The company owns six locomotives, two passenger and forty freight cars, with large and well-equipped machinery shops at the port, where also there are steam tugs and a fleet of lighters. Regarded as an investment merely, this enterprise may not appear a profitable one; but as an evidence of what pluck, energy, and British capital can do, it is an object lesson of the greatest value. To be sure, having no stock in the enterprise, we can view with equanimity these heroic efforts to plant the banner of civilization on the outer works; but I believe they will be successful, and that the manager's endeavors to turn the tide to his employer's advantage will be crowned with success.

The change that has been wrought in the customs of the natives is wonderful. Here we find, at the port, a colony, the nucleus and animating principle of which is Scotch virtue and thrift. One lesson Mr. McLelland has taught the natives is punctuality. Until the railroad was opened, they knew it not, neither did they regard the time-tables when they were posted. If the train was advertised to start at nine o'clock, they read it ten; they rode leisurely up to the station, hitched their horses to the nearest tree, saluted all their acquaintances within ear-shot, smoked cigarettes innumerable, and lounged about aimlessly, not regarding the warning whistle, believing the train would surely await the motions of distinguished *caballeros* like themselves; and the consequence was that they were left in the station, gazing hopelessly at the retreating train.

A few reminders of this kind taught them that they could not dally with the new manager, and if they really wanted to go to another station on the line they must be on hand, and in the car when the whistle sounded.

From the delightful hospitality of Mr. McLelland at Sanchez, I tore myself away with difficulty, and under his guidance made the trip to La Vega and the Cibao. The manager's house at La Vega was placed at my disposition, and thence I made preliminary trips to the places of interest, always, thanks to my friends, returning heavily laden with historic spoils for the Exposition.

## XV.

### THE HOLY HILL OF SANTO DOMINGO.

A RELIC FROM OLD VEGA

MY first visit to Sanchez was in June, 1891; my second in May, 1892; the third was in July of the same year. As I had all the islands of the West Indies to include in my province as Commissioner, and as inter-insular communication is desultory and unreliable, I could not always arrive at the most desirable points at the time desired.

It so happened that every visit to Santo Domingo was during or at the commencement of the rainy season. This was peculiarly unfortunate, since in this island of Santo Domingo more than in any other, I had before me the labor of exploration in a comparatively unknown field, where the roads were poor or non-existent, and the forests difficult to penetrate. At the time of my first arrival, a great flood had carried away the railroad bridges between Sanchez and Vega, and by the advice

of the manager, I continued on to Santo Domingo City, returning after the rains had abated a little.

La Vega, the terminus of rail communication, is a straggling town of mean houses set down in the midst of scenery perfectly beautiful. A great deal of business is transacted here, as it is the market town and railroad center for a vast region; but in the rainy season the roads are horrible, being merely broad mud-holes filled with filth, in which pigs are rolling and dirty children disporting themselves. The population is mainly colored, and the trade is controlled by a few shopkeepers.

Designed by a beneficent Deity for the abode of man, given a delicious climate, most delightful scenery and fertile soil — how man has abused these glorious gifts of the Almighty! Around the valley, which is level, and in the bend of the river Camu, is a range of pine-covered hills, the vegetation of two zones thus meeting and blending between the pine and the palm.

From the President of Santo Domingo and his ministers, I bore letters of introduction to the Governor of the province and to the Government Delegate, recommending me to their good offices and requesting their aid in my explorations. I gained a side glimpse of the peculiarities of Dominican politics in these letters, for I soon perceived that though the Governor was nominally the head of the civil body, yet the Government Delegate was really the man in power. In other words, the Governor had been appointed to please the people, and as a figurehead; but the real representative of the Government was the Delegate, who had been placed in position to watch the Governor.

My letters were received with the respect to which they were entitled, and with many assurances of an overpowering desire on the part of the recipients to serve me to the full extent of their powers. It was arranged that a body of gentlemen should meet next day at Mr. McLelland's house, and escort me to the hill

THE MANAGER'S HOUSE AT SANCHEZ.

of Santo Cerro, where the real work of investigation was to begin. They were to meet at seven, sharp; but I gave myself the benefit of my previous acquaintance with Dominican character to defer my preparations till nine, and about ten the *caballeros* came straggling along. There were ten of them, a gallant cavalcade, mounted on horses that, if not spirited, were made to appear so by application of the cruel bit and spur. We rode through the hall with great *éclat*, the horses of the Governor and the Delegate in friendly rivalry for the leadership, and cutting *muchas figuras* (curveting about) to the openly-expressed admiration of the fair ones in the doorways, as we swept along. The roads were deep and muddy, but that didn't matter; the horses must prance just the same, and we dashed on, regardless of the splashing mud, and forded the broad river at a run.

Some four miles more of mud-holes lay before us, but we kept well together all the way, and at last reached the base of the Santo Cerro, or Holy Hill. It is a stiff climb up the hill, even on foot, but our prancing steeds made nothing of it, and the black charger of the Governor dashed showily up, snorting, and pawing the slippery clay, and awaited us panting at the top. Some of our party were indignant, either because of the strain put upon a beautiful piece of horse flesh, or else because His Excellency had got ahead of them. However, we formed at the church, and then all dashed down the narrow street like a party of cowboys, only without their whoopings, making a brave appearance, I fancy, as we suddenly halted in front of the priest's house, throwing our horses upon their haunches directly in front of the *padre* and his pretty sister — for whose benefit, I doubt not, all this display was intended.

We flocked into the house, a dozen of us, at least — for such is the good old hospitable way they have in the island — and sat expectant while the ladies of the household prepared coffee for us. After an hour or two of friendly chat, during which the objects of my mission were duly set out, and hearty co-operation was promised, we wandered over to the church, and then into a *tienda*, where the old woman in charge promised to prepare a *san-coche* for us when my companions returned. For they were to return in a week or so and escort me back to Vega, with all the honors.

After half an hour of affecting leave-takings, my friends departed, and I was left in the hands of the priest, who was a young man of twenty-six, living in a little house with numerous relations, including his mother and an exceedingly pretty sister. They were kind, sympathetic, and hospitable, taking me, a perfect stranger, into their already crowded household, and making it evident that I was welcome. There was no room at the parsonage for me to sleep, but I was given the use of a hut adjoining, in which my things were placed and my hammock swung. It had a mud floor, to be sure, and a roof of *yagua*, or palm bark, and the hens, the cats, the dogs, and the pigs, walked in and out at will; but it was the best to be had, and if it had been a palace at their disposal, instead of a hut, I am sure it would have been mine.

Santo Cerro, or the Holy Hill of Santo Domingo, is one of the most remarkable of the natural attractions of the island. It rises some six hundred feet above the magnificent and extensive valley called the *Vega Real*, the Royal Plain, which extends almost across the island. It was in 1494 that, breaking through the mountain-walls of the Yaqui River, coming up from the coast of Isabella, Columbus gave this name to the glorious plain

VIEW OF THE ROYAL PLAIN.

before him, lying there like a vale of Paradise, shining with rivers, dotted with palms, above which floated the smoke from populous Indian villages, and over which spread a sky of purest ether. At the present day, the name is applied more particularly to the elevated plateau between the towns of Santiago and La Vega, and as viewed from this holy hill of Santo Cerro.

At the time of discovery, the island of Haiti — *Babeque* or *Quisqueya* as it was variously called by the natives, and *Española*, as Columbus termed it — was divided under the dominion of five caciques or chiefs. They held their office by hereditary right, and were absolute within their own territory. The first cacique to be encountered by the Spaniards was Guacanagari, who held sway in the northeast, over what is now Haiti proper, and on whose shore the flag-ship of Columbus was wrecked. His territory extended east to the Yaqui River, where began the possessions of Guarionex, which embraced all the valley of the Yaqui, and all the Royal Vega, probably as far as the Gulf of Samana. The third caciquedom was in the interior mountains, and comprised the Cibao (or stony) region, where the rich gold finds were. It was ruled by Caonabo, a chieftain of Carib descent, the fiercest and bravest of these Indians. This province was known as Maguana, and the seat of Caonabo, on the southern slope of the Cibao range of mountains, is to-day called San Juan de la Maguana. The fourth province was Higuey, including all the eastern portion of the island south of the river Yuna and Samana Bay, and was ruled over by Cacique Cotubanama. The fifth province, Xaragua, took in the southwestern and western part of the island, was very populous, and under the sway of Behechio, whose sister, Anacaona, was the wife of Caonabo, and celebrated for her beauty.

The subjection of the Indians began with that of Guacanagari, who was soon a fugitive; then Caonabo was captured, in 1494, and the Spaniards moved upon the rich cacique, Guarionex, in 1495. It was in March, 1495, that Columbus set out from Isabella to punish the Indians of the Vega for alleged outrages provoked by lawless Spaniards.

The army marched up the valley of the Yaqui to a point near the present city of Santiago, and there encountered the savages assembled, it is said, to the number of one hundred thousand. But, whatever the number, they stood no chance with the Spaniards; with their naked bodies and primitive weapons, they were almost defenseless against mail-clad soldiers armed with swords and pikes, cross-bows and arquebuses, and having the aid of horses that seemed to the Indians devouring beasts, and of fierce bloodhounds that tore them in pieces with growls of rage. They soon fled, of course, and the monsters that came here in the garb of civilization pursued them till they were weary with the slaughter. The province of Guarionex came under the hoof, and Columbus imposed exacting tribute that soon crushed out of these peaceful people the little life remaining. Gold was what he wanted, and gold he got, until the streams and superficial deposits were exhausted, and the Indians borne down into their graves.

The cacique offered to sow the entire Vega with corn,

and furnish supplies enough for the army for years; but Columbus would not hear to this proposition, and soon was experiencing the rewards of his short-sighted policy; for the Indians fled to the mountains, and famine spread over the land.

Then Columbus sent home to Spain as slaves, five hundred Indians, thus not only initiating the system of

SANTO CERRO CHURCH AND THE AGED TREE.

tribute that hastened their extinction, but laying the foundation for slavery in America.

After the battle, the Spaniards prowled through the Vega, plundering the natives, and shortly came to the hill now known as Santo Cerro. From its summit Columbus saw the magnificence of the country he had conquered, and by some historians it is told that the great battle was watched by him from this very spot.

He was here, at all events; and an aged tree is still pointed out near the church, beneath which he stood and looked out over the plain, and which is called the "*Nispero de Colon.*" The *padre* gave me fragments of it to take home; though I attach no importance to such relics as do not carry their value on the face.

Beneath, or near, this tree, Columbus erected a cross; and it is from a miracle said to have been performed anent this very cross, that the hill received its name of Santo Cerro — the Holy Hill. It seems that after the Spaniards had departed, the Indians espied this cross, and approached to revile it. As they did so, they saw a woman descend from the clouds and alight upon the cross. It was the Holy Virgin, but the savages did not know her, and proceeded to stone her away. She did not move; then they let fly their arrows at her, but the sharp barbs passed through her, and did not seem to affect her determination to remain and protect the cross. Seeing this the Indians recognized her saintliness, and fell down, and were converted on the spot.

Ever since, the hill has been a sacred spot; and the handsome chapel now erected there is the result of contributions from those who believe the tradition, and have faith in the efficacy of the saintly patron's charms. The people come from many miles around to pay their devotions here and perform their vows, and the little hamlet is entirely supported by the contributions of the faithful. It is a scant living they get, these dwellers on the Holy Hill, but there is a silversmith here who makes charms, a baker or two, and many hangers-on in general, who live in the *yagua*-covered huts, on the brink of the hill and of poverty.

The image of the Virgin contained within the chapel is a very beautiful one, and is said to date from the time of Columbus. The *padre*, one day, raised the curtain

THE SHRINE OF THE VIRGIN WORSHIPED IN THE TIME OF COLUMBUS.

that hid her from vulgar gaze except on certain feast-days, and granted me the privilege of photographing her in all her beauty of gold and tinsel, paint, silks and artificial flowers.

Although this island and this shrine are in the possession of colored and black people, yet they have generally white saints and virgins in their churches, and mostly white priests at the altars. The *padre* (to be exact, perhaps I should say the *cura*) is descended from white ancestors from Spain, and is a typical Spaniard. He and his family were goodness and hospitality personified — seeking ways to promote the success of my enterprise, and to enhance the pleasure of my stay. I doubt if the ecclesiastical revenues were vast, judging from the poverty-stricken people that congregated here; but there seemed no limit to his generosity and kindness.

Looking about for articles of interest for the Exposition, I espied in the church an old bell, dated 1777, cracked and useless, but of quaint pattern, and this I begged of the *cura*, who at once gave it to me. He gave it freely; but I noticed that in the belfry there was a small bell missing, and I resolved to supply its place. So, in the report to my chief, I recommended that another, and a good bell, be sent in exchange for this the *cura* had given us. And, a year later, coming back to Santo Cerro, I had the pleasure of assisting at the hanging of it. My dear *padre* had been transferred to another station, but another good man was in his place, and it was with heartfelt thanks to the executives of the Exposition, who had sent him this beautiful bell, that he received me. Miguel, the sacristan, took me up to the tower, and I had the satisfaction of ringing it.

Another, and yet more interesting relic of earliest times, I begged of the *cura* as a loan: this was an iron cross that had been dug up on the church site of the oldest city in this region, and had hung in the chapels here from time immemorial. It is of quaint and intricate pattern, and very old, probably coming to this country from Spain with the *conquistadores*. Still another relic was found in the shape of an old cannon, a small howitzer, or lombard, from the first fort erected by Columbus in this region. It had been burst in firing at some religious fête, but was still good for a noise, although the one that touched it off took his life in his hand. I promised a gun in exchange for this, also, and an amusing mistake at the War Department caused the

A VIEW OF SANTO CERRO.

sending to Santo Domingo of a fine bronze field-piece, though of an obsolete pattern, instead of the small yacht gun I had intended. When I reached Sanchez a year later, it lay in the warehouse of the railroad company, being so large and fine, and so altogether desirable for revolutionary purposes, that the manager hesitated to send it into the interior. In fact, rumor had it that several revolutionary leaders were anxiously awaiting its arrival, and the President was beginning to inquire about it. So it did not go in; but I saw the President afterward, and he promised me an ancient gun for it, from the arsenal at the capital.

Near the Cerro is an *arroyo* through which runs the stream Chancleta, the water of which has the peculiar

ALONG THE RIVER YUNA.

property of incrusting objects placed in it with a crystalline deposit. Bottles and other objects are sold at the Cerro covered with this deposit, which is ferruginous in color and vitreous in appearance. Within the chapel a sacred well is shown, from which at times gushes out a spring of water possessing wonderful efficacy when blessed by the priest; and half-way down the hill is another, supposed to have connection with this. The hill itself is half-covered with tropical forest-growth, and the path ascending is divided into stations for the devotees, indicated by crosses, while a group of wooden crosses adorns the crown of the hill.

As to the view from the church, I confess myself unable to do it justice in words, merely. It surpasses the view of the Yumuri Valley from Guadeloupe, in Cuba, and in some respects the outlook over Granada from the Alhambra Palace — both of which I have enjoyed, but each has a different charm. From a height of six hundred feet and more, one looks directly down upon tropical gardens occupied by palm-covered huts and flaming with the vivid crimson of the flamboyant trees, and beyond, over forests of palms, groves of cacao, coffee, plantains and bananas: a vast plain, bounded only by the hills of the Monte-Cristi range; populous, yet silent; fertile, yet half-cultivated; beautiful, yet with its beauties unenjoyed. Looking upon these visible charms which so moved the Admiral that he called it the Royal Vega, and recalling the immortal events of history that have transpired here, the heart swells with emotions difficult to express. With the witchery of the moon upon it all, it was inexpressibly beautiful, and I would that all who love the divine in nature could at least look once upon it.

The rainy season had caught me here; my plans were frustrated, and the work I had contemplated retarded. But I made excursions to the ruins of the earthquake-ruined city in the plain, in the intervals of the rains, and a journey to Santiago, returning with pleasure to my quarters with my good friend the *padre*.

320        IN THE WAKE OF COLUMBUS.

When the day came at last to depart, half the villagers descended to the plain to see me on my way. The *padre* was the last to leave me, and he sent along Miguel, in charge of a sturdy donkey groaning beneath the "plunder" I had collected for the Exposition — the bell, the lombard, and the cross, as well as numerous "curios" yet unmentioned.

WINDOW IN ROSARIO CHAPEL, SANTO DOMINGO.
(*The oldest chapel in America.*)

## XVI.

### THE EARTHQUAKE-BURIED TOWNS.

MY chief reason for establishing myself at Santo Cerro, was to be within working distance of the ancient *Vega Vieja*, Old Vega, which was one of the towns destroyed by the great earthquake of 1564. It has long been a tradition that beneath the walls a great deal of treasure lies buried.

But what was of even more importance to me was that many relics of the times of the *conquistadores* were yet to be found by search. After the subjugation of the Indians, Columbus erected a line of forts across the upland plain, the first being near the pass through the mountains at the entrance to the Yaqui Valley; the second farther up; the third at or near the present city of Santiago, and the last and most important near the hill now known as Santo Cerro. This was called Concepcion de la Vega, and being in a most fertile district, and also quite near the residence of Guarionex, the cacique of the Vega, it soon became the nucleus for a thriving settlement. A large town eventually surrounded it, and the ruins to-day indicate its extent, being scattered over a great area.

The most conspicuous ruins are those of the church, the fortress, and a large convent, the latter supposed to have been built by the bequest of Columbus. Owing to the richness of the country adjacent, in gold and agricultural resources, the town had the reputation of

RUINS OF THE CHURCH BUILT BY BEQUEST OF COLUMBUS.

being wealthy, at the time of its destruction, which occurred the twentieth of April, 1564, during the celebration of the morning mass. This was some seventy years after the founding of the fort, and when the town had become the chief settlement of this region. Miguel, the sacristan, who had assumed charge of me at Santo Cerro, and whose hammock hung in the only other room the hut contained, called me at six in the morning, and at seven we were descending the steep hill toward Old Vega. The path was filled with people coming to the Saturday mass, which is the mass of the Virgin, and is attended from far and near.

About two miles from the hill, we found four peons awaiting us, and at eight o'clock we were at work cleaning out the angle of the fort. This old fort is the veritable "Fort Concepcion" erected by order of Columbus, in 1495. There are yet remains enough to show its original plan, though it is entirely in ruins except the northeast angle, where its circular bastion is nearly perfect. Here, the walls are about ten feet high, six feet thick, with a space of sixteen feet inside. As near as one may judge from the remains, the fort was about two hundred feet square, with the circular bastions at the four corners, built mainly of brick, and in the thorough manner of the old Spanish architects.

For years and years, the residents of the Vega have been digging out the bricks, until nearly the whole structure has been taken away, except the northeast angle. The site is nearly overgrown with large trees, and the surroundings are attractive — the fields adjacent slope to the hills, and through the trees is a fine view of the Cerro. The site does not appear to have been commanding, some of the ruins of houses being higher up, but the surface features may have changed in the lapse of four hundred years.

After having given the peons another spot to excavate, I retired to the thatched tobacco shed on the crown of a low hill, and there superintended operations.

It is a most beautiful spot, in the midst of a clean-kept garden. Tall palms rise above the shed, a papaw-tree stands in front, sugar-cane, bananas, plantains, maize, tobacco, yucca, cassava, melons, and peppers, grow luxuriantly all around, while *cahuiles*, plums, cocoa palms, and calabashes, are sprinkled all about the garden.

RUINS OF FORT CONCEPCION.

Such a garden, with almost all these fruits and vegetables, might have had Guarionex, the cacique of the Vega, before the Spaniards came; and this spot was very near, if not on the site of his village.

The hills of the Cerro range rise near, and across the valley above Moca, others rise blue against the sky. Cool breezes sweep through, as I swing there in my hammock, and the simple people crowd around with bits of old iron and brass, from the ruins, to sell, and occasionally something better — as for instance, an original "hawk's bell," or *campanita*, which the first Spaniards brought here for traffic with the Indians, and which the natives treasured above all other things, bartering for these bells their most valued possessions, and giving in exchange great lumps of gold. With what I bought and what I dug out of the ruins, I brought away some hundreds of objects for the Exposition; most of them were small, but many of them were valuable for the confirmatory evidence they give on the early history of this region. The most valuable of all my "finds," perhaps, is a small bell, which, we have every reason to believe, was the first that ever was brought to America for religious purposes.

The only ruins of any importance whatever, are those of the fort and the old church. The latter are near the highway, and consist of great crumbling blocks of masonry, hung with vines and overgrown with the parasitic "fig-tree." This church was the first to be built after that of Isabella, and when, toward the last of the fifteenth century, that settlement was abandoned, all the ecclesiastical furniture of the first church was brought to the more recent settlement of the Vega — then a promising town around the fort called Concepcion. It is believed that amongst other things this bell was taken here and hung in the belfry of the church, and there seems little doubt that this was the first brought to America by Columbus as the gift of Isabella, placed in the chapel there, and later taken to the Vega. It hung in the tower till the great earthquake of 1564, when the church was tumbled to the ground. The tower remained almost intact, though cracked and shattered, but the bell was lost to sight. The dwellers of the city hastened to the site of the present Vega, and there settled, and the site of Concepcion was neglected and well-nigh forgotten.

Some years ago, a man observed a strange object in the branches of a "fig-tree" that had grown around the tower and penetrated the belfry. These "figs" are parasitic, and wrap themselves around any object within their reach, whether it be tree, wall or post. I have seen some with large trees of another species growing from their hearts, apparently, so thoroughly had they enmeshed them. They form a perfect network around the object enclosed, through which it can be seen; and their strength is so great that they sometimes lift stones and plants from the ground. This "fig" around the tower had entered the belfry, and emerged with the long-hidden bell in its ligneous arms, bringing it to the light of day, after the lapse of at least three centuries. Perceiving this, the simple people looked upon this re-appearance as nothing short of miraculous, and the "bell of the fig-tree" became famous throughout the island. It finally came into the possession of Father Bellini, a priest now deceased, whose good works are manifest in many things he did for the people of Santo Domingo. Father Bellini took it to the capital, where it hung for several years in the school he founded there, and where I first saw it. Through the good offices of Señor Galvan, at that time in Washington as plenipotentiary from the government of Santo Domingo to negotiate a treaty with the United States, this bell was obtained for the Exposition. At the request of the Chief of the Latin-American Department of the Exposition, Mr. W. E. Curtis, a letter was sent to the heirs of Father Bellini, requesting them to deliver to me, as Commissioner of the Exposition, this precious relic. After the customary felicitations, the letter goes on to say: "Mr. Curtis, interested in the welfare of our Republic, desires that this bell occupy the distinguished place in the Exposition which properly belongs to it from its historic importance, and has applied to me to assist in procuring as a loan the bell in question. I participate in his desire, and transmit it to you, begging you to associate your name and that of our Reverend Father Bellini (whom God guard) with this honorable exhibit of what our country once signified in the colonization of the American world — as also in the estimation of the catholic sovereign (Ferdinand) whose

A PRECIOUS RELIC.

monogram is engraved upon the bell itself. Mr. Ober, Special Commissioner of the Exposition to the Antilles, will place this letter in your hands, and I recommend him warmly to your attentions, doubting not that you will confide to his care the bell referred to, for which he will give a receipt, with a promise to return it at the close of the Exposition; and this you can do with all confidence, in view of the official and personal character of the gentleman named."

Armed with this letter, when at the capital I called upon General Bellini, nephew of the deceased priest, in whose charge the bell then remained, and, after a long interview, during which it seemed extremely doubtful if the bell could be secured, I was taken out to see it. I anxiously awaited the movements of the General, and was not happy until he finally placed it in the carriage we had in waiting, and drove with me to the American Consulate, where I put it in the safe. Next morning, bright and early, I took it on board the Clyde steamer, got a receipt from the purser, who placed it in the specie tank, and then had the satisfaction of seeing the steamer sail away. I say satisfaction, because I knew that the relic was not safe until well beyond the reach of any one who might wish to prevent its deportation to the States. It was held as such a sacred relic that the whole public felt they had an interest in it, and were it known that it was to be taken away, there would be trouble.

Indeed, I had barely finished my breakfast, before a messenger from the General desired me to return the bell at once, as his friends strenuously objected to its exportation. Happily, I could say that it was then impossible, since the bell was already on board the departing steamer, and beyond my reach. The General took the defeat good-naturedly, but was not satisfied until I had given, not only my personal receipt, but had insured the bell itself for a thousand dollars. This was done;

ONE OF THE MOST INTERESTING SPOTS OF JACAGUA.

and that is the manner in which I obtained one of the most precious of American relics for our great Exposition.

The house I was excavating at Old Vega was said to be about the only one that had not been opened since the earthquake, and I hoped to find something worthy of the undertaking; but an all-day search revealed very little. I suppose that there was little, if any, wealth at the time of its destruction, though the gold from the mountain mines was brought here to be refined before being sent to Spain.

The bright day came to an end at last, my men gave up the search, and we departed for the Cerro. It was my intention to spend several days in excavating; but that night the rains began, and as the downpour continued all the week following, I was unable to return.

A year passed before I could again visit Old Vega, and the rains were falling as before. Since the first attempt, however, excavations had been made, with little result, and my only object was to obtain a photograph of the ruined church, which I had not secured at my first visit.

The same earthquake that destroyed Old Vega laid waste another settlement, lying near the present city of Santiago. I intended to excavate on both sites, and, after waiting a few days in vain for the rain to hold up, I started for the other locality.

Miguel engaged a peon and two horses, and after breakfast one morning we started. It rained from the very start, and I had six long hours of misery on the road. The first hour was along and down the ridge of the Cerro, amidst lovely scenery, with a broad view of the Vega, and after descending the hill we crossed the three channels of the Rio Verde, a broad and beautiful stream overhung with great trees.

Beyond the Verde we encountered a stretch of road where the horses merely plumped from one deep hole into another. These holes extended as far as the eye could reach, and made the road one vast sea of mud crossed by regular ridges, like deep furrows across a ploughed field of richest soil. Through these mud holes women and children were struggling, from one slippery hummock to another, though just where mud left off and biped began, it would puzzle an expert to decide, so plastered and bespattered were all with the rich red earth.

This road was opened nearly four hundred years ago, and not a dollar has been expended in improvements since the first mail-clad *conquistador* rode through the forests between La Vega and Santiago, seeking a trail to connect the recently-erected fortresses. During all this time mules and horses, men and cattle, have set their feet in the self-same holes, until now they can hardly reach the solid earth beneath.

Rank and rich is the whole country between Vega and Santiago, yet it is not made to yield a thousandth part of its richness to the hand of man. It has the most fertile soil and the most beautiful forms of vegetable life, so enticingly luxuriant, so rankly regal, that it made my heart ache to think upon the waste of it all. Not one appreciative glance is ever cast upon this wealth of vegetation, not one effort is made at adornment, or any attempt to entice forth the dormant life that only needs encouragement to leap into grateful recognition.

There is not a house or hut, in all the twenty miles between Vega and Santiago, worth forty dollars; and around the doorways of these miserable hovels are crouched most miserable natives, the color of the mud that so plentifully bedaubs them. In the midst of plenty they are poor, and always on the verge of starvation. I was overtaken on the road by a boy who really looked half-starved, and who whiningly begged for a small coin. Not having one about me, I told him to await my return; and three days later, coming back, he was there in wait for me, looking hungrier than ever.

Reaching Santiago late in the afternoon, I paddled through its dismal streets in search of a hotel, drenched, and muddy to the chin, and after having been rained upon during the entire trip of over six hours. The regular hostelry was full, and I found shelter in an unfinished building on the plaza.

Santiago de los Caballeros, the chief city of the Cibao, or interior of Santo Domingo, was founded in 1504, by thirty *caballeros*, who obtained from the king of Spain permission to use the term above cited as the distinguishing appellation. Although it has been several times destroyed — first by the buccaneers, then by the Haitiens, and lastly by revolutionists — and has suffered from earthquakes, yet it is to-day a bright and flourishing city, the head of the province, which contains some forty thousand inhabitants. It has three churches, a fine plaza, a large cemetery, and is situated directly above the river Yaqui, on a commanding bluff.

As the center of trade for all the Cibao, Santiago controls all this vast interior traffic, the only outlet to the coast being by the way of La Vega and Puerto Plata. Two railroads are trending hither from the coast: one starting at Puerto Plata, and the other the road from Samana Bay, with its present terminus at La Vega, about twenty miles away. There is not traffic enough, either present or prospective, for more than one road, though it is quite certain that at least one is necessary, and will eventually reach this important place.

My arrival had been heralded, and the evening paper, *El Dia*, announced that the Commissioner for the

THE CEMETERY AT SANTIAGO.

Exposition had arrived, and that a party of gentlemen, the chief citizens of the place, would meet him that evening, at the house of Señor Jesus Mercado.

We met and discussed the prospects for an exhibit from the Cibao, and, after the discussion, we were entertained delightfully by the noble host. That was in July of 1891. Upon my return the next summer, I was grieved to learn that Señor Mercado had been suspected of conspiring against the Government, and was then languishing in the castle at the capital. Several other distinguished citizens were also keeping him company, and a feeling of great uneasiness prevailed, for it was not known who would be the next victim of the Dictator's suspicions. But I received the assurances of these gentlemen that I possessed their sympathies, and that all possible would be done to give the region a representation.

The one most interested in the work, and the one who gave substantial proofs of his interest, was Señor Hungria, the editor of the largest paper, *El Eco del Pueblo*. He not only presented me with articles of historic interest for the Exposition, but accompanied me, on my second visit, to the site of the second fortress erected in the gold region.

I was also introduced to a strange character, a gentleman of leisure, Señor Don Antonio Alix, known throughout the Cibao as the "Poet of the Sierras." He had a family of charming daughters, a wife devoted to him, and a muse who was always ready for a romp or a frolic in the fields of poesy; so what more could the heart of man desire?

Mounting his horse, the poet insisted on going with me to visit the ruins of old Jacagua, a league or two distant from the city. This town was destroyed by an earthquake in the year 1564. It was a lovely morning on which we made the trip, and we found a warm welcome at the hands of the proprietor of Jacagua, Señor Don

Ricardo Ovies, who spoke English fluently, and who placed the whole estate at my disposition. He had accumulated several articles of value, and these he gave me for the Exposition, while he promised to have the ruins excavated for our benefit. This promise I assisted him to fulfill, and on my return, a year later, left a sum

SITE OF THE OLD CHURCH AT JACAGUA.

of money for the purpose, by means of which many valuable relics were brought to light, and were sent to the head of the Department at Washington.

Jacagua was a flourishing settlement up to the time of the earthquake, when the people removed to the site of the present Santiago. It was founded soon after the great battle that decided the fate of the Indians of the Vega, and a fort was built here. There was a church, the ruins of which are visible, and the fine spring which is still flowing was the reason, probably, for the founding of the settlement here. I obtained a great number of relics of those ancient times, and through the good offices of Señor Ovies, the collections from Santo Domingo were largely augmented. Our host gave us a delightful dinner, including delicious wine of native fruits, and preserves of his good wife's making; he has since repeatedly proven the sincerity of his proffers by giving us the results of the excavations.

USED BY THE EARLY SPANIARDS.
(1. *Dominican Cutlass.* 2. *Old Toledo with Dominican hilt.* 3. "*Toledo*" *as brought over by a conquistador.*)

The poet found and gave me an ancient spur, called an *acicate*, and also an old Indian jug, with a whistle in its nose, while I purchased several of the old Toledo blades for which the section is famous. I do not mean, of course, that they are manufactured here, but that veritable Toledos are still in the possession of some of the old families, having descended to them from the *conquistadores*. As I have mentioned, the settlement was made by gentlemen of birth and breeding, the city receiving permission from the king of Spain to be known as the City of the Gentlemen; and to-day there are more people of white extraction here than in any other town in the island; the female types of pure and graded blood being quite pretty.

I have in my possession one of these old Toledos, which has all the flexibility for which the blades were noted in the time of the Moors, and which has been reset into a very quaint and effective hilt. Some of those I obtained went to Chicago, and doubtless many of my readers will have seen those veritable blades with which the half-barbaric Spaniards pricked and prodded the inoffensive Indians.

THE WHISTLING JUG.

There is no more interesting spot in Santiago than the cemetery, where the system of rental of graves still prevails, the remains being turned out after the expiration of time of lease. I saw here a most picturesque tomb that had been opened for that purpose, and the skull and coffin exposed.

Below the city runs the swift and turbulent Yaqui, which is crossed by a ferry owned and operated by an American. The citadel overlooks the city and river, and a glorious view of the country around is spread out before the observer.

## XVII.

#### IN SANTO DOMINGO CITY.

RETURNING from the interior of Santo Domingo, I resumed my voyage around the island, taking a Clyde steamer, and making the run from Samana to the capital in twenty-four hours.

Santo Domingo City lies west of south from the head of Samana Bay. It can be reached from that point either by an overland journey on horseback of two or three days, depending upon the state of the trails, or by the steamer sailing around the entire eastern end of the island.

Santo Domingo is the oldest city of European foundation in America. It possesses, doubtless, more attractions than any other on the continent, having within its walls so many relics of those early years of our history.

The town was founded in 1496, by Bartholomew Columbus, the intrepid brother of the Admiral; romantic interest and historic associations thickly cluster around it, and it is intimately identified with the career of Columbus himself.

Miguel Diaz, a Spanish soldier, fleeing from the punishment he had incurred by wounding a companion, wandered through the woods and over the mountains from Isabella to the south coast, where he formed an attachment for an Indian caciquess, who governed the tribe then resident along the banks of the river Ozama. The native queen retained him with her for a time, but seeing that he longed for the companionship of his fellow Spaniards, and learning that he was afraid to return to them without something with which to propitiate his commander, and that nothing would be so acceptable as gold, she informed him that within her own territory

A SANTO DOMINGO SEAPORT TOWN.

was an abundance of the precious metal. Diaz was conducted to the banks of the river Hayna, not far distant, and found such fine specimens that he ventured to return to Isabella, where the commander, Bartholomew Columbus, not only pardoned him, but gave him offices of trust, and soon after went with him to test the new deposits.

They were found to be so rich that a fortress was at once erected on the bank of the river, and soon the

Adelantado went around by sea to the nearest point on the south coast, and there founded the city that still bears the name he gave it. He called it Santo Domingo, and also after his father, Dominico Columbus, the weaver of Genoa.

The soldier's romance did not end here, so rumor tells us, for Miguel Diaz remained faithful to his Indian wife.

The mines, though rich at first, became worked out at last, though even at the present time gold is mined there, by means of improved processes. From that region some immense nuggets were obtained; they were famous even in those days of rich findings, one of them being so large that the lucky discoverers used it as a table, serving upon it a roast pig, entire, and boasting that never yet had any king of any land so rich a service of plate. The actual finder of the nugget was a poor Indian girl, but her masters, of course, appropriated it, and neither pig nor gold did she get. In fact, no one appears to have eventually profited by its discovery, for the great nugget went to the bottom of the sea, in the sinking of the fleet of Bobadilla, when twenty sail went down with all on board, off Santo Domingo in a hurricane.

On the eastern bank of the beautiful Ozama, Don Bartholomew erected his fort, and here first a settlement was commenced. It flourished a while, but was destroyed by a hurricane in the year 1502. Seeing then the superior advantages of the west bank of the river, the settlers removed thither, and the present city was begun, walls being built around it later, and about

HOMENAGE. — THE OLDEST CASTLE IN AMERICA.

the year 1509 the great tower, or castle, called the "Homenage."

This fine castle, the oldest in America, and one of the best specimens extant of the architecture of those times, stands in a commanding position at the mouth of the river, upon the right bank, rising grandly above a high cliff of coralline rock, wave-worn and cavernous. Extremely picturesque in itself, its position greatly enhances the effect, and it is well worth a journey thither to study. Around it, too, tradition and history have woven a tissue of fascinating stories, for it leads us back to those times when European civilization was wrestling with American barbarism, and the red Indians, now extinct, were in possession of the West Indian islands. The story oftenest repeated, however, that Columbus was once confined a prisoner within its walls, has no foundation in fact. The event of his imprisonment took place in the year 1500, when the settlement was on the east bank of the river, and he was confined in a small tower called afterward, from this event, the *Torrecilla de Colon.* This tower was situated at the extreme point of the eastern bank of the river as it reaches the ocean.

I myself have investigated this statement and the location, and have the support of the local authorities and historians. A few bricks and stones are the only remains of the *torrecilla;* but the chapel, at the entrance of which the usurper, Bobadilla, read the proclamation that announced the downfall of Columbus and his own elevation to power, is still standing, though in a half-ruined state, on the east bank. It is known as Rosario, and pertains to a large sugar estate on the side of the river opposite from the city, a conspicuous and beautiful plantation, with immense *cuisine*, and all the equipment of a first-class " plant " for sugar refining.

It is well attested that the great tower, the Homenage, was not built until, or near, 1509, eight or nine years

THE HOUSE OF COLUMBUS.

after the imprisonment of the distinguished explorer, and consequently could not have held him.

The most noteworthy object that attracts the attention of one entering the Ozama on the steamer, lies a little beyond the castle and on the same side of the river; this is the *Casa de Colon*, as it is called, or the House of Columbus. It has, like the castle, no connection with the great possessor of the name, except through his son Diego, who, succeeding to the titles and powers granted by the sovereigns of Spain to his distinguished father, came to Santo Domingo in the year 1509, and began the erection of a palace.

Having achieved distinction by his marriage with Doña Maria de Toledo, niece to the famous Duke of Alva, and arrogating the title of Viceroy of the colonies in America, Don Diego began his career in great splendor, and surrounded himself with all the dignities of a royal court. He erected on the bank of the Ozama a magnificent palace, fortified and defended with walls and cannon, and carried his pretensions to such an extent that the king became alarmed and recalled him to Spain to give account of his proceedings.

Beneath the bank, a short distance from the castle, the Syndic of the *Ayuntamiento*, or city council, once pointed out to me an old cannon, half-embedded in the sands, which tradition indicated as one that the city fathers of the time of Diego's reign had mounted and trained upon the palace, to bring the viceroy to terms. Upon investigation, this story was found to have support in local history, and, through the kind-assistance of the Syndic, I secured this ancient piece of ordnance for exhibition at Chicago, where it was sent. It was a very heavy cannon, and one of the river barges was sunk in the attempt to ship it on the steamer.

The fortified residence built by Don Diego rises directly above the wharf at which the steamer lands its passengers. It is a grand and gloomy pile of gray stone, roofless, and falling to decay; its pillared corridors are destroyed; its lower rooms are now occupied as stables for horses, goats and donkeys; squalid huts of palm-wood lean against its walls, and filth almost indescribable prevents the visitor from an investigation of the interior.

The city of Santo Domingo is walled, and still retains intact many fortified battlements, which were erected three hundred and eighty years ago, with numerous fine sentry-boxes, and *fortalezas*, especially such as those of "San Anton" and "Santa Barbara," directly behind the churches of the same name. A walk around the walls will well repay the exertion; for though they have stood nearly four hundred years, they are yet firm and strong, though in many places they are now being torn down to allow the city to spread out and beyond, as in Havana.

THE SUN-DIAL TO BE SEEN IN SANTO DOMINGO.

The present city is crouched beneath the walls and within the ruins of the past. Against the massive walls of neglected convents, that once sheltered learned and holy men, lean the worthless shanties of a despicable people, who even huddle in holes hollowed out of the walls themselves. Entering the city through a great gateway in the walls, you are brought face to face with the dirt and squalor of the place; with its horrible streets, its broken and dangerous sidewalks, and its languid inhabitants. You will find a shoemaker, or tailor, or vender of groceries, occupying a small room in a building originally intended for a palace, the remainder of which is vacant and falling to pieces. In every imaginable corner and crevice, under the arches by the city gate, and lurking in the corridors of once great mansions, the people dwell by day and sleep by night.

Not all the structures of the city are of the mean character of those around the walls, for several of the streets are lined with buildings that will compare favorably with some in Cuba, and are of the same Spanish style of architecture. Around the central plaza are the Government buildings, the city hall, and the cathedral. These are all excellent structures, and there are some scattered through the city that show evidences of wealth and attempts at adornment.

As the ancient buildings show us the architecture of Spain in the sixteenth and seventeenth centuries, so the modern houses are modeled after Spanish structures of the present time. Not so many have the inner courts, or *patios*, as in Mexico and Cuba, but all are massively built, with thick stone walls, heavy beams supporting tiled roofs and floors, grated windows, ornate balconies in the second stories, and long flaring waterspouts at the eaves, like batteries of guns; while heavy doors protect the entrances to the lower floors. In fact, viewing the houses along the streets of the city, and noting the unmistakably Spanish air of mingled decay and smartness about them, one might imagine himself in certain towns in Southern Spain.

Of the twelve or thirteen thousand inhabitants of this city, a very small number are white, most of them having African blood in their veins in greater or less proportion. The people are pleasant, alert, courteous, with all the Spanish and tropical vivacity of speech and gesture, as well as the indolence and love of pleasures.

Visiting the capital as the accredited representative of the Exposition, and having met the President at Puerto Plata some weeks earlier I was at once introduced to the best the city held, and every facility afforded for an examination of whatever of interest it contained. Our consular representative, Mr. Durham, was then absent on leave, but the courteous vice-consul, Mr. Juan Reed, a resident of the capital, but who spoke English like a native of the States, gave me the consular residence for occupation, and arranged with a small restaurant for my meals, so that I was at once installed and ready for business. The consulate was one of the old houses with thick walls and a balcony, one room on the ground floor and two above, that lined the principal street. I had complete possession, and at night no one but myself occupied the house—a small boy coming every morning to open the office, and a colored woman to take care of the rooms.

Living quietly in the consulate, in sole occupancy, I had time and opportunity to study the history of the island in the intervals of my official duties, and of becoming acquainted with the ruined structures within the city walls. Morning and evening, sallying out in

COLUMBUS IN CHAINS.

search of information, I gathered up the scattered threads of history, and found out just how much had been lost during the various revolutions and invasions through the past three centuries.

Of manuscripts and minor objects of antiquity, there are hardly any remaining, and their loss is ascribed to the invasions of the Haitians, and to the ravages of the buccaneers of the seventeenth century. Sir Francis Drake (whom they style "*el pirata Draakee*") comes in for the chief share of the blame, for he sacked the city and destroyed everything he could lay his piratical hands upon. After vigilant search, I could find nothing more ancient in manuscripts than the Baptismal Book in the cathedral, dated 1591. But few traditions did I discover that had not already been given to the world in general or in local histories. Not even of the great Las Casas, who once resided here, nor of Alonzo de Ojeda, nor Diego Colon.

I tried everywhere to procure antiquities, as well of the Indian days as of the early Spanish times; but I had not much success; an old cannon or two, an Indian drum, an ancient "Toledo," a few clay figulines, a canoe and other articles of this class, were the best I could do.

The best collection of Indian antiquities is in the possession of the archbishop, Monseñor Merino; but there is no local museum, nor any scientific society interested in the fascinating field for study afforded here at their very doors. No one appreciates the relics of the aborigines at their full value, but when any attempt is made to procure them for study or exhibition, the owners at once attach a fictitious and prohibitory value, as always happens where ignorance prevails regarding objects of ethnical or archæological interest.

Santo Domingo's chief claim to distinction lies in its connection with Columbus and the *conquistadores*, and the principal reminders of their times are the few structures remaining of their construction.

The center of attraction is, of course, the cathedral, but besides this there are at least ten churches and

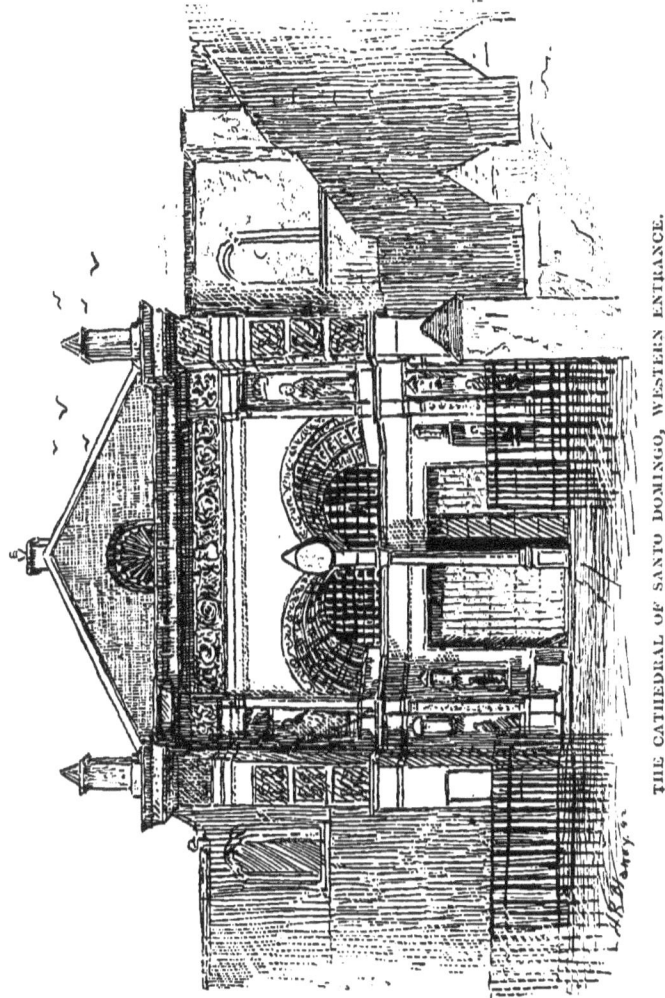

THE CATHEDRAL OF SANTO DOMINGO, WESTERN ENTRANCE.

convents of account in the city. The largest pile of ruins is that of the ancient convent, San Francisco, which stands conspicuous upon a hill behind the Casa de Colon, and about which cling all the traditions that fascinate the student of the times when the first missionaries came here to preach and to convert the Indians to the Catholic faith.

But a small portion of the convent is habitable now, and that is used as an asylum for the insane. About thirty *locos* are now immured there, in a wing of the vast edifice walled off from the ruins.

Entrance is freely granted to visitors, and one may wander at will through the deserted corridors, explore the labyrinthine mazes of the roofless cells, and seek for the burial-place of Ojeda, the lion-hearted soldier who lies interred at the walled-up entrance, and of Don Bartholomew Columbus, who is said to have been buried at the foot of the great altar. Arches, vine-draped and of magnificent proportions, towering walls with a forest of trees and vines growing on them and out of their crevices, deep holes where the treasure-seekers have dug for many years in vain — all these you may see in the ruins of San Francisco; but of the devoted missionaries who dwelt here, and who built the immense structure of which the crumbling stones alone remain, not a trace is to be found. Oblivion has claimed them all, save for their brief biographies in the annals of the order to which they belonged. There is said to exist a subterranean connection with another house of the order a long distance away, now used as a hotel, and known as the *Casa del Cordon.*

One of the oldest ruins here is that of San Nicolas, a convent church founded in 1509, the groined canopy of which, above the presbytery, is very beautiful, but destined soon to fall to pieces from decay.

The most famous of the convent churches is that of Santo Domingo; to it are attached the walls of the first university founded in America, and in which the celebrated Las Casas ministered. Deserted, ruined, and now in a disgraceful state of neglect and filth, the walls of this first of America's institutions of learning are a standing reproach to the people possessing this island. The interior of the church is most interesting, having been at some time carefully restored, and one should by all means examine its attractions.

INSCRIPTION ON AN OLD TOMBSTONE.
(*Convent Church.*)

The pulpit is supported upon a serpent carved of wood, the high altar is simple but chaste in the carving of its retable, and the quaint old tombstones in the pavement have interesting inscriptions. One, I recall, attracted my attention particularly from having carved upon it, besides an inscription with Scriptural reference, the *escudo*, or coat of arms, of the family to which it pertained — a shield containing thirteen stars. There was, of course, no connection between this heraldic device and the symbols we sometimes emblazon upon our country's flag; but it brought to mind the thirteen original States of our Union, which were probably first grouped about the time the remains beneath this stone were here interred.

A very beautiful church is Santa Barbara, near the river walls; it is old, simple in decoration inside, but with an exterior quaint and original. Another church, San Miguel on the hill, was built, it is said, by the king's treasurer, three hundred and fifty years ago; it is attractive, though small. La Merced is large and gloomy, and resembles Santo Domingo, while Santa Clara is quite handsome, having been restored, and a favorite with the ladies. This may be said also of the Regina, attached to which is a flourishing school, which was the care of the lamented Father Bellini. San Anton stands alone, and is only a shell of what was once a splendid church with fine arches.

Thus I might go on at further length enumerating the attractions here for the artist and the antiquarian, and especially the ecclesiologist; but I may, perhaps, have indicated enough to show that the old city is not devoid of fascinations, aside from its interest to the historian.

Although I do not intend to make this volume a guide-book, and certainly cannot follow my inclination to thread the paths of history that are constantly tempting one to diverge from the main track of explorations, yet I cannot refrain from indicating to one who may follow in my footsteps, the principal attractions here. Within the walls one may find numerous bits that will recall old Spain, Algiers, and the coast of Africa at Tangiers and Oran. One of the finest doorways is that of the old Mint, an excellent work in stucco, with fine and forcible medallions on the doorposts and lintels, and a beautiful window may be seen in an old house near the archbishop's palace.

The most famous structure in the capital is the cathedral, a long, low rambling edifice occupying one side

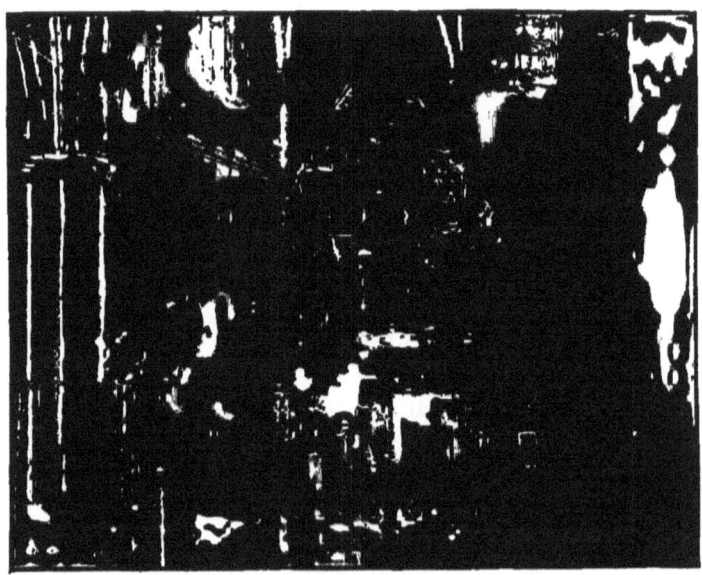

VIEW OF THE CATHEDRAL HIGH ALTAR AND RETABLE.

of the plaza; it is of a style of architecture that may be called composite, but peculiarly its own. Externally it is not particularly attractive, but its interior is worthy of detailed description, and I am going to ask my readers' attention while I make a tour of the chapels.

Entering by the great west doorway, before you lies

a nave of grand proportions, with high massive pillars supporting a groined ceiling. Walking down to the high altar, we find it apparently insignificant; faced with plates of silver of modern and poor workmanship, and with the customary adornments. Back of the altar is a splendid retable of richly carved and gilded wood, but temporarily hidden by an immense *silla* from the old coro, which was taken away some time ago. In front of the retable, and at the right of the altar (facing the nave), are the two vaults from which the two "remains" of Columbus were taken.

The first side-altar at the right is that of the Santa Reliquia; so called because in its sanctuary, closed by three locks, it contains a fragment of the cross of La Vega (mentioned in the chapter on Santo Cerro). This precious relic is set in gold and inclosed in a silver casket, and is shown only once a year. Here is a fine retable, richly gilded, and fortunately unrestored. The first chapel at the right is called Las Animas. It contains a fine painting of the Sanctissima Trinidad, and it has a *privilegio* from Benedicto XIV., of the year 1729, granting to any one here celebrating a mass, on any day of the year, the privilege of rescuing a soul from purgatory. Next to this is the chapel of La Virgen de Dolores, with the tomb of an archbishop who died in 1858.

Next beyond is the *Puerta de Perdon*, or Door of Pardon, so called because an escaping criminal who reached this doorway would be safe. Over the door is a tablet informing us that the cathedral was finished to this point in the year 1527, and through the doorway is a good view of the plaza, and the statue of Columbus standing there. The chapel next beyond the door has a tomb in it of the date 1524, a gory effigy of Christ, with real skull and cross-bones beneath it, and a *privilegio* dated 1727.

Two unimportant chapels come next; the sixth one contains a painting and the bones of a saint. The *capilla alta gracia* has a retable of mahogany and two modern tombs of Dominican patriots; opposite this chapel, beneath the nave, lies buried the celebrated historian Oviedo. The last chapel is known as that of Jesus Predicador, and beyond it is the great west door called the Puerta de San Pedro, with a statue of San José on the right and one of San Miguel on the left. Turning back toward the *altar mayor*, we find first the *capilla de Jesus en la Columna*, in which is an image of *la Señora de Buen Succsos*. The chapel next in sequence contains a painting said to have been brought here by Columbus, and presented by Isabella and Ferdinand. It is called *la Virgen de Colon*, and is very old, cracked and disfigured. There is also here a painting ascribed to a pupil of Murillo.

The chapel that the people regard with peculiar veneration is the next in order. It is called San Francisco de Paula, and contains the first cross erected in Santo Domingo, in the year 1514. This was on the site of the cathedral, which was begun at that time, but not finished until 1540. The cross is about nine feet high, and across its arms is an inscription setting forth the fact that it was planted here by the first religious men, and the date: "*Esta es la insignia primera que se planto en el centro de esta campo para dar principio a este magnifico templo, el año de MDXIV."* Wishing to secure a representation of such an important relic at the Exposition, and not caring to ask the loan of the cross itself, I had

THE PORTAL OF THE MINT. — SANTO DOMINGO.

a duplicate made by a local carpenter, which could not be distinguished from the original. Fortunately, at that time an old building attached to the castle was being renovated, and the governor of the castle, through the intercession of our Vice-Consul, gave me two old beams of mahogany, of the exact color of that composing the cross. These beams were over three hundred years old, and, as mahogany grows darker with age, they had the same rich hue as the cross. The carpenter worked most faithfully, and did credit to his profession, so that the duplicate was pronounced by the admiring natives to be the equal in every respect of the original. A native artist painted the inscription across the arms, and when dry, the cross was carefully wrapped in bagging and shipped to Washington, where it safely arrived and was sent on to the convent of La Rabida at the Exposition.

This, the first cross erected in the city, has been confounded with another and more famous one, which was planted on the hill of Santo Cerro, in the interior, and fragments of which are preserved as holy souvenirs in the cathedral and all the chief churches of the island. The latter cross, however, was set up about the year 1494 or 1495, nearly twenty years previous to this of the cathedral, and is venerated on account of its connection with an apparition of the Holy Virgin—as related in the description of Santo Cerro.

The eleventh chapel, in the order in which we have taken them, is that of the *Sanctissima Sacramento*, and in it are portraits of the twelve apostles, ascribed to the great Spanish artist Velasquez. High above the altar is a Virgin, said to be by Murillo, but perhaps a copy, and if so a good one. Regarding the authenticity of these pictures, the Archbishop expressed some doubt, but said that there was much in favor of their genuineness. But I present them without comment, at the same time believing it very probable that they are genuine, for there is no motive for deceit, and they have all the appearance of the pictures by the same artist, which I myself have seen in the museums and churches of Spain.

The *sagrario* of this chapel is of silver, and contains a figure of Christ, well carved from the horn of a deer. In the pavement is a tombstone over ten feet long, with a magnificent *escudo:* casque and helm with flowing plumes; date 1551. Adjoining, is the *Puerta de Bautismo* (Door of Baptism), with beautiful figures above it modeled in plaster. The *capilla de Bautismo* succeeds, with a fine retable and paintings, but the last and largest is the *capilla del Adelantado Rodrigo de Bastides*, who, a one-time commander in Santo Domingo, now lies interred here, with his wife and child, as attested by a quaint inscription on the wall. This chapel is extremely fine and old, with domed ceiling, and the *azulejos*, or Moorish tiles, are the most beautiful I have seen here.

There is a tomb of an early archbishop here, with his figure, *jacent*, sculptured in marble. Back of this tomb is a small cell, in which at present are held the alleged remains of Columbus. The two-leaved door of this cell is so fine that I had it reproduced in plaster and sent to the Exposition as an example of the wood-carving of the time it was made. At the left of the chapel is the altar "Ave Maria," facing the nave, with a gilded retable and excellent painting of Ave Maria, flanked by the kneeling figures of King Ferdinand and Queen Isabella, similar to those in the royal chapel at Granada, in Spain. Back of this altar is the vault from which the remains of Don Luis Colon were taken, on the side of the chancel opposite to that from which the ashes of the great Admiral were removed.

Thus having again reached the presbytery, we have made the tour of the cathedral and have noted everything in it, nearly, except the remains of the immortal Colon, which I shall reserve for another chapter. I trust it will appear that the cathedral is worthy the minute description I have given, and that the long journey has not been wearisome.

THE HOMENAJE.

## XVIII.

#### WHERE IS THE TOMB OF COLUMBUS?

IN the center of the plaza of Santo Domingo City, opposite the great door of the cathedral, stands a heroic figure in bronze of Christopher Columbus. It is dignified, commanding, impressive, and points with one extended hand toward the West, as though indicating to Europe the region of his discoveries.

At the feet of the statue crouches the Indian Anacaona, an aboriginal queen, whose subjects were massacred by the companions of this same Columbus, and who was burned at the stake by one of his Spanish successors. Yet, with an irony born of ignorance of historical facts, the artist has represented this unfortunate princess as tracing an inscription in praise of one who, more than all others, aided in bringing about the extinction of her race. The irony of truth, indeed; at one stroke presenting the character of one whose exalted sentiments were often at variance with his deeds.

The life of Columbus shows him to have had a dual nature: two towns claim the honor of his birthplace; two nations hold the luster of his deeds in reverence; two continents unite in laudation of his greatness; after his death two convents in Spain held his remains in charge, and now two islands lay claim to the absolute possession of his ashes.

One of the features of my mission to the West Indies, as Commissioner of the Columbian Exposition, was to resolve this doubt concerning the present burial-place of Columbus.

The great Admiral died on the twentieth of May, 1506, in the city of Valladolid, in Spain, and his mortal remains were deposited in the convent church of the Franciscans.

The last rites were celebrated with great pomp and ceremony in the church of Santa Maria la Antigua. But a few years later the body was given sepulture in the *Cartuja* of Santa Maria de las Cuevas, in the city of Seville. "It would seem," says the Spanish academician who investigated the subject, "that the interment at Valladolid was an act of piety, merely, accorded at the time; but that in las Cuevas was in accordance with the expressed wish of the Admiral or his relatives." In the same convent, some years later, were deposited the remains of Diego, his son.

The second removal of the body of Columbus had for its object the perpetual sepulture of his remains in the island of Española and the city of Santo Domingo. It was made in accordance with the petition of Doña Maria de Toledo, widow of Don Diego, who stated that it was the expressed desire of the Admiral himself; and in consequence a royal *cedula* to that effect was issued by the Emperor, Charles V., giving the requisite authority to the grandson of Columbus, Don Luis Colon. Permission

ONE OF THE DISPUTED BIRTHPLACES.
*(House in Cogoletto in which it is claimed Columbus was born.)*

was given to the family of Colon to occupy forever the great chapel (*capilla mayor*) of the cathedral of Santo Domingo; and this donation by Charles V. of the chapel as a place of interment, converted that part of the presbytery into private property, and no one unauthorized by them had any right to remove or efface even an inscription.

There is no record of the transfer of the remains from Seville to Santo Domingo; but the probable date was about 1540, as the first *cedula* giving the use of the chapel was issued in 1537; a second, confirming the first, was issued in 1539, and a third, confirming the second, in 1540. It is thought that there was some delay in granting sepulture in the cathedral, after the arrival of the remains; but that they were deposited there finally, concurrent evidence proves. In 1549, for instance, the first archbishop of that diocese writes: "The tomb of Don Cristobal Colon, where are his bones, is much venerated in this cathedral." The historian Herrera says: "From the Cuevas of Seville the bones of Columbus were removed to the city of Santo Domingo, and are in the great chapel of the cathedral;" and agreeing with him are the historians Alcedo, Navarette, and Washington Irving.

But although it would seem probable that some record should exist in the archives of the cathedral itself, it is not known that any has ever been discovered. The total absence of all early manuscript is attributed to the ravages of the pirate Drake, who was such a terror to the Spanish West Indies, and who sacked the city; embedded in the roof of the cathedral to-day is a cannon-ball, half-protruding from the masonry, which is said to have been fired from a gun on board one of Drake's vessels. Nor is there any tradition of records preserved by the oldest inhabitants of the city, derived from their ancestors, or from people who lived in the latter part of the last century. It cannot be shown, either, that there was ever a stone, tablet, or monument, to mark the place of interment; and this seems the more strange as there are magnificent memorials of the early archbishops, of the military governor, Rodrigo de Bastides, who died in 1527, of his wife, who died in 1552, and others of that century, several of them contemporaries of Columbus.

But that Columbus was interred in the great chapel of the cathedral, there is no room for doubt, as it has been proven by tradition and by contemporary evidence. Aside from the testimony already cited, we have also the record of over a hundred years later, that when the English invaded the island the archbishop ordered the tombs to be covered with earth, to prevent their desecration, "especially that of the old Admiral, which is in the *evangelio* of my holy church and chapel." And when the church was nearly ruined by an earthquake, the archbishop mentioned among other reasons for restoring the temple, that "in the *capilla mayor* is interred the illustrious Don Cristoval Colon." Again, in 1683, the diocesan synod of Santo Domingo states: "The bones of C. Colon are there in a leaden case, in the presbytery . . . according to the tradition of the old inhabitants of the island."

Just a hundred years later, the historian Moreau de

BRONZE STATUE OF COLUMBUS BEFORE THE DOOR OF THE CATHEDRAL IN SANTO DOMINGO CITY.

St. Mery, states that the dean of the cathedral affirmed that there was a box of lead, inclosed in one of stone, which tradition, constant and unvarying, pointed to as containing the bones of Columbus. Thus through two hundred years we have accumulative evidence that the last mortal remains of the great Admiral rested in the cathedral of Santo Domingo, and it might be assumed that in the course of human events they would be likely to remain there to the end of time, had not an event occurred that necessitated, the Spaniards thought, their removal.

In 1795, by the treaty of Basle, Spain ceded to France "the cradle of her greatness in the New World;" but there were those who remembered that the ashes of Columbus were yet in Santo Domingo, and felt that it would be unworthy the greatness of Spain to allow these relics of the man who had made her first among nations to pass under another flag.

The delivery of the colony into French possession was not accomplished until 1801, but the project of transferring the ashes of America's discoverer was executed in 1795. As already remarked, there was neither tombstone nor inscription, nor any indication whatever as to the resting-place of the remains; there was not a native of the country who remembered having seen such, nor any tradition extant directly derived from their ancestors. Therefore the Spaniards, in proceeding to the examination, had to be guided solely by traditions of the ecclesiastical authorities of the cathedral, and residents of the capital.

And what did these tell them? Simply what has

been quoted for generations: that the relics of Columbus had been deposited in the cathedral, on the gospel side of the altar, at the place where the canopy of the archbishop used to stand. On the twentieth of December, 1795, a group of distinguished gentlemen, including commissioners deputed by the Duke of Veragua, the lineal descendant of the Admiral, opened a vault above the presbytery on the gospel side of the altar, which was a yard in depth and breadth. According to the report signed by the clerk of the Royal Court of Justice of Santo Domingo, there were found therein some plates of lead about a foot long, bearing evidence of having been part of a box or casket of that metal, and some fragments of bones and dust. These were gathered together on a plate, and afterward placed in a leaden box, and with great solemnity taken on board the man-of-war *San Lorenzo*, on which they were transported to Cuba. Arrived at Havana, the revered relics were borne in procession to the cathedral, and there deposited in a niche opened in the wall of the presbytery, on the evangelist side, and the spot designated by a marble slab, with a bust and elegant Latin inscription, bearing date 1796.

Thus far I have followed the *Informe* of the Royal Academy of Spain, which exhaustively investigated the subject of the last resting-place in 1879, and the members of which were of the opinion that the remains of five members, at least, of the Columbus family were interred in the presbytery of the cathedral, namely: Christopher, Diego his son, Bartholomew his brother, Luis his grandson, and Cristobal the second grandson.

In the year 1877, while repairs were being made in the chancel of the cathedral of Santo Domingo, a vault was discovered on the left side (facing the nave) containing a small box of lead that fell to pieces on removal,

THE COLUMBUS VAULTS IN SANTO DOMINGO CATHEDRAL.
(*I. Vault from which ashes were removed, 1795. II. Vault opened in 1877.*)

but which had an inscription that read: "*El Almirante, D. Luis Colon, Duque de Veragua, Marques de*" — (presumably of Jamaica).

It was not known that the grandson of Columbus had been interred here — but this was indubitable evidence; it revived the tradition that his grandfather was buried on the opposite side, and it was decided by the bishop to search the alleged resting-place of the bones of the Admiral while the repairs were progressing.

After a preliminary excavation, the investigators opened the spot indicated by tradition as that from which the remains transported to Havana had been taken; a small vault was brought to light, which was entirely empty. This, without doubt, was the vault from which the ashes taken away in 1795 had been removed, and Canon Bellini, in charge of the investigation, believed that this would only tend to prove the truth of the Spanish account. But the next day the space between this empty vault and the wall of the cathedral was sounded, and some indications of another tomb were discovered. A piece of a large stone slab that had been partly revealed, was broken off, and through this opening it was seen that there was indeed a vault, and that it contained an object which appeared like a square box.

Instantly all was excitement. The chief vestryman hastened at once to inform the archbishop of what had occurred, while the foreign consuls, notably the Italian, M. Cambiaso, were notified, and came to the cathedral, where the canon was awaiting them with the workmen. The men were working under the direction of Sr. J. M. Castillo, a civil engineer who had charge of all important works in the island, and with whom I myself have frequently conversed. Sr. Castillo died in 1892, and his loss has been severely felt in Santo Domingo, where his distinguished talents as an engineer and his genial presence were highly esteemed.

The canon and the engineer guarded the vault until

the arrival of the civic and ecclesiastical dignitaries, when in their presence the opening was enlarged, and the object inside revealed to be a box of lead, resting upon two bricks. The top was covered with dust and small pieces of stone, but it was apparent that there was an inscription on it. Everything was then left as found, the cathedral doors locked, and a guard placed around them, the keys being left in the possession of Canon Bellini.

THE COLUMBUS CASKET.
(*End View.*)

On the tenth of September the box was taken out, in the presence of the civil, ecclesiastical and military authorities of the capital, of the consular corps, and a great number of natives and foreigners. Only a superficial examination of the bones could be made at that time, but it seemed patent to everybody present that at last the veritable remains of Columbus had been brought to light, and no one there doubted.

The enthusiasm manifested by the people bordered

on delirium, and so, says the local historian, "If it be permitted to those who have left this vale of tears to enjoy what afterward occurs on earth, then Columbus must have felt unbounded satisfaction, almost equal to that when his eyes for the first time contemplated the shores of America, in seeing that the discovery of his

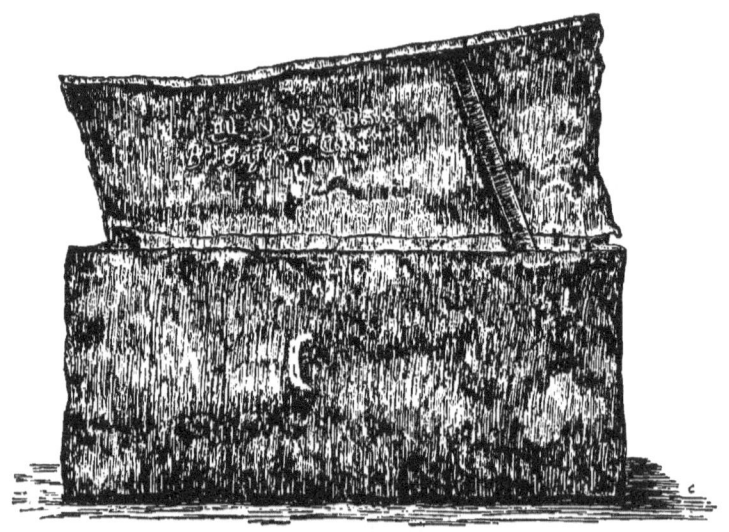

THE COLUMBUS CASKET.
(*Front View.*)

remains, forgotten during so many centuries, caused such deep emotion in the hearts of so many people."

An examination of the contents of the lead case revealed human bones crumbling and fragmentary, and only a few parts of the skeleton complete, the skull entirely reduced to dust; even those bones appearing entire at the discovery were found to have rapidly decomposed at an examination some six months later. Besides the bones and dust, a bullet was found in the case, and a silver plate.

The box in which the remains were found is entirely of lead, and when closed is twenty-three centimeters high, forty-four long, and twenty-one wide. The lid is forty-four centimeters long and twenty-one wide, with an overlapping edge in front and on the sides, and like the box is made of a single sheet of lead. The box is in a good state of preservation, and it is impossible to state whether it had been buried one, two, or three hundred years, as it is well known that lead after long exposure becomes covered with a thin coating of protoxide, which preserves it for centuries without other alteration. The color is dark gray, or of oxide of lead, such as would naturally result from the exposure. As to its preservation: the vault in which it was found is entirely of stone and brick, very dry, and without wood or any other substance that could affect the metal.

On the outside of the lid was this inscription: *D. de la A. Per Ate,*" which was interpreted to mean, "Discoverer of America, First Admiral." It has been advanced, as an argument against the authenticity of these remains, that the term "America" was not in use at the time the remains of Columbus were brought to Santo Domingo, and hence the inscription must be spurious, and fraud was implied, if not alleged. Regarding the "fraud," no one acquainted with the circumstances of discovery and the high character of the people concerned, will for a moment admit it; and it has been satisfactorily shown that the term America was in use as early as 1520, or sixteen years at least before the translation of the remains. On the inside of the lid were the words, "*Illtre y Edo Varon, Dn Cristoval Colon.*" On the right end of the case was the letter *A*, on the left end and on the front, *C*. The silver plate found in the case also had inscribed on it the name and

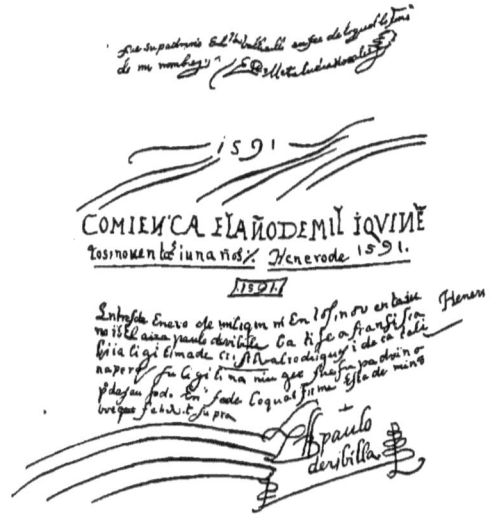

FAC-SIMILE OF OLD BAPTISMAL BOOK.

titles of Columbus; and it was held by the Dominicans that the proof of genuineness was overwhelming: in the inscriptions, and in the locality in which the case was found.

Regarding the writing on the silver plate, an objection has been raised that the *s* in the spelling of Cristoval was not of the kind in vogue in the sixteenth century, and could not be genuine; but this I myself

D. de la A. D.ra A.te

Facsímile de la inscripcion que tiene la urna de D Cristóbal Colon en la parte esterior de la tapa.

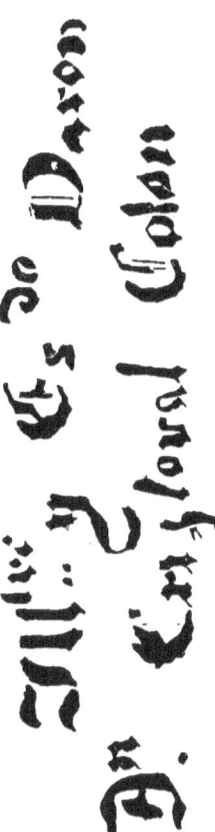

Facsímile de la inscripcion que tiene la urna de Don Cristóbal Colon en la parte interior de la tapa.

proved to be an error, for in the oldest record in the cathedral, the Book of Baptisms, bearing date 1591, this same form of *s* is used. I photographed the page on which it occurs, in order to show that it was authentic. Having orders from the chief of my department at Washington to obtain a fac-simile of the caskets in which the remains found in 1877 were held, I had a perfect duplicate made, with ancient characters and all, and this was sent to Chicago for exhibition, with other relics of Columbus, in the convent of La Rabida. After the identification of the bones, they were deposited in a cell behind one of the chapels in the cathedral, and eventually the leaden case was inclosed in one of satinwood and glass, so that everything is visible to the observer — case, bones and inscriptions.

The alleged discovery of these remains, of course, as soon as the startling information became public, attracted the attention of Spain; for her claim to the true relics was in danger of being invalidated. The Royal Academy at Madrid discussed the question at great length, and finally published a book containing the results of their investigations. The subject was treated elaborately and exhaustively, but with evident heat and some prejudice, and while it sums up the evidence against the validity of the Domingo bones, yet it offers nothing to prove that the *boveda* (or vault) opened by the Spaniards in 1795, contained the true relics of Columbus; in fact it is all of a negative character.

But the conclusion reached by the Academy is that "The remains of Cristoval Colon are in the cathedral of Habana, in the shadow of the glorious banner of

Castile. . . . It is most fit that over his sepulcher waves the same flag that sailed with him from Palos in the *Santa Maria*. . . . There rest the bones of the First Admiral of the Indies; there is his last abode."

I sincerely desire to assent to this opinion, feeling how much more fit it were if the remains still reposed under the flag Columbus himself adopted; but after having sifted all the evidence carefully, after having seen the place selected by the Admiral for his last abode, after having examined the men who were present at the discovery, the casket, the inscriptions, and even the relics themselves, I am forced to admit that the Dominicans have a stronger case than the Havanese. As already shown, the Spaniards found absolutely nothing to prove that the ashes they removed in 1795 were those of the Admiral, and no claim is advanced that they did. The only tradition they had to guide them was that the remains were on the gospel side of the altar, and this is equally applicable to the vault opened in 1877. The error of the Spaniards lay in their ignorance of the fact that there were two vaults, closely contiguous; that only a few inches distant, in fact, from the one they opened, was another. Both vaults are under the chancel, both on the gospel side; but the one containing the remains alleged by the Dominicans to be those of Columbus is nearer (close to) the wall. The Spaniards in making their excavation, by chance opened a vault wherein were the fragments of a leaden case, and vestiges of human remains; and as they could not presume that close at hand, even within the same chancel, there was another vault, they concluded that what they found was what they wanted. Such a mistake might have occurred to the Dominicans themselves; but is it not strange that the tomb of the discoverer of a world did not bear an inscription, not even the common cross, which is not denied the meanest of the poor?

Whose, then, were the remains carried to Havana in 1795? It was at first thought that they were those of Don Bartholomew, Christopher's brother who died at Santo Domingo in 1514; but finally it was concluded that they pertained to Don Diego, the son and Viceroy, who was, according to history, and at the expressed wish of his wife, interred in the chancel of the cathedral. It must then (says the chronicler I have been following) be acknowledged that, while there is no evidence to the contrary, the relics taken to Havana with so much pomp must have been those of Diego Columbus, son of the great Discoverer, and who, during his first term as governor of Hispaniola, greatly promoted the colonization of Cuba. This being true, it seems, after all, most fitting that Cuba should have secured (even though unwittingly) the relics of one who was so closely identified with her colonization, and that Santo Domingo should have retained (though unconsciously) those of the great man who founded the first city on her soil, and whose last wish it was that he might rest forever in her embrace.

Since the discovery, accusations of fraud have been made, but no evidence has been adduced that such was perpetrated; in truth, nothing could be sustained against men of such blameless lives as the archbishop, then the Apostolic Delegate of the Pope, Monseñor Roque

Cocchia, Bishop of Orope, and the canon of the cathedral, Bellini.

I have followed, in writing this account of the last burial-place of Columbus, first, the *Informe* of the Spanish Academy, and second, the work published in Santo Domingo by Emiliano Tejera, whose words even I have sometimes used, as translated from the original

THE TABLET AND THE VAULT AT SANTO DOMINGO.

Spanish, and to whom, as a friend and an author, I am indebted for his impartial statements. Several other pamphlets have been published on this question, but the two cited above suffice to give one all the facts on both sides. Tejera closes his work, "*Los Restos de Colon*," with an impassioned appeal to the world for a just and impartial verdict. After reciting the trials and sorrows of Columbus, he says: "And what did Fate reserve for the discoverer of America in return for so much faith, and a life devoted to a realization of the soul's ideal? Sad to confess, the hatred of the envious, the sorrows of a faithful servant, the crushing weight of insult, shipwreck, disappointment, and finally a sad and solitary death, filled to overflowing with the bitterness of one who, after having consecrated his whole life to the cause of humanity, goes down to the grave seeing that mankind has for him only a Calvary. Nearly three hundred years after the death of the great Admiral, posterity gave evidence of a desire to pay their debt of gratitude, and it was decided to transfer his remains from one Spanish colony to another. But those in charge of the removal made a mistake, and homage was paid to a stranger, while the great hero remained forgotten in his stone vault in Santo Domingo. Another great wrong may be inflicted to-day: for his authentic remains are on the eve of being disowned, and thus the oblivion of three centuries will be perpetuated."

It may seem trivial to the outside world, but to the Dominicans the question is a vital one, and they desire, of all things, to prove to the world that the ashes of Columbus remain in the cathedral, and the island in which he himself desired they should finally rest.

In view of the difficulties in the way of an adjustment of differences between the Dominican and the Spanish governments, perhaps it might not seem presumptuous in me to suggest that they effect a compromise, and one of them resign to the other the ashes in its possession, depositing them in a common vault, erect above them a monument commemorating the many virtues of their erstwhile owners; and thus the admirers of the great Columbus would feel quite certain of their hero, and not be harassed by doubts that they were paying their devotions at the wrong shrine.

Shortly after my arrival at Santo Domingo, I was taken to the cathedral and was shown the alleged remains of the great Admiral. Since their removal from the vault in which they were discovered, in 1877, they have been inclosed in a casket of satin-wood, and are now guarded in a little cell at the left of the great altar in the cathedral. To obtain permission to view the remains, it is necessary to secure the sanction of the ecclesiastical, municipal and national authorities. Each body holds a key to the cell, and a delegate from each must accompany the visitor. As Commissioner from the Exposition, I was given the extraordinary privilege of viewing the *restos*, the Minister of Foreign Relations accompanying me to and through the cathedral, and Señor Pichardo, a local historian of renown, explaining to me all the details. I was shown the vaults, the fragments of the leaden case out of the grave of Don Luis Colon, the cell, and finally the remains themselves. I photographed everything appertaining to the relics and the things having a bearing upon their authenticity, and while in the thick of it a register was brought me, in which I was requested to inscribe my signature and my opinion as to the legitimacy of the bones. But it did not appear to me that I was there to give an opinion, having been sent by my Government merely to collect data for others wiser than myself in historical lore to elaborate. So I took council with myself, while the eyes of the eager officials were upon me, and, instead of committing myself to an irrevocable opinion, I quietly walked all around the question of legitimacy, and wrote how happy I was to view this grand cathedral, this onetime resting-place of the ashes of the great Columbus, etc., etc., having seen so many places identified with his life and grand achievements in other lands. When this was translated to the officials in waiting it did not seem, somehow, to satisfy them, and a deep silence fell around us, broken at last by the indignant exclamation of my guide, that I had not pronounced upon the authenticity of the relics at all.

Concerning this question of the present resting-place of the bones of Columbus, I may say, however, that I have declared myself in favor of Santo Domingo; but it was not until after I had resigned my position as Commissioner, and when my declaration would not convey with it an official sanction. My mission merely was to collect everything pertaining to Columbus, not only in Santo Domingo, but in Cuba and throughout all the Antilles, that this historical material might be presented at Chicago for inspection by a competent committee, who would then perhaps determine as between the claims of the two islands. To give an opinion while then in the performance of my duty, as above stated, would seem at least an impertinence, and could not be entertained.

## XIX.

PUERTO RICO AND PONCE DE LEON.

ARMS OF PUERTO RICO.

THE island of Puerto Rico was discovered by Columbus on his second voyage to the New World, in November, 1493. Sailing northwesterly up from the Caribbees, leaving behind him the attractive group of the Virgins, he had scarcely lost sight of these before another and larger island came to view. Coasting its southern shore, the Spaniards feasted their eyes upon a succession of hills and mountains covered with glorious forests, and sailed in and out of beautiful harbors fringed with tropical trees above beaches of glistening sands.

*Borinquen* was the native name of this large and fertile island, but the European discoverer called it San Juan Bautista, afterward changed to Puerto Rico.

Columbus landed at a harbor which he called Aguadilla, or the watering-place; here he filled his water-casks, and, after remaining a couple of days, sailed thence over to the island of Santo Domingo, only sixty miles distant. Arriving eventually at Samana (the *Golfo de las Flechas*), an Indian who had been taken from this spot to Spain on the previous voyage, and been baptized and instructed in the faith, was sent ashore in a boat. The Indian was then set at liberty, bearing many trinkets and kind messages to the cacique, but nothing was ever heard of him again. One Indian still remained with Columbus; he was a young Lucayan, a native of Guanahani, and he had been christened Diego Colon, after the brother of the Admiral; he served the Spaniards as interpreter.

On the twenty-fifth of November the peaks of Monte-Cristi appeared to the eyes of the anxious Spaniards, and they came to anchor in the mouth of the Rio del Oro, where they found the dead bodies of some of their countrymen who had been killed at the time of the massacre at Navidad. Next day they discovered that all the garrison had been killed, and saw that the friendly chieftain, Guacanagari was wounded and ill.

At first they distrusted the cacique's story, but he was at length taken on board the ships, and his wondering eyes beheld the various plants and animals brought over for the settlement. The Indian then saw, for the first time, cattle, sheep, swine and horses; and, as the largest native quadruped of Haiti was no bigger than a raccoon, he was astounded at their size. The horses, in particular, excited his wonderment to the highest degree; they were the first ever brought to America, and he shrank from them as terrible monsters, that would devour him at the Spaniards' commands.

If anything further were needed to impress the simple Indians with the prowess of Columbus, it was presented in the persons of the Carib warriors, taken prisoners in the Southern islands, and from whom the timid Haitiens shrank in affright. But there were other captives to whom the cacique was attracted. These were certain Indian women from Puerto Rico, whom Columbus had rescued from the Caribs; but who were detained by him in captivity. Among them was one woman of fine presence, whom even the Spaniards admired and had named Catalina. Guacanagari was at once enamored of this princess from Puerto Rico, and conveyed to her the information that she and her friends would find liberty and a warm welcome awaiting them, if they could but join him at his village on shore. The women made the attempt, dropping overboard about midnight and swimming for the shore. It was three miles distant, and the sea was rough, but they all reached the land in safety, though four of them were recaptured on the beach. A beacon light was burning, and the cacique was in waiting. Catalina and her companions escaped with him to the forest, and when a search was made, next morning, all the Indians had disappeared.

Guacanagari, henceforth, was regarded as a fugitive, to be dealt with as a felon, and was eventually hounded to death by the men he had most benefited. Catalina disappears from view with her flight into the forest.

GENERAL HEUREAUX.
(*President of the Republic of Santo Domingo.*)

The Island of Borinquen, or Porto Rico, from which the Indian maid was taken, was left undisturbed for fifteen years after its discovery; but in 1508 Ponce de Leon, the Governor of the eastern province of Santo Domingo, had his attention called to it by reports of its rich soil and mineral wealth. He sailed across the channel and landed at Aguada, with a caravel of soldiers. He was hospitably entertained by the cacique of that province, Agueynaba, who showed him some rivers with golden sands.

The bay of Aguadilla is broad and beautiful, with

miles of cocoa palms sweeping its sandy shores, and with a background of the rounded hills that distinguish the island of Puerto Rico. Both Columbus and De Leon were charmed with these peaceful shores, and with good reason. The Admiral watered his ships at the spring of Aguadilla, which to-day still gushes forth from the earth in great volume, and gives the spot its name: Aguada, or Aguadilla; good watering-place.

Leaving here some of his men, De Leon returned to Santo Domingo, and came back with an armament, finally locating at a spot near the present capital of the island, San Juan. Not long after he commenced the distribution of the natives of the island as slaves, to his followers, in *repartimientos*, as the custom had prevailed in Santo Domingo. The gentle Indians had never before been subjected to any restraint, and they soon revolted, killing many Spaniards before they were subjected.

During this revolt some of the Indians tried an experiment to ascertain if it were true (as the Spaniards told them) that the white strangers were immortal, and could not be killed. Two of them found a Spaniard in a lonely place, took him to a river, and held his head under water two or three hours, after that watching the body for two days. Well satisfied from this experiment that the Spaniard was really dead, these conscientious Indians reported to that effect to their chief, Agueynaba, and the massacre was begun. But as the Spaniards were being constantly re-enforced by soldiers coming in caravels out of the sea, the simple Indians did finally believe that those they had slain revived, in some mysterious way, and so submitted.

Ponce de Leon has a name for gentle deeds and chivalrous actions; but he did not hesitate to employ the most barbarous methods for the subjection of the natives. To this day has survived the fame of his great bloodhound "Berezillo." The great dog was a terror to the Indians, springing upon them and tearing them to pieces, and his services were so highly valued that he drew the pay of a cross-bowman. After years of fiendish work in the Spanish service, this Berezillo was finally killed by a poisoned arrow, while swimming a stream in pursuit of a Carib.

The first city founded, Caparra, was located across the bay southwest from the present capital. Caparra was abandoned in 1522, and nothing of consequence remains to indicate its site. San Juan de Puerto Rico, founded by De Leon in 1511, became the capital, and is now the chief city, though not leading in population.

The chief ports to-day are San Juan and Arecibo on the north coast, Humacao and Fajardo on the east, Arroyo, Ponce and Guayanilla on the south coast, Mayaguez and Aguadilla on the west.

The island is mountainous, the interior being a vast sea of rounded hills, yet with such gentle slopes and fertile soil as to be cultivable to their summits, and possessing great possibilities for the agriculturist. The highest mountain, the nucleus of the central chain that traverses the island from east to west, is Luquillo; it is about four thousand feet high. There are many rivers, large and small; numerous caves, in which the Indians formerly lived; several hot springs, good roads between the chief cities, and an improved cultivation throughout the island. "The cattle on a thousand hills" is an expression that may well be used in speaking of Puerto Rico, as the hills are to be counted by thousands, and the island is famous for its fine breeds of live-stock. All the islands south of Puerto Rico send to it for its horses and cattle, which are shipped thence in large numbers.

To conclude these statistics (which are only given because so little is really known of this island), Puerto Rico is nearly square in outline; it contains some three hundred and fifty Spanish square leagues, with a population of about seven hundred and fifty thousand.

The largest city is Ponce, with a population of perhaps thirty-five thousand; it is on the south coast, in the center of the sugar region. San Juan, the capital, has but twenty-five thousand inhabitants, and there are several cities with populations numbering at least twenty thousand each.

The capital, San Juan de Puerto Rico, is most advantageously situated on an island connected with the mainland of the north coast by a bridge and causeway. A magnificent high road (the *camino real*) connects it with Ponce; a line of railway has been projected and is partially constructed, that will eventually traverse the whole island along the coast, connecting all important towns and cities, and short lines now run out into the country. San Juan is as compact a city as ever was built; it is on a peninsula terminated by a fortress, surrounded by massive walls of hardened stone and mortar, with a height in places of from fifty to one hundred feet. Behind the citadel is a broad parade ground, but except for this open space the houses cover the area within the

THE HARBOR OF SAN JUAN SEEN FROM THE CASA BLANCA, OR HOME OF PONCE DE LEON

walls, from the eastern to the western fort. The houses are of stone, with iron balconies, and of all colors: pink, gray, blue, yellow, drab—but none white. These mingling tints produce a harmony of tones most gratifying to the eye. All have shutters and jalousies, but no windows, and all are chimneyless. The cathedral, theater, city hall, the Governor-General's palace, and several churches, are the principal structures. Below the walls are the wharves, about which and on the *Marina*, only, wooden houses are suffered to be built. Through the *Marina* is a broad concrete walk lined with seats, adorned with rude statues, and with an ornamental garden of flowers and tropic trees lying between it and the high walls, which are gray and stark, with ornate and antique sentry-boxes projecting at intervals.

Through an arched entrance in the lower wall runs the only street into the city when the gates fronting the sea are closed; from this entrance a road leads out into the country, at first through open pasture, then dipping toward the shore of the bay, where it is bordered with cocoa-palms that increase in number as the distance lengthens from the town. Here and there is a little village, full of shops and drinking booths, where the people come from the city to drink and pass the time in the afternoon and on Sundays. Beyond, is another broad waste, then the outer fort at the bridge is reached, where the stream and shore are bordered with mangroves. In the distance is a misty mountain, some two thousand feet in height, and from this circle around hundreds and hundreds of hills and hillocks, forming a panorama of exceeding loveliness. These hills approach the shore, growing smaller and smaller as they near it, flecked with every shade and shadow of cloud, and gleaming in the sun. A village shows here and there in a valley; the cocoa-palms stand in long golden ranks on the shores of the bay. There are few trees, however, in town, save in the plaza, a palm on the *Marina*, and at the *casa blanca*, the house of De Leon.

My arrival at San Juan, with the invitation from our Government to participate in the Exposition, was during Christmas week, 1891. The whole city was in festivity; there was grand mass in the cathedral, music continually in the plaza, and a special view of the holy patroness *la Virgen de Providencia*, whose cloak is said to be worth fifteen hundred dollars, and her jewels twenty thousand dollars. In response to a cablegram from St. Thomas, Mr. Hayden, the American Vice-Consul, met me on board the steamer and took me with him to quarters in the consulate. His good offices and the hospitality of our Consul, Mr. Stewart, were freely placed at my disposal, and through them I was at once enabled to communicate with the authorities.

The consular residence was in a large and noble structure on the bluff above the fortifications, and in the healthiest part of the city commanding a glorious view of the harbor and distant mountains. It is important, in securing residence in San Juan, to find, if possible, a spot elevated above the dirty streets and houses, that are crowded and swarming with a careless population. For every year the yellow fever attacks the foreigners here, and many succumb to its dread ravages. At the time of my arrival the Consul was at home on sick leave,

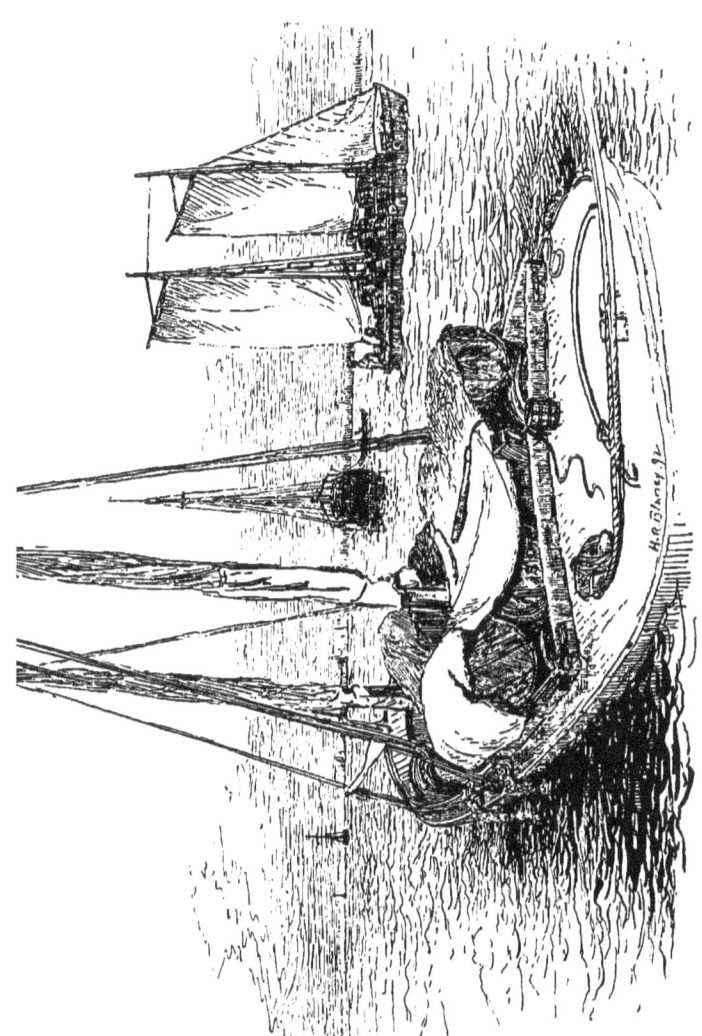

A SUGAR LIGHTER IN PUERTO RICO WATERS.

having been prostrated with fever from which he barely recovered. Most of the foreign residents live in the immediate suburbs, like Cangrejo, where there are gardens of palms and fruits, and where the air is pure.

The Governor and Captain-General, Señor Don José Lasso y Perez, received me graciously and acted upon my suggestions with promptitude. A commission was soon appointed, consisting of gentlemen identified with the island's best interests, and after my departure they had charge of the Exposition matters and seemed alive to the demands of the occasion. Although a Spanish island, one of the few possessions yet remaining to Spain in America, yet there is the same discontent with the home government, so manifest in Cuba. Excessive taxes and an alien soldiery, together with extensive and expensive office-holdings by foreigners, have contributed to wean this once loyal island from its attachment to the Spanish crown.

The social life of San Juan, though foreign and Spanish in its features, is delightful to one allowed to visit in the families; it is there that may be seen the true courtesy, the gentle breeding, of these descendants of the Old World hidalgos. One cannot fail to note the gracious beauty of the ladies of Puerto Rico; they possess all the features which make their Spanish sisters so famous, and have a languid grace all their own.

From the living types of the present inhabitants to the ancient dwellers here, may seem a violent departure, and those in the flesh are certainly far more interesting; but the aborigines have their claims, and I would not leave the island without a brief reference to them.

NATIVE HUTS AND DOVE COTES.
(*Island of Puerto Rico.*)

The aborigines of this island have left behind them some very unique antiquities. There are no others like them in the world, and they present most interesting subjects for study. In our national museum is the finest collection of these Indian relics, the gift some years ago of the late George Latimer, of San Juan. It has been described in a valuable pamphlet by Professor

Mason, of the Smithsonian Institution, and it is a possession envied by all the museums in the world. There is now in the island a collection of these antiquities that may rival that in our museum, owned by a learned doctor residing at Bayamon, and I secured the promise of this collection for exhibition at Chicago.

Without going into a description of the many unique specimens found in Puerto Rico, I may mention two, at least, that are peculiar to the island: these are a stone collar and a carved stone shaped like a pointed mountain. The collars have been found in great abundance, and it was conjectured that they were made for war or sacrificial purposes. But the explanation given me by a Jesuit professor seems to me to be the correct one. He held that these stone collars, which are in shape like a horse-collar, and elaborately carved, were made by the Indians for use after death. Each Indian of importance, with no tools other than stone knives and chisels, would spend the greater part of a lifetime laboriously carving out this great stone, and when he died it was placed in the grave with him, resting upon his breast, to keep him in place forever, so that the Devil could not take him away.

But the Indians have long since disappeared, and no one can tell us their motives in making these queer things; the antiquarian can only indulge in blind guesses as to their uses.

If one would gain knowledge of the common people he must go to the market, which is situated on the hill near the ocean skirt of the city. In the court, wnich is flagged with great stones, are rude booths containing

ALONG THE RIVER.

meat, vegetables and country produce of every sort. A little stall now and then had a parrot for sale, but most conspicuous of the fowl kind on exhibition, was the game-cock, tied to the stool of its owner. Outside the court, in sheds, dozens of these game-cocks were scratching and crowing, each one confined by a little length of string. Asking some questions about them, I was shown a room in which there were from thirty to fifty, each one in a square open box, and every one crowing defiantly at the top of his lungs. Every cock had the feathers shaven from his back, and plucked from head, neck and tail. They were very pugnacious between themselves, but easily handled. One was shown me which had won a purse of one hundred dollars the Sunday before, and the average price for a good game-cock was from ten to twenty-five dollars.

Expressing a desire to see the cock-pit, where the fights took place, a man conducted me to the *Marina*, where I was shown a tumble-down shanty with corrugated iron roof covering a circular inclosure some thirty feet in diameter. The floor was of hard earth inclosed within a fence three feet high, outside of which were seats placed around the arena, and numbered. There is a cock-fight here every Sunday, and a great deal of money is lost and won. Outside the structure, on the sidewalk, were a number of cocks in a row, taking an airing, tied to pegs a few feet apart. The man in attendance took up every fowl in succession, and after filling his mouth with water squirted it in the eyes and under the wings of the bird, as a "refresher." In various parts of the city, these fighting-cocks may be seen every day, taking their airings on the sidewalks, strutting up and down to the length of their strings, and making the air resound with their crows of defiance.

Beneath the walls of the Morro — the great fort that guards the harbor — the heavy surf comes tumbling in, thundering at the cavernous cliffs, and rolling in great white-crested billows over the coral beds. For the perfection of sea views, comprising waves and breakers, one should go out to the windward side of San Juan.

Permission was given me to visit the Morro. It is not unlike the fortress of the same name at Havana. Within its great walls is a small town by itself, with

SENTRY BOX AND CEMETERY GATE AT SAN JUAN.

chapel, houses and barracks, and there are deep dungeons, covered ways and antiquated guns. A lighttower rises above the fort within the walls, equipped with a first-class light, and a signal station.

Relics of the early days of Puerto Rico are not plentiful here, and although I persistently searched, I found few objects of interest. Perhaps the Indian relics lead in interest, but only to the antiquarian, while to the numismatist the old coins of the island are valuable. These are called the *macuquina*, and are clipped coins of Spain, generally of the last century, cut and counterstamped, in order to keep them in the island for local barter. They are now very scarce, and can only be found in the pawnshops and in the hands of private collectors.

The most picturesque structure in San Juan de Puerto Rico, leaving out portions of the fortifications, is the building occupied to-day by the Royal Engineers, and known as the *Casa Blanca*. It is also the most valuable to the historian, for it was built and occupied by no less a personage than Juan Ponce de Leon, the *Conquistador* who, as has been said, was the first governor of this island, coming here in the year 1508.

The *Casa Blanca* is protected toward the bay by a crenelated wall of ancient aspect, backed by a garden full of tropical plants, with a double row of cocoa-palms making it conspicuous. From the seaward looking windows and the garden, the view spread out below, of the bay and harbor, is most entrancing. Immediately beneath is the great gray wall of the line of defense, with its quaint old cannon, its projecting sentry turrets hanging precariously over the waves, and its massive battlements; beyond, is the blue-tinted water of the bay, the palm-fringed coast of the mainland; the low and jagged hills in ranks and rows, growing darker and mistier, till, merged in the clouds above and well-nigh piercing them rises majestic Yunque, the mountain with an Indian name.

The site lies midway between the palace and the Morro. In Ponce De Leon's time, doubtless, all the space was open, and the old *Conquistador*, ensconced in his white castle, could sweep the surrounding sea clear to the horizon's brim. It was here, after the island was subjected, that he sat and planned the

THE CASA BLANCA.
(*The ancient castle of Ponce de Leon the Conquistador.*)

voyage that made his name so famous. Looking out upon the northward-stretching ocean, he speculated upon the unseen wonders that lay beyond his sight, turning over in his mind the stories told him by his Indian servants of the mysterious island to the north, in the Lucayan chain, that held in the bosom of its deep forest the wonderful Fountain of Youth. So we may say that the voyage that resulted in the discovery of Florida and the upper Bahamas was planned in this very *Casa Blanca*, the ancient castle of Ponce de Leon.

It was in the year 1512 that Ponce de Leon sailed out of the bay of Aguadilla for the discovery of Bimini, where, the Indians of Puerto Rico told him, was to be found the Fountain of Eternal Youth. Sailing northwest he cruised the Bahama chain, and landed on San Salvador, or Guanahani, the first land discovered by Columbus. Leon was there just twenty years after the landing of the Admiral. Thence, sailing northwardly, he sighted a coast banked with flowers hanging from lofty trees; this he called Florida. He thought it an island, even after he had been named, by the king of Spain, Adelantado of Florida and of Bimini. He did not stay here, but under the guidance of an old woman, whom he found on one of the keys, searched the chain for the famed Bimini, and finding it not returned disheartened to Puerto Rico; one of his officers following him with the tidings of its discovery.

He received from the crown of Spain the elevated title of Adelantado of Bimini and Florida; but his attention was so drawn to affairs in the island of Puerto Rico that he paid no attention to his new provinces, until the great discoveries of Cortez, in Mexico, roused his dormant energies, and he again essayed a voyage to the northward.

He had previously, in 1515, made an expedition against the Caribs of the Southern islands, but was disastrously defeated, many of his soldiers were killed, and he returned without booty to his own island. Here he staid as governor until 1521, when he fitted out two ships and sailed for Florida. There he was attacked by the Indians, severely wounded, and retreated to Cuba, where he died. His body was brought to Puerto Rico and deposited beneath the altar of the Dominican church of San Juan, where it rested until 1863, when it

THE LAST OF HIM WHO SOUGHT ETERNAL YOUTH.
(*Lead case containing the bones of Ponce de Leon.*)

was removed, the intention being to erect a monument to his memory, and place his ashes beneath it. This monument has not yet been erected, and the ashes still lie unsepultured. The lead case in which they are contained can be seen to-day, in the chapel attached to the church. Here I saw it, in 1892. It is about three feet long, bound with ribbons sealed with the municipal seal.

The church itself, in which the ashes at present lie, is one of the oldest in San Juan, and in its decorations quite attractive. Here, then, is the last resting-place of one of the bravest of the *conquistadores*, the subjugator of Puerto Rico, discoverer of Florida, and the seeker for the Fountain of Youth. The inscription on his monument reads: "This narrow grave contains the remains of a man who was a Lion by name, and much more by his deeds."

His deeds, indeed, live after him; the island he discovered is still in possession of the descendants of the conquerors; but the people he found so peacefully dwelling here have long since passed away.

Facing the western sea, looking out over the waving palms, the *Casa Blanca* recalls to us those great deeds of the lion-hearted Spaniard. There is no spot in San Juan more picturesque, and no outlook so attractive, especially at sunset. One memorable sunset I shall never forget. As the sun went down, the mountain, great and solitary Yunque, was left cold and green, with spirals of smoke circling around its crown from hidden valleys in its cool recesses. Its peak was left outlined against a clear and amber sky, though now and then obscured by smoke-colored clouds. After the sun had fairly set, banks of rose-colored clouds remained along the horizon, ascending in the east, even to the moon, which, "in full-orbed splendor," round and silver white, looked down upon the lonely island in the bay. In the west, flecking a sky so clear and hard that it seemed as if cut from an amethyst, lay fleecy lines of golden clouds. As though jealous of the splendors of the sun, that night the moon disported a lunar rainbow, rivaling in beauty anything I have ever seen in the tropic sky.

Thus I left the island of Puerto Rico; the propeller again shook the steamer, and soon the calm waters of the sheltered bay gave place to the rougher waves of the turbulent Caribbean Sea.

The clouds faded out of the sky as the open sea was reached, and the breeze was so cool that I could easily imagine myself in Northern waters in the month of May. And those mountains might be Northern, too, for aught one might note to the contrary, were it not for their carpet of deepest green, and the border of palms that caresses their feet before they plunge into the sea.

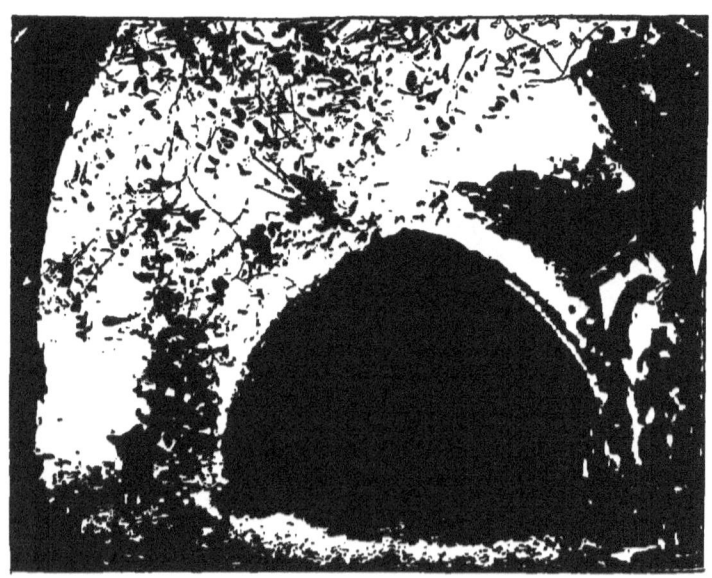

ARCHES OF SAN FRANCISCO CONVENT. — SANTO DOMINGO CITY.

## XX.

AMONG THE SAINTS AND THE VIRGINS.

LYING directly east of Puerto Rico is the Danish Island of St. Thomas; near it is another, St. John's, and south of these lies Santa Cruz.

All these Saints at present pertain to Denmark; but north of them, and northwesterly, is a cluster of isles and islets belonging mostly to England, and known as the Virgins. Columbus named them all, as he came through this archipelago on his second voyage in 1493. The latter group he called after the lamented and revered Saint Ursula and her hapless eleven thousand virgins, so cruelly put to death by the Huns. Saints and Virgins, all, are now nearly as dead as the great and holy men and women after whom they were named; moribund, every one, and awaiting the touch of American enterprise to revive them.

All but Santa Cruz lie within the parallels 18° and 19° north latitude; 64° and 65° west longitude, and are purely tropical in character and surroundings. The only port of call is that of St. Thomas, where the steamers of the "United States and Brazil Line" touch on their way to and from South America. The voyage thither from the United States consumes five days from the port of Newport News, and six from New York. Leaving the Northern port with the decks covered with snow and ice, the second day the ice has disappeared; on the third one may wander about without wraps, and by the fifth, when the island desired is sighted, the mercury has climbed to 80°, where it persistently stays all day, when allowed to remain in the shade.

It may be night when the steamer arrives at the harbor of St. Thomas, but the sweet land-breeze brings off the fragrance of a thousand flowers, and the strange, pungent odors of the terrene tropics, and you know that a new land is reached at last. New scenes await you, if it be your first trip to the tropics, and they cannot but interest and delight you. Arriving at the harbor in the night, one might well imagine he had by mistake been brought to the borders of the infernal regions, for flaring flambeaux illumine the dark waters, dusky forms glide about with strange and discordant cries, yells and whistlings. A weird procession of black and hideous hags, clad in ragged raiment, bearing upon their heads great baskets, and shuffling clumsily up and down the gang-planks, has established connection with the shore, and is supplying the steamer with coal. It is merely an episode in the life of the voyager; but it is a matter of great importance to those wretched negresses, who get but a penny a basket for their toil, and who are always ready, by night and by day, to respond to the blast of the great horn blown by the contractor from the parapet of Blackbeard's castle, on the hill across the harbor.

As daylight comes, it is seen what a beautiful harbor is this of St. Thomas, worthy of all the adjectives one can heap upon it — magnificent, glorious, gem-like; it is everything except hurricane-proof. Hills on all sides surround it, save toward the southern sea, where the entrance lies between two high promontories guarded

THE HARBOR FROM THE FORT.

by ancient forts. Hills behind it, sun-burnt and bare, look down upon a charming town, itself built upon three elevations, and one of the most picturesque places in the Caribbean Sea. One rarely hears the name of this town, the port of St. Thomas, but it is called Charlotte Amalia, and is a good old-fashioned settlement, clean and pretty, with straight streets, good though decaying wharves, street and harbor lights, a fine police force, a stable government and most delightful situation. There is not another just like it anywhere for comfort and convenience, and it fitly supplements the advantages of its royal harbor as a place of call, and even detention, for the naval vessels cruising in these seas.

Almost entirely landlocked, the harbor of St. Thomas has room for two hundred vessels to lie at anchor; it contains a marine railway and a floating dock, and is the last resort of all the distressed vessels in this region. It has often been spoken of in connection with the establishing in the West Indies of a coaling station for the vessels of the United States navy. Two other points have claimed attention: Mole St. Nicolas, on the coast of Haiti, and Samana Bay in Santo Domingo. The first-named has some advantages not possessed by the others; namely, contiguity to the great channel between Cuba, Haiti and Jamaica, and the consequent command of the traffic passing through, which will be immensely augmented after the construction of the Nicaragua Canal; but it is in a barren and barbarous country, and there are many difficulties in the way of its acquisition, the most important being the aversion of the Haitiens to the alienation of any of their territory.

Samana is farther east, but has almost equal value as a strategic position, has a magnificent harbor with deep water, and healthful situation. It can be more easily acquired than St. Nicolas, and there is little doubt that the whole peninsula could be purchased outright.

St. Thomas, however, is not only available, without

any danger of international complications, but it is eager and anxious to come under the protection of the United States. For the acquisition of St. Thomas, it would only be necessary to appropriate a few million dollars, treat with Denmark in a frank, open manner, and the island (as well as Santa Cruz and St. John's) would become American property. Unfortunately, our Government once treated with Denmark for this very possession; the treaty was not only ready for ratification, but the king of Denmark had taken farewell of his loyal subjects and virtually given up the island, when occurred one of those humiliating episodes that have more than once made America a byword in diplomatic circles.

The treaty intention was ignored; the king of Denmark had the humiliation of recalling his loyal but disappointed subjects, and the attitude of the home government toward us cannot but be that of deep resentment. As it stands now, Denmark, though anxious to dispose of her West Indian possessions, cannot take the initiative, having been once insulted, and has every reason to view with distrust any proposition emanating from the Government of the United States, even should our legislators have the wisdom to move for their acquisition. Among the people of the islands themselves, there is a strong desire for annexation to the United States, for they realize that such union means renewed life and prosperity, in the place of the present death-in-life existence they are forced to lead. Even among the officials there is the same strong feeling in favor of the possession of the islands by our Government, for the higher officials would then be retired on pensions, and the soldiers would be relieved from dangerous and irksome duty so far from home. At present the government is expensive, somewhat oppressive, and the annual deficit to Denmark rises from $50,000 to $100,000. For these reasons, the inhabitants of St. Thomas, St. John's and Santa Cruz would hail with joy any movement looking toward their becoming citizens entitled to the protection and benefits of the United States. They do not expect the rights of elective franchise, and would be content with a form of government somewhat like our territorial administration, desiring only to participate in our prosperity. Such a government as we should give them would lessen their oppressive taxes, allow of greater freedom, and permit of their unlimited expansion; whereas they are now bound by the fetters of European domination.

The society here in Charlotte Amalia is most enjoyable, though the few members composing the *élite* are necessarily exclusive, and restrict the privileges to the Danish office-holders and leading merchants. But it is a quaint and enjoyable society one meets here, and if, perchance, the island ever should pass under the American flag, it will be a long while before the social status will be adjusted on the prevailing harmonious basis and along the present lines.

The island is thirteen miles long by three wide; deserted plantations and barren fields cover the hills and line the shores, but there is no other settlement than Charlotte Amalia, with its population of some twelve or thirteen thousand. Most of the inhabitants are black or colored, and the few whites live on the hills of the town. Government Hill is the center, and here are the best houses, though there are fine structures on and about the others. The only level street runs around the shore and out into the country, while the other thor-

OLD FORT AT ST. THOMAS.

oughfares, aided by flights of stone steps, climb up and down the hills, that give such beautiful views over the harbor, and where the breezes always play.

Although Danish is the official language, yet English is universally spoken, even the officials using it; while reminders of what St. Thomas used to be when the ships of all nations came here, and trade was carried on with foreigners of every kind, are constantly met with in the linguistic attainments of all classes. Scarcely a trader or merchant here that cannot speak at least three or four tongues beside his own, and even the boys in the streets are polyglots. The old days, when this island was the entrepot of all the others, when merchants sought it coming from Puerto Rico and Santo Domingo with their vessels ballasted with Mexican dollars to be exchanged for goods, and silver was often seen wheeled in barrows through the streets — those days have departed never to return. And yet, the fortunate position of St. Thomas in relation to the easternmost West Indies and the South American ports has remained unchanged; only the methods of doing business have altered, and the increased number of steamers running to different ports have taken from the island the importance of being a distributing center.

As a valuable site for a coaling-station, however, commanding the Caribbean Sea and the approaches to the east coast of South America, it still possesses the great natural advantages with which the Creator originally endowed it; and wise will be the Government that takes advantage of the opportunity afforded for its acquisition.

The only drawback to the purchase of the Danish islands is the fact that with St. Thomas must go the island of Santa Cruz, which, though rich and picturesque, with good roads, large plantations, and a population in need of nothing but money to make them prosperous, yet would not be a desirable possession. St. John's, though poor and comparatively uninhabited, has at least one good harbor in which large vessels can find shelter, and has an importance that for centuries has been overlooked.

The history of St. Thomas, of its perils from the pirates of the sea, from the roving buccaneers and the adventurers of various nations, is written on its face. Upon the crests of two hills above the town stand two towers, called respectively "Bluebeard's" and "Blackbeard's" castles. They may have once been occupied by those famous pirates, who certainly sailed the adjoining seas, and tradition has it that vast treasure lies hidden underneath them; but history states that they were built by the Government, about the year 1700. Perhaps the finest view of the harbor and the island is to be obtained from the castle known as "Blackbeard's," the property of Mr. Edward Moron, whose house, adjacent, is the abode of a generous hospitality.

It was my desire, of course, to obtain the co-operation of the Government in the Exposition, and to this end the American Consul, genial Colonel Horne, presented me to the Governor, General Arendrup. I found His Excellency a pleasant and shrewd gentleman, with the Danish desire for thrift, who listened with evident interest to the statement of my case; but who was opposed to the granting by his Government of any appropriation for the display of the resources of the islands. Although drawing a princely salary himself, and having many officials under him magnificently reimbursed for their absence from home comforts, he yet professed to see no way by which even a few thousand dollars could be raised for an exhibit at

Chicago. Finally, being convinced of the niggardliness of the Government, and the total lack of concern for the welfare of the colony, I appealed with some success to the merchants of the town. It was true, as the Governor urged, that the island had little to send, having few native products, and no industries. But, knowing the desire of the people to make known the advantages of their island as a winter resort, and its desirability as a coaling-station, I recommended that a large model, or relief-map, be prepared, showing the glorious harbor, the surrounding hills, the town, the tropical vegetation—in a word, a small exposition of the island visible at a glance, that should convey to the world at large an adequate picture of its beauty and advantages. This idea was applauded, and several of the merchants promised the necessary funds for the purpose. It was next necessary to secure the talent for producing the map: a difficult thing in a community where there is no uplifting public sentiment and example for the encouragement of art or literature.

Fortunately, there was one in whom the divine spark of genius was glowing with fervor, whose life had fitted him for the very work I had projected, and whose patriotism was equal to the demands about to be made upon it. Dr. C. E. Taylor, though an Englishman by birth, and a Dane by adoption, who had the only bookstore in St. Thomas, and who was a member of the General Council, came to my assistance. He volunteered to reproduce the harbor, drawn to a scale, and in such a shape as to be attractive to the general observer as well as valuable to the scientist. With the assistance of his son, a boy of sixteen, but who had already given proof of artistic ability, he set to work, and after six months of hard labor, in the intervals of his business, he produced a relief model of the hills and harbor that will challenge the criticism of the world. Thus, without the aid of the impecunious Government, and by the unassisted effort of native talent, my friend has evoked a work that will comprehensively show the many and varied attractions of the island at a glance.

Dr. Taylor, as I have indicated, is a genius, having turned his hand to many things, during his varied and checkered career, and having accomplished things that would have discouraged any one of less heroic mold.

If one will climb the hill behind to its crest, he will have before him, and in fact all around him, such a panorama of sea and water views as is opened out to one very seldom in a lifetime. The whole island is in sight—a perfect gem; its facets almost gleaming beneath the intense light of the tropical sun. Brown and bare as it is, yet the island has a beauty of an appealing sort, and one delights in the visions of the others of the Virgin group, rising at varying distances from this, out of the sapphire sea. Santa Cruz is forty miles away, and cloud-like on the horizon; nearer by is St. John's; beyond are Tortola and Virgin Gorda, all islands that have played no inconspicuous parts in the world's history, yet now neglected and alone, lying there lifeless on the bosom of the shining sea, wrapped in the memories of the past.

I went to St. John's one day, and there revisited the scenes of some old hunting excursions made in 1880, when I was investigating the bird-life of these islands. It is a beautiful island, covered all over with fragrant bay and spice-trees, with countless beaches of snow-white sand, and with every requisite that nature can furnish for a free, wild life; yet this island is now well-nigh abandoned. My friends of twelve years before had departed, and, except the police justice and local magistrate, there is scarcely a white inhabitant on the

BUCCANEER CANNON. — ST. JOHN'S.

island. In the scant woods are beautiful birds, and in the ravines I used to find wild pigeons and doves. Over on the windward side is a secluded bay, where the ancient Caribs lived, before the white men came here, and who left evidences of their one-time residence in rude carvings on the rocks; such as the figures of men, a rudely incised cross, and strange characters.

Scattered about the island are old cannon, relics of

the buccaneer times, when the landlocked and hidden bays gave them shelter from French and Spanish cruisers. Over in the forsaken island of Tortola I found two small cannon that once belonged to the pirates, and sent them to the Exposition. In this latter island are but two white inhabitants, the Governor and the doctor, and the only cultivation of any importance is the recently undertaken industry of raising the Sisal hemp. Tortola once had a peculiar coinage of its own, created by stamping the coins of other countries with its signature, a rude counterstamp that makes a very effective and distinctive mark. These coins are now scarce, but I secured a few, notwithstanding that the Governor had made a "corner" in the market, and it is over a hundred years since they were produced.

There comes an end to all things, and even a sea voyage is no exception; but when you are cruising among islands, one sea voyage only begets another; your steamer leaves the waves of the turbulent Atlantic only to disturb the bosom of the Caribbean Sea.

I sailed into St. Thomas only to sail out again, after a short stay. But I made the most of my opportunities, and learned the many good points of this island. I found out the cool and sandy beaches for my early morning bath, where I could disport myself unmolested beneath the cocoanut-trees. I found the best points of view on the hill-summits, and I soon ascertained that a pleasant stroll of an afternoon was out toward the tennis grounds between the hour of five and the cool interval just preceding dusk and dinner.

## XXI.

AN ISLAND QUITE OUT OF THE WORLD.

SABA, the northernmost sentinel of the volcanic islands composing the Caribbean chain, lay right abeam at last. The sloop that had brought me thus far from St. Thomas was to continue on to St. Kitt's, but the captain had promised to drop me at Saba, as he passed. Preparations were hastily made; the boat was swung over the side, my luggage stowed in it, and this, with the three men at the oars, filled it to overflowing.

By that time it was dark, though a silver semblance of a moon had caught enough of the sun's reflections to light us dimly on our way. The great billows heaved me up and down, the wind blew fitfully from out the gorges that split the mountain-island, and a sea-bird shrieked shrilly as it flew by on its way to land. Black and frowning walls rose straight up ahead of us, with a narrow rim of bowlders at their base over which the sea dashed in great black waves. Nearly a thousand feet above us a light gleamed from a hut, but beneath all was darkness, for not a soul lived below the cliffs.

It was impossible to run the boat through the billows unaided; for all the fishermen had retired to the hills to sleep, so my crew lay upon their oars and sent their voices out into the darkness. "Come down! Come down! Come down!" they shouted. No one replied. The waves alone sent back a hoarse refrain, and a night heron, fishing among the rocks, answered with derisive croaks as he flapped his heavy wings and sped away. Each man tried his best, and then all united in one great and prolonged shout. Hark! Was that merely the echo of the last effort? We repeated the cry, and immediately there followed a faint response — faint and hoarse, but most unmistakably a reply.

For nearly half an hour longer we lay there on our oars, listening to the waves, and to the signs of life and approaching deliverance, manifested in the showers of gravel and stones rattling down the cliffs, disturbed by those who had answered our hail. By this time the moon had followed the sun in his descent, and had buried herself in the same watery grave, sharing with him the embraces of the ocean. And when the moon retires she leaves no light this side the curtain of night, save that of the stars. These were all out to keep their vigil: stars of the North and stars of the South — Orion and the Southern Cross; yet their united gleams were not more than sufficient to show us the figures of two human beings, indistinct as ghosts yet black as demons, awaiting us in the surf.

"Come in, now. Steady! Out with you, quick! Run to the bow, sir. Jump, jump! don't wait! Here!" All this was uttered in a breath by the waiting negroes on the rocks, as we turned our boat head on, and shot with terrific speed upon the shore.

In an instant the waves were foaming round us as the boat touched the stones and rested a second, quivering; another, and strong hands had seized her, strong arms lifted and guided her in, as the next wave hurled her on.

I leaped to the bow, as directed, scrambled over guns and trunks, and a mighty wave came rolling in just as I started, the crest of it striking me sharply on the back, and assisting me so well that I landed high on the rocks without other help. But at the same time it deluged my goods, and this promised to be of more serious moment than the injury to my person. In a twinkling, those stalwart blacks unloaded the boat, and carried my things beyond the reach of the sea; in five minutes or so the boat was back on the breast of a wave, and I was left alone with two strange black men, whose faces, even, I had never seen.

Then, in the darkness, with the wind and waves roaring in my ears, I began to realize the situation I was in, the exigencies of which had prevented me from adequately comprehending it.

During the past two days I had eaten but one meal, of sea-soaked biscuit; I was so weak I could hardly stand, now that the excitement of the landing had passed; hence, I was not in the most favorable condition for climbing to the top of the precipice, where alone I could find shelter and a bed. In fact, in my weakness, I preferred to sleep on the rocks till morning; but the urgent appeals of the negroes finally induced me to change my mind and try the ascent.

This island of Saba owes its reputation chiefly to the

difficulty of reaching it. It has no harbor, no roadstead, even, and no landing-place that in any civilized country would be dignified with that name. The people who inhabit this half-submerged mountain take their lives in their hands oftener, I presume, than those of any other island in these seas. They dare the sirens of the sea, tempt fate, and run the risk of a watery grave, nearly every time they leave or return to their island home. There are but two points at the base of this mountain at which a boat can land: one is called the Fort, used only when the wind is well to the north and west; the other, at which I had landed, is known as the Ladder; this, though worse than the other, is oftenest used, as it is sheltered from the prevailing wind.

I had heard fearful stories about this Ladder. It was said to be so steep that only the natives could climb it; that all visitors had to be carried up on their backs; that the ascent could only be accomplished by the aid of ropes, and that some even required to be pulled up in a basket. These stories vaguely flitted through my brain as I thought of the terrible ascent before me, in my exhausted state; and it was with some trepidation that I committed myself to the guidance of one of the men, and set my face skyward.

I will not detail the events of that dreadful climb. It was one continued, laborious effort for nearly an hour, up an incline so steep that the roof of an ordinary house would have been easy walking in comparison. The stones loosened by my feet fell straight down to the beach; and this sort of climbing continued to the bitter end, the trail zigzagging and doubling upon itself, beneath impending rocks seemingly all ready to fall, and along the brink of precipices which I afterward saw by daylight only to shudder at. After a perpendicular lift of over seven hundred feet, I felt like rolling over the cliffs, and long before the top was reached I could have wished old Saba sunk in the sea. The darkness was dense, but the steady hand of my guide prevented me from slipping, and at last we reached a point whence the narrow path wound among the rocks at an easy grade.

THE LADDER.

At the first house we passed a large crowd had congregated to learn the news. My guide committed me to a boy in the crowd, and returned to the seaside. This boy led me to the house of the harbor-master of this port without a harbor, and he, after a long catechising as to my business, my intentions and my respectability, permitted me to remain and to sleep on the floor. Previous to retiring I walked out with my host into the little garden, and in doing so stumbled over a long, low, white object, which proved by daylight to be a tomb of mason work, covering a shallow grave. This custom of interring their dead in their gardens is a touching proof of affection, in a place where soil is so scarce, and garden-space so valuable. For I am sure if all the people of Saba should die at one time, there would not be enough soil to bury them in. It may be considered fortunate that the majority of the inhabitants are seafaring men, and die away from home.

In the morning I went out for a walk, and was surprised to see, directly in front of me, a very steep hill; east of it another, and to the west another. In truth, this little town of "Bottom" is completely surrounded by hills, with one opening to the east and one to the west, through which only the inhabitants reach the ocean. It is eight hundred and sixty feet above the sea, and occupies the leveled surface of a vast mass of débris that ages since filled the crater of an extinct volcano. I do not know how many houses there are, but there are not many. Each one is painted white, with low, red roof, and each is in the center of a diminutive garden filled with rocks. The streets are merely narrow foot-paths, walled in between great piles of rocks and stones, so that in many places the walls o'er-topped my head. A profusion of cactus, vines and prickly-pears covered these walls, among which, and across these most devious lanes, darted tiny gilt-capped humming-birds, yellow-breasts and sparrows, playing at hide-and-seek.

The captain and myself (all old men are captains here) walked out in the cool of the morning. We went down one lane and up another, around one corner and then another, but never in a straight line, nor ever over a level path, until we came to a neat little cottage, with its front yard filled with limes, crotons and trumpet flowers, and along its flagged entrance were wooden benches, most inviting to sit upon. A meek and melancholy woman bade us enter, and with her the captain quickly arranged for my board. Then he went with me to visit the Governor, who was a Dutchman, but spoke English. He received us kindly, and speedily granted me permission to hunt in the island, waiving the customary payment of two guilders for such a privilege. The good man thereupon retired to his private room, after a little while returning and handing me a paper that would, he said, be my protection from the police, who, four in number, ranged the island, seeking what they might devour.

It was a passport; it was in Dutch, and it sufficed.

I lived for ten days in this quaint little town, in the bed of the crater, nine hundred feet above the sea. From its elevation the heat is never very oppressive, though a walk from the landing to the top, with the sun pegging away at your back, is likely to create a contrary impression. But the thermometer maintains a steady pace, from about seventy degrees at night to eighty at noon, and it was rather monotonous writing down the record, one day was so like another.

One cannot walk in any direction without going up or down hill, hence the numerous ladies of Saba rarely take exercise. There are some even who have never left their crater home, or ever been to the seaside. For them a voiage to St. Kitt's, some forty miles away, is a

TOWN OF BOTTOM. — ISLAND OF SABA.
(Eight hundred feet above the sea.)

great event; though their husbands, fathers and brothers voyage to every part of the navigable globe. Such love have these sailors for their sea-girt home that they return to it whenever opportunity offers, and after they have earned a competency rarely take up their residence anywhere else. The white people of Saba are in greater number proportionally to the blacks than in any other island of the West Indies. They all have fair skins and rosy complexions, with some freckles, but with little tan, while there is a predominance of tow-heads among the juvenile population. White boys, with flaxen hair, pug noses, wide mouths and sky-blue eyes, showing their Dutch origin, mingled freely with the blacks, all on terms of perfect equality. With them also were those of other complexions: brown, yellow and chocolate; these form the connecting links between the two races, and are by far the most insolent and haughty in their bearing.

Notwithstanding all its difficulties of access and its isolation, this island possesses, with its cool climate, its tropical fruits growing in a temperate atmosphere, and its pretty maidens, with clear complexions and flaxen hair, so many attractions for the Saba sailor, that he never elsewhere finds a land he likes so well, and ever returns to it at the end of his voyages.

I made the ascent of the peak of Saba the first day that it was free from the fog-clouds that poured over and enwreathed it from the Atlantic. With its grand sweep from peak to ocean, the brown rock-ribbed hills that rose higher and higher, the great gorges that extended from its lateral ridges down to the broadening ravines, and, finally, its perpetually-verdant coronet of tree-ferns, mountain palms, and all the moisture-loving plants that inhabit this tropical border land, it was a picture for an artist to view.

At daylight it rained; it was cold, and the fog swept over the ridges in volumes of mist that obscured the trail. We passed from the town underneath jutting cliffs, crossing a narrow ridge and entering a little valley where the fertile washings from the cone had accumulated in pockets in and among the great volcanic rocks that had been shot down, or upheaved, ages ago. If one should need a lesson in the economy of soil, he would find it here, where every available foot was cultivated. The little vale was apportioned into diminutive gardens, by walls of stones gathered from the surface; even the path through which we walked was walled in, leaving a walk like a ditch, between high embankments, covered with a host of beautiful plants, growing wild. It was a pleasure to walk there, not only to view the varying flora, but to contemplate the primitive simplicity in which man here lived and carried on the cultivation of the earth. These people, thought I, are to be envied, for they are in perpetual possession of the pleasures of childhood — these small gardens being scarcely more than the little spots tilled by children in other lands, and to which man in his memory continually reverts as to a time when he owned the riches of the earth. Here in this valley, hemmed in by hills and in a measure protected from hurricanes, are raised the principal vegetables used in the island, and shipped to St. Thomas. The great elevation of more than fifteen hundred feet

A TROPICAL SUNRISE.

above the sea, with its consequent coolness and moisture, gives it a climate equal to that of a remove of twenty degrees farther to the northward, where potatoes (which cannot be raised below), cabbages, corn, and even strawberries, may grow in perfection.

Inquiring about a trail to the mountain-top, we were promptly assured that there was none, and that nobody knew the way to the summit. This I regarded as an encouraging reply, because the very ignorance in respect to the high forest argued no end of possibilities in the matter of new birds and plants, so dear to the heart of a naturalist. Leaving the last house, we ascended through the ever-deepening gloom of fog, through gardens fertile as those below, and again across ravines choked with wonders of tropic growth, and through gullies thick with wild bananas and plantains, that could be traced in lines up the mountain side. Every available inch was planted, clear to the forest, and even the pocket of earth caught in the hollow of a rock displayed its broad caladium leaf, or gave root to the vine of the sweet potato, with its flower like that of a morning-glory. From an inclosure here and there, a cow looked out, or a calf, sleek and well-fed, from eating the wild grass and leaves of the plantain and trumpet-tree.

Climbing a steep slope, we entered a wilderness — not a parched and barren one, but a wilderness of plants. Words of mine cannot describe the scene that the partially-lifted veil of fog disclosed to me. It was a view that repaid all the exertion, that checked my murmurs at the unpropitious weather, and drew from me exclamations of wonder and joy. I had been somewhat prepared by the sight of occasional clumps of tree-ferns and picturesque masses of broad-leaved "China" plants, for an exhibition of something beautiful, but had not thought it possible to find grouped together such a variety of ferns and mosses, air-plants, begonias and arums.

Here the tree-ferns, which could be seen from town, forming a long line against the sky, with their graceful groups delicately outlined, or massed together in the gorges, in undistinguishable greens, rose above and around us. The tree-fern is one of the few plants that preserves its beauty everywhere and under all conditions, at all distances. There is, in my opinion, hardly anything so lovely in nature, that is not dependent solely upon color for effect, as the tree-fern. It has an exquisite delicacy of form and airy tracery of filminess in those glorious fronds that are spread between one and the sky; the supporting stems possess such graceful curves, bending apparently to the breezes, yet ever bearing their fretted crowns securely aloft. They give one only the perfect outline of their stems, at times, and again are clothed from head to foot in a wealth of air-plants that add, if possible, beauty to beauty, yet always retaining the best attainable pose, full of expression and animation.

I hastened on, up through the deepening forest. Every tree and vine was dripping great drops; my legs, despite their canvas leggings, were soaked, and my hat of papyrus pith, made only for fair weather and the sun, was soon soggy, and drooped about my ears. We halted for a bit in a little opening where the mountain palms formed a perfect canopy above us, and then I was first made aware of the absence of one of our number, a colored man, who had joined himself to me the first day of my arrival, and had followed in the rear of every excursion since. He had an unpronounceable name, but as it sounded somewhat like that of the great French naturalist, I called him Cuvier. Cuvier, then, was absent, and though we shouted, and disturbed the leafy sanctuary to the extent of our lungs, yet no response came to our cries. It may as well be remarked that Cuvier was not lost, for it later developed that he had descended a more facile path to the ravine, in search of snails, rather than climb the rugged cliff to the top of the mountain.

Then the real labor began; the guide went ahead and slashed with his cutlass a narrow path, while I broke down with my broad, hobnailed shoes such bushes and limbs as were left. Progressing painfully and slowly, we passed through such collections of orchids as would have driven a botanist wild, and through such effects of leaf and vine and flower as made me despair of adequately depicting them to my friends, and caused me to sigh for sunshine and my camera; in fact, I resolved to return and enrich myself with negatives of this glorious vegetation.

Finally we saw a glimpse of light ahead — a little speck of fog-covered sky, through the tops of the palm-trees — and pushed for it. There was more cutting and slashing, more neck-deep plunges into pitfalls covered with wet and slippery broad-leaved plants, and frantic scramblings over quaking beds of orchideous vegetation, then, mounting upon a great rock, we looked down the mountain side. We reached the peak, as the roar of the windward surf informed us, but it was in vain that I sought to penetrate and look beyond the billows of fog that surged against the mountain side, condensing now and then into vapor. Below and immediately about us, we looked upon a level-topped sea of verdure, spread over the cone like a wonderfully-tapestried carpet, embossed with the fronds of magnificent palms, the laced witchery of tree-fern leaves, brown rocks and the broad leaves of wild plantains. The great mountain swept up from below in waving lines, drawn to a focus at the point on which we stood.

CACAO FRUIT.

What an added value would this achievement have possessed, had the day been clear and the islands in sight that gem these northern waters of the Caribbean! From occasional views at lower elevations, I knew what I should have seen: east of me lay St. Bart's, with St. Martin's and Anguilla forming an isolated group of islands, and lying between the Virgins and St. Eustatius. The latter island was right beneath me, and not far from St. Kitt's, which in turn nearly joins the cone of Nevis, and this, again, backed by the purple clouds of Montserrat, though eighty miles to the south; while away north might be descried, perhaps, St. Thomas and Santa Cruz.

From all appearances, we were the first, at least for years, to visit this spot, for there were no traces of a trail, no scarred trees, no limbs broken by the hand of man; all was in the primitive state that might have existed since the first throes of the volcano. Soon a tremendous burst of wind and rain drove us to the shelter of the palms, and, as there was no promise of a clearer view that day, we reluctantly began the descent. Emerging from the wood of mountain palms, we reached at last the upper "provision grounds" of a deep ravine called "Martinique Gut," where the dwarf bananas struggled with decaying trees and picturesque parasites.

The most conspicuous tree here was a great "trumpet," clothed from root to crown in an immense envelope of vines, forming a whole forest by itself, with its attendant vines, air-plants and parasites. Among its branches were humming-birds, thrushes and "trembleurs," that came down to earth at my call; some of them now form specimens in the Government museum, at Washington. I here determined the limit, or northern range, of the beautiful garnet-throated humming-bird, and on another day I hunted down a curious bird called the "Wedrigo," which I think is identical with the *Jablotin*, or Devil Bird, of the islands to the south.

BREAD-FRUIT.

As we descended the ridge leading to the hamlet, we met a long line of negroes climbing the hill, bearing upon their heads the cargo of a sloop that had just arrived. Everything from abroad comes up to the village on the heads of the people. Each man carried a hundred pounds on his head, climbing the steep cliffs easily, and taking his load to the farthest hamlet, a distance of three miles, and with a perpendicular ascent of one thousand three hundred feet. A barrel of flour is divided, one half put into a sack, and thus carried from beach to village.

One day I went in search of the famous sulphur mine, on the windward side of the island, wending my way eastward and northward, always climbing up or scrambling down, around angles in the path that revealed the grandest of sea views, skirting precipices that rose above and descended far beneath us, until I reached a deep and narrow gorge.

Here was the gateway to the sulphur mine and the entrance to Inferno. Impressed upon the rock was the shape of an immense hand, which the natives declare is the Devil's hoof, and, near by, they show the "Devil's heating-iron"—a smooth, flat stone that is always hot, no matter how wet the weather or how hard the rain.

Descending by a well-worn footpath — there are no horses or other large quadrupeds on the island — we came to the door of a small two-roomed building, strong and new. The owner was absent in the mine, but our little colored guide descended to notify him of the arrival of strangers, and in an hour or so he came up. As I sat there looking out over the sea to the island of St. Eustatius, dim in the east, and gazing up at the peak of the volcano that reared its cleft summit directly above me, and the time slipped by, I wondered why the proprietor was so long in coming; but when, later, I went over the same ground he had traversed, I wondered why he had come at all.

Cornwall Henwood, part owner and principal worker of the sulphur mine of Saba, was a man of about forty, robust and handsome, who had spent some twenty years in and about the West Indies. Educated as a miner, he had prospected in nearly every island of the chain, for precious metals and phosphates, and at last his years of toil seemed about to be rewarded, in this apparently exhaustless deposit of sulphur. "I will show you," he said, "the only mine of pure, cool sulphur in the Eastern hemisphere; the only one of any extent outside Sicily."

Then he led the way down the hill toward the sea, and we walked and walked, all the way down hill, until it really seemed as though we should eventually reach the nether region just mentioned. High above us, the everlasting cliffs were seamed with great veins of sulphur, and even down below, where they were lapped by the waves of the Atlantic. At this place a derrick had been erected, and a wire rope ran down from it to the sea, six hundred feet below. Down this rude tram the sulphur was shot in buckets to a platform, whence it was taken in boats to a vessel in waiting near the shore. Owing to the purity of the crude sulphur, as it is blasted from the face of the perpendicular cliffs, and the facility with which it can be dumped from the mine to a vessel below, it was found more profitable to ship direct than to refine on the spot, though works had been erected for that purpose.

Mr. Henwood explained to me the dip and breadth of the veins of sulphur, and invited me to inspect a tunnel he had begun at a lower level. It was then twelve o'clock, the sun was attending strictly to business, and the latitude of the place was only eighteen degrees north of the equator. We had already descended some five hundred feet, and the tunnel was four hundred feet farther, so at first I hesitated, but finally we went down. We crept along ledges that seemed scarcely wider than picture-moldings, and down a path which no sane person in the world, if forewarned, would have attempted to descend. But we safely reached the bottom, about two hundred feet above the beach, and there found several black men working, under the direction of a fine-looking white man, laboring at pick and shovel with a will that would have been creditable in a more northern clime. The sun beat down with tremendous force, and the thermometer must have been at the boiling-point. We examined the indications, saw the wisdom of Henwood's reasonings, and agreed with him that the sulphur must lead to the very center of the volcano.

The less said about the ascent the better. In going up I learned a lesson from this veteran climber of West Indian mountains. He made almost a full stop after every step, and by this leisurely mode of progression we reached the summit without great fatigue.

The history of the Saba sulphur mines is short, but eventful. When the mineral was first discovered no one knows, but the first specimens were taken to America many years ago.

I wish I could put on record a successful issue to these herculean efforts of the indomitable Cornishman; but the labors of Mr. Henwood never received their reward. Going to New York, shortly after the time of my visit, in order to interest capitalists in his venture, this generous and talented man was murdered, in a hotel. His death brought disaster to the enterprise, and I am not aware that it was ever resumed; for few men could be found of the courage and ability necessary to success.

ST. PATRICK'S ROCK, SABA.

## XXII.

### THE SECOND VOYAGE TO THE NEW WORLD.

THE islands discovered by Columbus in his second voyage to the New World, lie mainly in the Caribbee chain, which sweeps around from Puerto Rico eastward and southward, between the Greater Antilles and the north coast of South America.

Every island is a gem; nearly every one is a mountain clothed in green, thrust up from the depths of the sea, with white strand encircling it, blue waves embracing it, and silvery clouds caressing it.

Sailing from the Dutch island of St. Eustatius, where, in November, 1776, the stars and stripes were first saluted by a foreign power, a few hours took me to the north end of St. Kitt's—as the English now call that island Columbus named St. Christopher. This island, with its great central peak astride the lower hills, reminded him, perhaps, of the good giant, St. Christopher, who bore the infant Christ upon his shoulders, and from which, it is said, his good mother took the future admiral's own name. At all events, he had this legend in mind when he so named it: and, as I drew near the beautiful island, and saw its grim old mountain rising above its supporting hills and furrowed slopes, I was struck with its beauty, if not impressed with its resemblance to the historic saint.

Mount Misery is the highest peak in the island; and near its center it has a crater in its bosom, and a silver wreath of clouds at all times plays around its head. Seen a little ways out at sea, the whole island lies before you: the dark mountain masses towering above the broad-breasted hills, with deep ravines running down to the spaces cultivated in sugar-cane, which are of a lighter green, and opening upon the sea. The estate houses are scattered here and there, some of them surrounded with palms, and all with groves of cocoas; near them are the "works," where the cane is converted into

THE ISLAND OF ST. EUSTATIUS, SEEN FROM ST. KITT'S.

sugar, their tall chimneys rising high into the air. The belt of cane land is broad and far-reaching; it surrounds the island entirely; extends from the sea as far up the mountains as possible, while above stretch the pasture-lands and the "provision grounds" of the laborers. These latter, where the common people raise all their provisions, such as taniers, sweet potatoes, yams, bananas, etc., and which they cultivate only on one or two days in the week, are a long ways from their dwellings. They build here little watch houses, to which they retire in the heat of noon to eat their frugal meals, or when the rain falls heavily. On no account, however, would they sleep there at night, for they are afraid of the evil spirits, known to the black man as "jumbies," which lose no opportunity to do harm to the black man who may be caught in the mountains after dark.

In St. Kitt's are some of the most hospitable people in the world; they are mostly descendants of the old planters who have owned property here ever since the buccaneer period, when the Spaniards drove away the first piratical settlers. Like Barbadoes, that other loyal island away to the south, St. Kitt's has been in English hands so long that there is a stability and thriftiness about the population most refreshing to note. I recall a visit made here some years ago, when the planters seemed to vie with one another to do my pleasure, each one entertaining me at his house, and passing me entirely around the island, from one beautiful estate to the other, until I had made the complete circuit, consuming several weeks in making the journey. There is a road around the island, some forty miles in length, broad, smooth and macadamized, which opens up to the traveler glorious views of estates, mountains, sea, and distant isles half-hidden in cloud.

If I were to descend to details, and attempt to describe the island of St. Kitt's, I should, of course, begin with its capital and only town of importance, Basse Terre, which shows in its name the trace of French occupancy, centuries back. But you must look to the guide-books for that; my dealings are with the people, and also with things remote from the active life of to-day.

Basse Terre is a pretty enough town, with a fine central square and tropical garden, where tall palms wave rustling leaves above an elegant fountain, and in the harbor of which is a beautiful view of the near island of Nevis, its one mountain rising above clouds that are ever changing and always fascinating. Here the Governor-in-chief of the Leeward Islands has one of his residences, and here I was entertained at dinner by him, and met some old friends of years ago.

Across a narrow channel lies the island of Nevis, between which and St. Kitt's a little steam launch makes frequent trips. The natural charms of Nevis are many, but its memories are sad, for it is now living in the recollection of its past. Ruined estates and tumble-down dwellings are scattered over the slopes of its beautiful mountain, and its few white people, though hospitable (as are all West Indians), cannot readily be found. When I was there, in 1880, I was entertained by a well-known West Indian baronet, Sir Graham Briggs, at his plantation, Stony Grove. But Sir Graham is now dead; his vast properties in Nevis and Barbadoes have passed into other hands, and things have changed for the worse all over the island. All Englishmen know that it was here that Lord Nelson married the Widow Nesbit, in the year 1787; and all Americans ought to know that Alexander Hamilton was born here, and went from hence to the States, to become foremost among men of his time.

Southwardly from Nevis lies Montserrat, which is

now entirely devoted to plantations of limes, thousands of acres bearing the fruit from which the now famous "Montserrat lime juice" is expressed. I have tested the hospitality of the few white inhabitants of Montserrat, and can assure my readers it was genuine. Like all the islands in the Caribbean chain, Montserrat has its crater, or sulphur hole, which is a miniature Vesu-

WASHERWOMEN OF NEVIS.

vius, though no longer active. In this island, when on one of my ornithological trips, I discovered a new bird, a species of oriole, with beautiful plumage and well-defined characteristics, which the naturalists at Washington (with the sanction of the British ornithologists) named in my honor. It is a pleasant thought: that one may have a namesake at large in the world that cannot bring him discredit; but I often recur, with a pang of tender solicitude, to my feathered children, flitting through the depths of the tropical forests of this far-off island, and pray that no harm may befall my beautiful *Icterus Oberi*.

Montserrat was thought by Columbus to have been the abode of the famous Amazons of the Caribbees, who dwelt here in this island called Madanino, though the great navigator never found those fierce females, nor is it known that any such existed.

East of Nevis is the island of Antigua, the capital of which, St. John's, is the seat of government of the Leeward Islands. Here resides the present Governor of the Leeward group, Sir W. F. Haynes Smith, K. C. M. G., whom I had the pleasure of meeting several times, and who is locally known as the "Yankee of the Caribbees," from his activity and his benevolent desire to improve the condition of his people. He has initiated a movement looking to the establishing of a regular line of steamers between New York and the Lesser Antilles, and the building of hotels in the islands of Dominica and St. Kitt's.

There is, and has been for some years, a line of good steamers between these islands and the States, the "Quebec Line," which has given much attention to the development of tourist travel hither, and has provided as regular a service as the travel and traffic would warrant. Many have taken advantage of their excursion tickets, in the few years past, to visit these islands, and all speak with delight of the trip afforded by voyaging on such steamers as the *Caribbee*, which makes a leisurely tour of the chain, stopping a few days at the principal ports, giving ample time for excursions into the country, and providing a comfortable home for its passengers, to which they can retreat as occasion demands. I had the good fortune to meet one of these excursion parties, and to spend a week in their company, and the memory of the event remains with me as one of the pleasantest of my life.

In Antigua there is little to see except sugar plantations, where the cultivation has been carried to perfection; but here also one meets with those splendid people I have already mentioned, who maintained the prestige of the West Indian hospitality. In the center of the island is a valley of petrifactions, where beautiful specimens of silicified woods are found by the cartload. I secured many of the best for the Exposition, including some perfectly silicified sections of the boles of the cocoa palm.

But I could not prevail upon the Governor and his Council to send to the Exposition a representative exhibit from the Lesser Antilles; though I am sure it was not so much the fault of His Excellency as of the local councilors, whose insular ideas need not only polishing, but a vigorous rasping.

In memory, I continually revert to a little island north of Antigua, where I once had the best hunting for small game that I ever enjoyed. The island of Barbuda once belonged to the famous Codrington family, one of whom established that flourishing seat of learning in Barbadoes, Codrington College. Away back in the last century, they stocked the island with deer, sheep, guinea fowl and goats, which increased abundantly, and now their descendants swarm here, affording the best of sport to one inclined to dally with the huntress Diana. Permission must first be obtained at Antigua, but that once secured, a whole island is open to the exploration of one who can appreciate the pleasures of the chase of small game beneath an ardent sun.

Directly south of Antigua lies the largest island of the Caribbean group — Guadeloupe. It is really two islands in one, being divided into two parts by a shallow salt-water river; the larger and mountainous one is called Guadeloupe, and the low-lying portion Grande Terre. Guadeloupe and its dependencies, Marie Galante, the Saintes and Désirade, belong to the French, although the islands were discovered by the Spanish. In truth, the mention of them brings me back to the text of my narrative: the wanderings of Columbus, on whose trail we are supposed to be.

We have seen that the fleet prepared for the second voyage to the New World, left Cadiz, and steered for the Canary isles. Taking his departure from the Canaries, a more southerly course was pursued than on the first voyage; by this the fleet escaped somewhat the seaweeds of the Sargasso Sea, and the trade winds wafted them steadily onward.

On Saturday, the second of November, 1493, Columbus noted signs of land — at least, of its proximity — and early next morning a blue and beautiful island rose to sight. Having been sighted on a Sunday, this land was called Dominica, by which name it is still known. The

Spaniards did not land on this island, as the windward, or Atlantic shores of all the Caribbees are, in general, rough and difficult of approach. They kept on, and first touched shore at another and smaller island, of which the Admiral took possession in the name of Spain, calling it Marigalante, after the ship which he commanded. Sailing on toward a still larger island, above which towered a cloud-capped volcano, they landed at a point on its eastern shore, finding there an Indian village, and for the first time seeing evidences of the Caribs — the fierce man-eaters of whom they had heard such wonderful stories on the previous voyage. Fortunately for some of the Spaniards, who later were lost for several days in the forest, most of the warriors were away, on a predatory expedition to the northward; but even the women were difficult to capture, and fought like demons.

It is recorded that Columbus found in Guadeloupe the stern-post of a vessel, and other indications of extraneous civilization, that had probably drifted upon this shore from the Atlantic currents; and here he first met with the pineapple. A party of the Spaniards having strayed into the forest and lost their way, the valiant Alonzo de Ojeda was sent in search of them. On his return, he gave the most enthusiastic account of the rich and beautiful country, the forests filled with aromatic trees and shrubs, which he believed produced precious gums and spices. He declared there was no country like it, or so well watered, for he had forded and waded twenty-six rivers in the distance of six leagues; and as for the forests, the trees were so tall, he said, as to obscure the light of day.

Sailing onward, the voyagers saw island after island rising above the waves : those that I have described as lying between Guadeloupe and St. Thomas; and finally they reached their destination — the island of Santo Domingo.

Having followed Columbus throughout his voyagings thus far in the West Indies, let us complete our investigations by seeking to identify the places connected with his landings at Guadeloupe. In pursuance of my plan to visit every island of the Antilles of importance, and present to every government the invitation from our own to participate with us in celebrating the Columbian anniversary, I touched at Basse Terre, the seaport on the Caribbean side of Guadeloupe, in April, 1892. Basse Terre is the most picturesque port of the island, but the roadstead is open, and the chief harbor is that of Pointe á Pitre, in the Grande Terre portion.

I was presented to the Governor, M. Nouet, and invited by His Excellency to visit a while at his "hotel" at Camp Jacob. Behind two powerful American mules we rode up the steep hills to the Governor's country seat in the mountains, near the hamlet of Camp Jacob, which is a retreat for the people of the coast during the heat and sickly season of the summer. Here are vast coffee estates, winding roads and lanes lined with tree-ferns and plantains, and all the rank and luxuriant vegetation of the tropic belt. The air is deliciously cool, and at night it is a delight to be abroad. The Governor's house is a large and handsome building, perfect in all its appointments, and planted in the midst of a gloriously beautiful garden, with every kind of fruit and flower. Bamboos clashed their spears above trickling rills, long avenues of *pomme-rose* trees gave dense shade and secluded walks, kiosks under broad mango-trees looked out upon the plains and distant sea, and above the myriad flowers hovered living gems in shape of humming-birds. I was offered a little cottage in one of the gardens, for as long a time as I would occupy,

GREAT TREES OF THE HIGH WOODS.

and it has been my regret ever since that I could not accept the Governor's offer to tarry a while in this terrestrial paradise.

His Excellency is a Frenchman, born in Paris, though long resident in foreign lands on service for his country; and, having made the tour of the United States, speaks our language perfectly. He not only provided for little excursions about the hamlet, but one morning took me up into the high woods — those glorious forests in which I dwelt for months some fourteen years before.* It was a joy to re-visit the scenes of my adventures, to ride through the somber high woods, with their wonderful vegetation, with the mighty gommier-trees towering aloft, hung with cable-like lianas, and completely enveloped in orchids and air plants. There is no more attractive ride accessible to the traveler anywhere than that over the paths opened by Governor Nouet through the high woods near the Camp. At the base of the highest hill near the foot of the volcano, is a hot spring which has been walled up and converted into a bath, where the Governor and myself had a refreshing dip, ere we descended to the Camp again. Below, and running up into the forest, are old coffee estates, one of which belongs to an old friend, M. Colardeau, director of the Jardin des Plantes, and where I was entertained while hunting these forests for rare birds.

My friends would have kept me long, but my work demanded my presence elsewhere. At an attractive place some ten miles from Basse Terre, I saw and photographed a large rock with carvings upon it, said to be Carib, near a little bay where the aborigines are known to have lived. But the most interesting spot was at Carbet, near the point of Capesterre, on the eastern coast of Guadeloupe, for this was the first landing-place of Columbus, where he found the first evidences of the Caribs. A stream drops down to the coast,

---

* My descriptions of the vegetation, the birds, and an ascent of the volcano, or the great sulphur mountain, have already been given in my book of adventures, entitled "Camps in the Caribbees," and published in 1879. I need not repeat them here.

forming an entrance from the sea suitable for canoes, and the rich land slopes back toward the distant hills. At the mouth of the river is a gnarled native "banyan" tree, on the beach, and this I photographed, as a distinctive object for the identification of the spot.

My guide to the place was M. Charles Hyot, a wealthy planter resident at Capesterre. He had informed himself thoroughly upon the evidence, and had identified the

BANYAN-TREE. — GUADELOUPE.
(*Where Columbus first landed on his second voyage.*)

spot as that of the first landing of Columbus on the second voyage. I spent a night and a day at his beautiful plantation, and he also took me to the bay at which Columbus remained several days while awaiting the return of his soldiers lost in the forests. This is the Bay St. Marie, where another river forms a wide though shallow harbor behind a line of reefs, and about which the scenery is as delightful as at the time of the first arrival of white men in this region. Beyond the palms that adorn the estates, beyond the plains and swelling hills, and beyond the shoulders of the volcano, which rises to the clouds, is the great waterfall, described by Columbus. It is so distant as to seem a mere thread drawn against the rock; it drops, white against the somber background of the forest, and to-day, as when first observed by Columbus, it appears, to use his own expressive language, to be falling from the sky.

The Caribbee islands, which form the crescentic chain between latitude twelve and twenty, north of the equator, possess every variety of climate between temperate and tropic, and every beautiful aspect of vegetation, from the sugar-cane of the coast to the feathery tree-fern of the cool and pleasant high woods, with their giant trees and tangle of vines and bush-ropes.

Along the coast are all the fruits for which the West Indies are noted: custard-apples, sapodillas, guavas, mangoes, soursops, and the score or two of others more familiarly known to the North.

In the high woods are many rare plants and trees, such as the great *figuer*, or wild fig; delicate ferns, and their big brothers, the magnificent tree-ferns; the most conspicuous tree being the *gommier*, or giant gum, the *bursera gummifera*, from which the Carib Indians hew out their large canoes. Climbing higher, the ground is seen carpeted with a curious lycopodium, unlike anything of its family found elsewhere.

There are at least four islands in the Caribbees that

nearly realize one's ideals. These are: Guadeloupe, Dominica, Martinique and St. Vincent. The first is grand and gloomy, yet with shining shores; the second equally somber as to the mountain region, but breaking out into broad smiling tracts of sugar-cane; the third combines the features of the other two; the fourth has all the beauty of the three combined, and less of somberness.

Dear old Dominica, however, has for me the greatest charm, for in this island I first tasted the delights of adventure in tropic forests. Here I first camped in huts with thatch of palm; here I made the acquaintance of strange forms of animal life; here I found my first new bird, and here I lived a free, wild life for many months.

My visit to the Caribs of Dominica was for the purpose of ascertaining how many of them, of pure blood, could be prevailed upon to go to the Exposition; it being the intention of the managers to gather there all the representative Indians of North and South America.

The Caribs, as the last living representatives of the Indians found in these islands by Columbus, possess a peculiar interest for the ethnologist, and it was my desire to secure from them not only an exhibit, but the best types of the people themselves. There are very few of pure Indian blood remaining, as, in the course of generations, they have become mixed to a great extent with the blacks.

Altogether, there may be two hundred Caribs in Dominica, and of this number some fifteen families are uncontaminated with negro blood. They live in the same

primitive style as did their ancestors when found by Columbus; dwelling in huts of palm, tilling a little land, making cassava bread from the manihot plant, fishing when the sea is smooth, hewing out canoes from the great gum-trees, and weaving baskets.

Their life is a careless and happy one, but altogether devoid of the diversions of a civilized state of existence. There are now among them about ten expert canoe makers, and twenty basket weavers; these pursue their vocations contentedly, under the thick shade of the mango-trees, in fair weather, and retreat to the huts when the rain comes down.

A very few of them speak the ancient Carib tongue, and my companion, who is a linguist, is preparing a vocabulary of the last remaining words as spoken by the older Indians to-day.

Their speech is a compound of English and French *patois*, and I can no better illustrate it, perhaps, than by quoting the remark of an old Indian whose wife was ill, and about whose condition he had great solicitude: "Eef he make sick some more I must to geeve heem some peel (pills) *porchi*, I not want to lose heem, like my ozer wife, who die and have same *com*-plaint." This Indian spoke English better than French, but there are others who speak the *patois* entirely, and others again who use the mixture.

It was in the distant mountains back of the Indian country that I had the good fortune to find specimens of a most magnificent parrot, known to the naturalists as the *Chrysotis Augusta* — the Imperial, one of the largest in the world. That was on my first exploration, and on the third I obtained a live specimen, which I took to the States. Although one of the most beautiful of birds, and apparently intelligent, the *Chrysotis* has never been known to talk — that is, to learn words or phrases and repeat them by rote.

All birds, however, speak in their own fashion. Jean Baptiste used to assure me that some of them were polyglots. One of the birds seen frequently in the woods, is a species of grosbeck; this he called the "*Priez-Dieu*," because, he said, it repeated these words. One would cry, "*Priez-Dieu, Priez-Dieu!*" and its mate would reply, "*Pierre, priez pour nous!*" "Pray for us, Peter, pray for us." Another bird he called the "*Oiseau Bon-Dieu*," or God-bird, because it led a harmless life, and did no evil. This bird was a species of warbler, but in the other islands the wren is known as the God-bird.

The Imperial Parrot, to which I have alluded, is confined to the island of Dominica, as a species, but there are others of the genus in several islands. There was one, formerly, in Martinique, only thirty miles away; there is another in St. Lucia, and yet another in St. Vincent. All are beautiful; all large and strong of wing; yet no species of any one island has ever been found in any other. This fact may serve to throw a little light upon the question of the ancient contiguity of these islands, and there are many other items of interest in connection with the study of the avi-fauna of the Caribbees, that may sometime serve the investigators.

Half a degree of latitude south of Dominica lies the mountain island of Martinique, some fifty miles in length, with deep-water bays, grim promontories, fertile valleys, and possessing a vegetation unsurpassed for beauty and exuberance. Its principal port is St. Pierre, situated on a broad bay some three miles in length; the water in the harbor of St. Pierre is so deep that vessels at anchor have to run out all their chain. Its houses of stone and brick were formerly covered with tiles, mel-

VOLCANO ON ST. LUCIA.

low-red in tone; but since the hurricane of 1891, the roofs are hideous in tin and galvanized iron. The sidewalks are mere cat-paths separated from the streets by deep gutters, through which, every morning, swift streams course from the hills and lose themselves in the bay. These living waters serve to cleanse the city and carry away the garbage, and every morning hundreds of black and yellow servants emerge from the dwellings with tall earthen jars on their heads, the contents of which are dumped in the gutters. Babies are washed in these watercourses, held by their hair or their girdles, lest they be swept away, and even dishes may be seen piled upon the curbs.

It is in the morning that the servants thus disport themselves in the streets, but in the afternoon their masters and mistresses may be seen on the promenade leading to the river, or strolling through the avenues of the *Jardin des Plantes*, which is more than locally celebrated for its horticultural rarities. The high-class creoles of Martinique are dressed in the height of fashion; but those lowlier born wear garments more gorgeous, yet decidedly more becoming. There are perhaps one hundred and sixty thousand people in Martinique; the great majority are colored, and many of the quarter and eighth castes women (quadroons and octoroons) are noted for their beauty. With their dresses of the last century — high-waisted, loosely-flowing, and bright of color, and their superabundance of ornamentation, the octoroons of the island are attractive and striking.

In my last visit I found that Martinique had changed greatly in the fourteen years since I first made its acquaintance — and for the worse. The white people have either died out or have moved away, and the island population is taking on the hue and habits of the African. There was formerly a fine society of whites, and it was a pleasure to promenade of an afternoon, as one always felt sure of meeting some interesting person. But latterly all this seems to have changed. It may have been the hurricane, which swept over the island in August, 1891, destroying all the crops, sweeping away forests, and killing many people. Becoming discouraged at the appalling losses, the white inhabitants may have given up the fight against the elements, and have sought other fields for enterprise.. At the time of my last visit, the shore was still lined with wrecks, half of the houses of St. Pierre were roofless, and nearly the

NEGRO BOYS OF MARTINIQUE.

whole of Fort de France, the capital of the island, had been destroyed. It was a grievous sight, and I did not expect a hopeful answer to my invitation to the Exposition. I met the Governor at Fort de France, and found him very amiable. He was a Frenchman, and was domiciled in one of the few houses still standing in the ravaged city. Fourteen years ago I photographed and described the birthplace of Josephine, at one time Empress of the French; but I was assured that the last ruin of the habitations had been swept away by the hurricane. Around the beautiful statue in the savane of the capital the tall palmistes stood erect, like masts divested of their sails, with hardly a shred of leaf remaining.

Against the hurricane and earthquake, the white people of the West Indies have ever had the courage to fight, and hopefully; but against the black inundation from Africa which has swept their shores they are powerless.

## XXIII.

#### CARIB ISLANDS AND LAKE DWELLERS.

ALL these Southern islands of the West Indies, at the time of their discovery, were in the possession of the Caribs; but in two of them only, are there any remaining Indians at the present time. These are Dominica and St. Vincent, lying about two degrees apart, and between are the islands of Martinique and St. Lucia.

Sailing south from Martinique, the first object claiming attention is an isolated rock, some five hundred feet high, at a distance from the coast, and commanding the channel into Port Royal. It is a rock with a unique history, for it has had the honor of having been entered on the books of the British Admiralty as a ship. It was when the French and English were at odds, a little less than a hundred years ago, that Lord Howe took possession of this great rock, sent some guns to its summit, manned it with a dozen sailors and a midshipman, and then sailed away, leaving the gallant fellows with a year's provisions and any amount of pluck. They did good work in annoying the Frenchmen, and it is said sent several vessels to the bottom of the sea; but at last their provisions gave out, and they were obliged to surrender. So it was that the good "ship" the *Diamond*, though she surrendered her crew, was never sunk, but left where her captors found her, and there she may still be seen.

It cannot be said that the island of St. Lucia is attractive, though its only town has a perfect harbor, which

THE DIAMOND ROCK OFF MARTINIQUE.
(*As seen through the steamer's port-hole.*)

the English are fortifying, and attempting to convert into a second Gibraltar. The harbor and town of Castries have an unsavory reputation for fever and smells. I was in the harbor at one time, on board our cruiser the *Philadelphia*, when the horrible odors came off at night so strong and fever-suggestive, that orders were given to up anchor and seek another station.

Castries has improved greatly in late years, and may eventually become an attractive spot; but it is hot and sometimes unhealthy.

Like all these Caribbee islands, St. Lucia can boast of its "Soufriére" or sulphur basin, in the heart of an extinct crater. To reach this one it is necessary to take passage in a small coasting launch that goes down the leeward coast in the morning, returning at night to Castries. The trip is well worth the while, for the crater is still smoking and steaming, and the sulphur is being gathered from the vent-holes where it is deposited and sublimated. Beautiful streams pour into this basin, one of them being half-concealed in ferns and broad-leaved plants. In exploring this sulphur deposit, one must be careful, as the crust is thin, and accidents sometimes happen. We saw an old man who had lost one of his feet by having broken through the crust and plunged into a caldron of steam and hot water. The sulphur is carried out on the heads of negroes and negresses, and shipped from the bay of Soufriére, where there is a most attractive village, nestled under the Pitons.

The Pitons are the most symmetrical mountains in the world. They lie at the southern end of St. Lucia, detached and isolate, a pair of pyramids, the higher one three thousand feet in altitude, clothed from base to summit in living green, and so steep that no one has ever climbed them, and returned to tell the tale.

It is related that four English sailors once attempted

the feat, but that all died before they accomplished it, either of fatigue or, as is more probable, from the stings of the terrible serpent the "Iron Lance." St. Lucia, like Martinique, is infested with this poisonous reptile,

THE PITONS OF ST. LUCIA.

and has not yet been able to cope with it, though it is said the introduction of the mongoose has somewhat diminished its numbers.

From the vicinity of the Pitons can be seen another island, still more beautiful than any we have visited. This is St. Vincent, than which none can be found more complete in charms of scenery. The capital of St. Vincent is Kingstown; and its inhabitants are as particular that you put in the "w" in the spelling of "town," as the residents of Arkansas are that you pronounce their State's name with a "saw." There is another Kingston, they say, in Jamaica, but only one Kingstown, and that is in St. Vincent.

At any rate, there is no prettier town to be found anywhere in the islands, if we take its surroundings into the picture, bordering as it does a wide bay, with tossed and jagged hills rising behind it. The people resident here are friendly, and the whites are in greater proportion to the blacks than in the other islands. This is shown when there is a ball or a tennis meet, for then all the pretty girls — and St. Vincent is noted for them

KINGSTOWN, CAPITAL OF ST. VINCENT.

— assemble in force, and, as it were, carry the visitors by storm.

Back of the town is the botanic garden — the oldest botanical station in these parts. Here was introduced first the bread-fruit, nutmeg and other valuable trees. Here resides the Administrator, or resident executive; the Governor of the Windward Islands, to which St. Vincent belongs, lives at Grenada. That the white inhabitants were exceedingly attentive to strangers, when I was here on my first visit, I myself am a living witness — having experienced their kindness while very sick with fever. Luxuries that money could not buy, and attentions grateful to an invalid, they lavishly bestowed, and the very name of St. Vincent awakens tender recollections.

I did not linger long in town, as the remoter parts of the island beckoned me away to explore them; and taking seats one day, in a "passage boat," a friend and myself left for the north end, skirting the leeward shore. The "passage boat" was about thirty feet in length, with five rowers and a "captain;" and was piled high amidships with merchandise and great Carib baskets.

Our boat trip ended at the little town of Chateaubelair, which we reached at dusk, finding the sea running so high that the boat could not be beached. So it was backed in as near as possible, and held there, while three of the boatmen plunged into the sea and carried us severally ashore in their arms. They were knocked down three times before they had landed the luggage; but finally all was safe on the sands, and we were taken to the estate house at Golden Grove, which had kindly been placed at our orders by its owner. This estate was but one of many owned by the proprietor, Mr. Porter, who has in his possession nearly two thirds the sugar plantations of the island. The house was vacant, but in charge of an old lady who provided us with a good dinner, and made up comfortable beds; and here we met some friends of the past, who had been managers of estates and were managers still, with little hope of ever securing properties of their own.

It was at Chateaubelair that a most curious discovery was made, a few years ago, of Carib relics. In opening

PALMS OF THE LEEWARD COAST. — ST. VINCENT.

a road near the beach, a *cache* was uncovered of stone weapons and agricultural implements, some two hundred in number, that had been buried there at least three hundred years ago. There were hoes and axes, hatchets, celts, and several huge battle-axes. I myself secured, at another point, two great battle-axes, one weighing six pounds and with a breadth of ten inches. These relics of the aborigines were exhibited at the Jamaica exposition of 1891, and there attracted much attention. No one knows who hid them there, or for what purpose, but they were probably concealed by the ancient Caribs for use in any need at time of war, or sudden irruption of their enemies from South America. Although found on private property, the stones were claimed by the Crown, and may eventually become the nucleus of a collection for a valuable local museum.

The air was cool that night, and the ensuing morning was cool and sweet, as we rode to Richmond, the next estate, where we breakfasted. This estate lies in a pretty valley, and contains some eight hundred acres, planted in sugar-cane, and managed by Alexander Frazer, another old acquaintance of times past. Hence, mounted on horses loaned by the manager, we rode over to Morne Ronde, where the Black Caribs live. Their huts of palm are half-hidden in natural groves of mango, cacao and bread-fruit. All were at home awaiting me, as the Royal Ranger, Mr. Musgrave, had sent word from town that I was coming, and old François, whom I had met in Jamaica, had prevented any one from leaving the settlement. We assembled in the great hut where the basket makers worked, who pursued their vocation industriously. Gathered outside were the girls and boys, separating of their own accord into groups. They are all dark, and many with curly hair —for these Black Caribs are the result of the intermixture of the real, or Yellow, Caribs and negroes.

They have a fine reservation, extending from the

sea far up into the mountains, and containing over four hundred acres. In all they number about two hundred; old François went out and took the census, while I waited in the hut. They drank the spirits sent them, and with great enjoyment smoked the cigars we brought, giving us in exchange cocoanut water and poached eggs. There was but one of them who could speak, or

THE TEN LITTLE CARIBS.

pretended to speak, the Carib tongue, and as no one else knew the sense of his lingo, it had to pass as that.

The small boys and girls frisked and played in the water, deriving much enjoyment from capsizing an old canoe, and then going to its rescue before it was carried away by the waves.

The baskets made by these Black Caribs are in such demand that they are kept busy filling orders, and seem much more industrious than their Indian brothers of Dominica. Their reservation is owned in common, but each family possesses its plot for individual cultivation.

Peaceful and quiet as they now are, their ancestors made a great deal of trouble for the planters here a hundred years ago. At the house on the Richmond estate I was shown an old table hacked by the cutlasses of the Indian rebels of that time; and it is a matter of local history that the manager of the adjoining estate of Wallilabou was captured by them, and killed by being crushed between the rollers of his cane mill.

Having seen the Blacks, my next visit was to the Yellow Caribs, on the other side of the mountain; to reach them we were obliged to climb the volcano, and descend the eastern slope to the windward coast.

Mr. Frazer loaned us a horse and a mule, and we cantered across the Dry River to the hills, where we overtook two jolly priests, with whom we kept company to the top of the volcano, making, with our attendants, a long procession, winding up the narrow trail. Glorious were the views on every side, increasing in beauty and extent as we got higher, and the woods shut out the prospect, though giving us in exchange rare effects in leaf and shade. We halted at the "Maroon-Tree," for rest and refreshment, and at noon were at a cave under the brim of the crater, where we gathered for lunch. The priests were well provided with provender, and we mingled our cheer in the cave, lunching *al fresco*.

Fourteen years before I had spent the greater part of four days and nights in this same cave, having as company an old negro, my object being to secure a rare bird that inhabited the upper slopes of the volcano. The people of the island called it the "Invisible Bird," because, though they heard its song, they could never discover the singer. I secured several specimens, but only by living on the crest of the volcano for four days, and camping with the old negro in the cave. The exposure also gave me a fever which lasted several months, and thus the bird cost me dear — even though it proved to be a species new to the world.

And to return to this lone place, many years after the event, and have my photograph taken in the very cave where I had passed some very dreary hours — this was one of the strangest things that ever happened to me. I heard the strains of the Soufriére Bird (the "invisible" one) all along the trail; but on this visit I carried no gun, and the little creature was not molested.

Just back of the cave is the crater-brim, and far below it lies a pearly lake, slumbering in beauty, two thousand feet above the sea. The volcano peak is three thousand feet above sea-level, and is only attained after hard struggle and climbing. Here the priests parted from us, at the fork of the windward trail, and as it was so bad that no horse could descend, we sent our animals back and essayed the remainder on foot. It was deeply gullied and almost impassable, plunging deep into the ferns in its descent until the heat was well-nigh intolerable. The last mile or so was through thickets of ferns and mountain palms, but emerging from there we entered the open pasture-lands of Mahoe, thickly studded with great bread-fruit-trees, and then descended into the cultivated lands of "Lot Fourteen;" we passed through immense cane fields, and finally reached the "works," where the boilers were in full blast, and numerous negroes were feeding the rollers.

The manager was away, but the overseer gave us two mounts — one on a mule, having a saddle without girth or stirrups — and we were soon cantering off for the "Carib Country," a two hours' ride distant. Striking across the fields, we followed the main road along the windward coast; it dwindled finally into a bridle-trail beyond Overland Village, and then climbed the steep hills that guarded the Carib lands. We reached the settlement, Sandy Bay, after dark.

I had taken the precaution to send on boxes of provisions, two days ahead; but they had not arrived, and so an old Carib friend, Rabacca, volunteered to go in search of them. He returned late in the night, and then we swung our hammocks, opened our canned provisions and feasted in the hut that a good Indian widow had vacated in anticipation of our coming.

In the morning the Indian friends of past hunting adventures came to see me, and I heard the same sad stories that all the world is familiar with — of sickness and death, and struggles with poverty. The former chief of the settlement, Captain George, had lost his good old wife, but was now rejoicing in a handsomer new one, and living high up in the hills. One of the girls, whom I remembered as the prettiest Indian child I had ever seen, was now changed into a coarse, but comely woman. She took me to the site of her mother's hut on the hill, and described to me the terrible hurricane that had blown the hut away, and destroyed every vestige of their carefully-kept garden. Disaster had overtaken them; one by one her family had gone away, until she alone was left with her old mother, and

BEACH NEAR THE BOCA. — TRINIDAD.

obliged to cultivate with her own hands the little strip of arrowroot ground on the hillside, the only resource that lay between them and absolute starvation.

Sandy Bay is the central settlement of the Yellow Caribs. These people have no reservation of their own, but hire land of the Government. They live by the cultivation of arrowroot, mainly, with occasional forays upon the sea, and working now and then upon the sugar plantations. Their habits are similar to those of the Dominica Caribs, and there are about the same number of the pure-blooded Indians here as in the northern island. Altogether, in both islands, there may be about three hundred descendants of the Indians discovered in the Caribbees by the first Spaniards, and equally divided between the two.

St. Vincent was discovered, it is believed, by Columbus, on his third or fourth voyage to America, but it was for a long time overlooked, and the Spaniards never made a settlement here.

Lying three degrees farther to the south is another and vastly larger and more important island, that of Trinidad, between ten and eleven degrees of north latitude, which was first seen by Columbus on his third voyage, in 1498. He had been two months at sea, and was suffering from the dreadful heat of this latitude, with nearly all his store of water gone, when the watch at the mast-head descried the peaks of three mountains in the distance, which a nearer approach revealed to be united at their base. The land to which they appertained Columbus at once called Trinidad, or the Trinity, having previously promised to name his next discovery after the sacred Triad, in token of his gratitude at sight of land. He approached the island from the southeast, coasting its southern shore, and entering the Bay of Paria through the passage which he named the Serpent's Mouth; the *Boca del Serpiente*.

Coming up under its western shore, he was surprised to observe the verdure of its forests and the beautiful trees that came down to the water's edge; for he had reasoned that, being so near the equator, he should find the vegetation parched from the heat, with little water and moisture. He also thought that the inhabitants of this country would appear like the negroes of Africa; with skins black from exposure to the sun, and woolly

THE PITCH LAKE. — TRINIDAD.

hair. Instead, he found the people who came out to his vessels in their canoes to be like the Caribs in the islands to the north, and equally as comely.

His reasonings and conclusions are quaintly set forth in the writings of Pietro Martire, one of the first chroniclers of his discoveries:

"So that, as he (Columbus) saith, it (the earth) is not round after the form of a ball or an apple, as others think, but rather like a pear as it hangeth on the tree; and that Paria is that region which possesseth the super-eminent or highest part thereof, nearest unto heaven. Insomuch that he earnestly contendeth the Earthly Paradise to be situate in the top of those three hills which the watchman saw out of the top-castle of the ship; and that the outrageous streams of the fresh waters which did so violently issue out of the said gulf, and strive so with the salt water, fall headlong from the tops of the said mountains."

He coasted the inner shores of Trinidad, delighted with the scenery, and discovering troops of monkeys sporting in the forests; then he stood across for the peninsula of Paria, where he found the most agreeable Indians the Spaniards had ever seen. Here he saw the first pearls, and gained information of the Pearl Islands, which he later sailed to, and from which he brought away some valuable specimens. He found oysters growing on trees, and recalling what the learned Pliny had written regarding the formation of pearls from dew, inferred that they hung there with their mouths open to receive the dew that was to be transmuted into the precious pearls. Oysters may be seen there now, growing in the same manner, suspended from the twigs and roots of the mangroves; but no one has yet found pearls in any quantity in the Gulf of Paria.

It was about mid-August that he sailed through the Serpent's Mouth (which he so named because of the terrible currents he encountered there), and steered northwardly, first visiting the Pearl Islands, Cubagua and Margarita, and thence making for Hispaniola.

Arrived there, he found the island in turmoil, and

eventually he was made prisoner by Bobadilla, an official sent out by the king of Spain, and returned home in chains. Columbus would have remained longer among the Pearl Islands, which gave such promise of wealth, but a malady of the eyes made him nearly blind, and he was obliged to seek the island of Hispaniola, where there was promise of relief.

During the year that followed, he sent home to Spain an account of his discoveries and specimens of the finest pearls, by which other adventurers became aware of the richness of the newly-discovered land; and one of his old companions, Alonzo de Ojeda, a brave soldier, obtained the king's permission to fit out an expedition to explore where Columbus left off. With Ojeda was another adventurer, then unknown, but who subsequently became famous, through his narrative of the voyage, and through having his name given to the country discovered by Columbus. This man was Americus Vespucci, and he arrived at the Gulf of Paria and the Pearl Islands in the year following the visit of Columbus, 1499.

It has been denied by some investigators that our country was named after the Florentine, but that it derived its name from an aboriginal word in use on this very peninsula of Paria, *Americapan*, which is applied to a settlement there. This may be so; let the geographers decide it; but one thing is certain: Vespucci gave the name to the richest country on the north coast of South America — Venezuela.

Sailing beyond the Pearl Islands, these purloiners from the fame of Columbus discovered Curaçao, which they described as inhabited by a race of giants, and then proceeded still farther to the west, and entered the great Gulf of Maracaibo. On its eastern shore they saw a more surprising sight than any that yet had greeted their eyes, for, standing out into the waters of a placid bay, at a distance from the shore, was an Indian village. It was built on long piles driven into the

SUNSET ON THE VENEZUELAN COAST.

bottom of the lake, and consisted of palm-leaf huts, bell-shaped, and perched on platforms, with slight connecting drawbridges between them. Numerous Indians sported in the water, and darted about in their canoes, but as soon as they saw the great vessels of the Spaniards coming toward them, they fled to their habitations, raised their drawbridges, and prepared for fight. This village in the water, so different from anything previously seen, struck Vespucci so forcibly that he called it

PLOUGHING UNDER THE PALMS.

"Venezuela," or Little Venice — a name that has since been applied to the country adjacent to the gulf and the sea he was navigating.

The Caribs, then, and the Lake Dwellers discovered by Vespucci, are about the only Indians whose descendants still live in the places where originally found. I have grouped them together in this chapter on that account, having myself visited them all at various times.

In the spring of 1890 I went to Maracaibo, on the gulf of that name, and from that city took a boat for the settlement of Lake Dwellers, which is known as Santa Rosa. I found them living in huts made of reeds and palm, erected upon piles in the lake, in water about waist deep, and exactly as described by Vespucci, four hundred years ago. These Lake Dwellers are mild and good natured, differing from the Guajiros on the main, opposite, who are ferocious, wild, unsubdued, still ruled by their own chiefs, and governed by their own laws.

The Lake Dwellers live as lived their ancient prototypes of the Swiss Lakes, and, together with another settlement higher up Lake Maracaibo, are the last survivors of a most interesting people.

WASHING CLOTHES AT CURACAO.

Being only ten miles distant from the large city of Maracaibo, they all speak Spanish as well as their own tongue, and find a market for their fish and small articles in that city. They still retain the fondness for white men that so captivated Ojeda and Vespucci, and mothers regularly sell their children to strangers for as long a period as may be desired. The market price for an Indian girl at the Lake settlement is all the way from twenty to sixty dollars, and they go into service virtually the property of their purchasers, making faithful servants and devoted adherents. Boys command a lower price, and can be got for ten and fifteen dollars each. It seems to be an understood arrangement that the mothers shall sell their children, and does not diminish filial affection at all, if one may judge from appearances.

They are peaceable now, though their ancestors were warlike, and gave battle to Ojeda, at first, finally becoming reconciled, and parting from him the best of friends.

The voyage terminated in June, 1500, when the adventurers finally returned to Cadiz, but a few months previous to the arrival there of the great Admiral wearing the chains placed upon him by Bobadilla. Summing up the results of the voyage, they found it had been unprofitable; although a small vessel, that had started after they had sailed, and returned two months before, brought home great quantities of beautiful pearls, and from the very islands they themselves had visited.

## XXIV.

#### JAMAICA AND THE WRECK OF COLUMBUS.

A BEAUTEOUS island is Jamaica.
I arrived there on the twentieth of March, from Havana, *via* the north coast of Cuba and Haiti. On the afternoon of my arrival I called on our Consul, who generously placed his services at my disposal, and the next day visited by appointment the Governor, Sir Henry Blake, who received us cordially, listened attentively to my statement, and assured me that personally he was strongly in favor of the representation of Jamaica at Chicago. He promised to bring the matter before the Council at the earliest opportunity; meanwhile I was at liberty to consult with representative citizens, and make my mission known as widely as I chose. Acting upon this suggestion, that same day I visited the offices of the newspapers, the editors of which courteously received me and placed their columns at my disposition, later proving their sincerity and good-will by advertising the Exposition to the fullest extent.

There are four papers published in Kingston, the capital of Jamaica, three of them of a high order of merit.

The same evening I was present at a dinner given by the General Manager of the Jamaica Exposition (then open at Kingston) to the officers of our cruiser, the *Philadelphia*, and had the privilege of proposing as a toast, "Chicago," which was drunk with acclaim by all present.

Two days later the Consul and myself lunched with the General Manager of the Exposition, as the guests of the day; my consular flag was flown from the central dome of the great building, and a salute of seven guns was given us at our arrival and departure. Two days after that Admiral Gherardi, of the *Philadelphia*, placed his launch under our orders; in this we proceeded to Port Royal, across the bay, to lunch with Commodore Lloyd, of H. M. S. *Urgent*, who received us with a salute from his ship, and entertained us delightfully at his quarters on shore.

Port Royal is not an attractive place for residence, and has never recovered from the great disaster of two hundred years ago, when the city that was here erected, and which was the rendezvous of pirates and buccaneers, containing vast wealth, was sunk by an earthquake. Beneath the sea may yet be seen, it is said, the roofs of sunken houses. That tremendous catastrophe occurred in 1692, at the same time the Salem people were putting to death their kin for witchcraft; and in 1693, just two hundred years ago, the frightened remnant of the population abandoned a place of such disaster, and settled on the other side of the magnificent bay that forms the harbor of Kingston.

Within the week of my arrival I dined at the "King's

House" with the Governor, meeting there several distinguished ladies, and also officers of the British army, and later had all I could do to attend the calls of the hospitable citizens of the capital. Thus was inaugurated the good feeling that has distinguished our relations with Jamaica, and which resulted in her sending an exhibit to Chicago. It was anticipated that I might have difficulty in inducing the Government to participate with ours in the Exposition, because there had been a misunderstanding by which it had seemed as though we had ignored their own invitation to join in theirs. To obviate any misconception I had been furnished with a letter from Mr. Blaine, then our Secretary of State, which was to be produced only if absolutely necessary; fortunately, I had no necessity to use it.

Through the courtesy of the Governors of the Jamaica Institute, I was invited to read a paper before that distinguished body on "The World's Columbian Exposition," in the lecture hall of the exposition building. The Jamaica Institute is a literary and scientific institution, endowed by the home Government, and acknowledgedly in advance of any other of the kind in the West Indies. The time allotted me was short, but I prepared a comprehensive statement of our great undertaking, taking a wide survey of the field, assuming and holding an advanced position for our Government, and delivered my lecture before a select and appreciative audience, on the eleventh of April.

Ten days later I repeated it before the Chamber of Commerce of Kingston, and, like the first, it was well

THE HEART OF THE COCOA PALM.

received, and the substance of it published in all the papers the next morning. A full report of my first lecture was printed in the *Post* the day after it was delivered. It filled eight columns of that paper, and I mention the fact to show that there is enterprise and activity in the reportorial staff of a Tropical paper that would do credit to a Northern journal.

In truth, I have never found the people of the Tropics lacking in either energy or enterprise; the reporters are as assiduous in gathering news, and the boys as frantically athletic at cricket and baseball, here beneath the blazing sun of the Tropics, as in the far-distant North.

I spent seven weeks in Jamaica, and nearly every day was a busy one. Upon arrival, I secured quarters at the new Myrtle Bank Hotel, which was admirably situated, both for business and pleasure, on the shore of the bay, and yet in or near the center of the town. The hotel has broad piazzas, surrounded by rows of cocoa palms, and affords fine views of the distant hills. The cocoas were just high enough to permit inspection of their crowns, and one could study the growth of flower and leaf, and watch the development of the great clusters of nuts, from the first appearance of the blossoms, protected by the overhanging spathes, to the ripened fruit ready to drop to the ground. It was an interesting process, this evolution of the cocoanut, and the heart of the palm was a never-ending source of pleasure to me.

By moonlight, the bay and the palm groves were as beautiful as the most critical artist could desire. One night, as an experiment, I pitched my camera on the upper veranda, focused upon a grove of palms illumined by the moon, and after a half-hour's exposure with a rapid plate, secured a perfect picture by moonlight, which is one of the most interesting of the thousand or so that I took in my travels through the islands. Kingston, the capital of Jamaica, although it has a fine situation, on one of the best harbors in the West Indies, cannot be called a handsome city. It may contain some forty thousand inhabitants, has a few good public buildings, many comfortable private residences, and latterly has become possessed of two or three excellent hotels; but its streets are dusty, and at times filthy, through open drainage; the general run of houses are poor and squalid, and it is not an attractive place of residence at all. Strange to say, the country districts of Jamaica have better roads, and are more desirable for winter quarters than the capital.

But with Kingston as headquarters, delightful excursions may be made in many directions — as to Rio Cobre and the entrancing scenery of the Bog Walk River, to the hills and the Blue Mountains, and into the interior. Around the entire island is a system of excellent roads, smooth and hard, leading always to most beautiful places, and even over the mountains run regular lines of stages.

The island itself is some one hundred and forty miles long, by fifty broad in its widest part, and contains about four thousand square miles, with hills rising everywhere; it has one mountain seven thousand feet in height.

It is a beautiful island, and when a good line of

steamers shall be running regularly and frequently between it and the United States, it will become one of the most frequented of winter resorts. A few years ago there was passed an "hotel act," by which capital was encouraged to invest, on Government guarantees, and the result has been the erection of several first-class establishments: one in the city, the "Myrtle Bank," the "Constant Spring," some six miles out, one at Rio Cobre, and others in the interior.

After I had been assured that the Governor would recommend, and the Council would pass an appropriation for Jamaica's representation at our Exposition, and had filled the papers full of information regarding the enterprise, my presence seemed no longer necessary at the capital, for a few days; I therefore accepted an invitation from the Director of the Public Gardens and Plantations to go with him into the mountains. The Director, Mr. W. Fawcett, author of the "Economic Plants of Jamaica," and a botanist of ability, took me to the Government experimental station in the mountains, called Cinchona, which is about six hours' ride from Kingston, and situated at an elevation of five thousand feet above the sea. Such an opportunity for consulting with an acknowledged authority on Jamaica's resources was not to be neglected, and I eagerly embraced it. It was an opinion of mine, and in this Mr. Fawcett concurred, that Jamaica's strong point for an elaborate display lay in her natural resources and attractions, and especially in her botanical products. She could hope for little in the way of display from such things as sugar, coffee, rum, bananas, etc., and it was impressed upon me that she should try to elaborate what one might term a foliaceous exhibit of her vast wealth of tropical shrubs and trees—so strange to Northern eyes. I would have had the different climatic zones represented by the varying vegetation, as for instance: the exuberant tropical forms of the coast belt, such as plantains, bread-fruit, cocoa palms, etc.; the higher temperate region by the cacao, mountain palm, tree-fern, and trumpet-trees; the mountain, or sub-alpine district, by the cinchona, gums, locopodiums, etc. Thus the entire range of vegetation could be shown at a glance.

I would have had, also, a panoramic display as a background, such as the view of Kingston harbor from the sea, with the golden foot-hills, the purple mountains, and the distant Blue Mountain peak, with its circling wreath of clouds. By massing the tropical forms in front, and by assigning Jamaica a space long and narrow, for perspective effect, a most grand and effective picture would be presented to the beholder; and the instructive nature of such an exhibit is self-evident.

Regarding the numerous tropical plants to be removed, Jamaica, lying nearest to the United States of any tropical country having a perfected system of botanical stations, and with every resource of the kind available, could afford an inexhaustible supply. And regarding the removal of the larger shrubs, and even trees, the Director was of the opinion that it could be successfully accomplished. In preparing for the Jamaica exposition, he superintended the removal of palms over forty feet in height, transporting them three miles, and then planting them in the park, without the loss of a tree. He assured me that he could remove successfully to Chicago, provided direct transportation were afforded, palm-trees over thirty feet high. A palm of that height, such as is the native *gru-gru*, would weigh some six tons. The chief objections would be climatic: they should be transported at midsummer, and guarded against the night temperature at Chicago. In this connection, I might mention that the only other island in the West Indies possessing a botanical garden worthy of mention is Trinidad, which is several days' distance farther from the States than Jamaica. Also, that while the island of Cuba has essentially the same flora, yet there is no reliable and organized department similar to that presided over by Mr. Fawcett; and that, while the palms of Cuba would be equally worthy of representation, it would be impossible to obtain them, there being no good roads into the country districts, etc. In a general way, Chicago must draw upon Mexico and Central America, to some extent, for strange plants, such as orchids, etc.; the north coast of South America, particularly Maracaibo, and also the Amazons; but it is from such places as Trinidad and Jamaica, where gardens of acclimatization have been established for nearly a century, that the strangest and rarest plants may be obtained ready at hand. Jamaica, with its varied flora — with, for instance, four hundred varieties of ferns, situated at the very gates of the Gulf of Mexico — offers therefore greater attractions to the managers of the botanical department than any other country.

I would like to describe the Government garden at

Cinchona, with its exotic plants, its plantation of cinchona trees, coffee, tea, its wild strawberries and treefern walks; but I have not sufficient space for it; nor, indeed, for doing justice to the thousand attractions of this glorious island. One of the oldest of the English islands, its charms have been sung many a time, and its resources fully exploited.

In January, 1891, there was opened here an exhibition that approached the dignity of a World's Fair, and which continued four months. It was not financially a success, nor did it serve the full purpose of an exposition of Jamaica's resources; yet it was far from proving a failure. England sent, as her representative, Prince George, the second son of the Prince of Wales. Great enthusiasm was manifested at the opening; the buildings and grounds were crowded, and from the moment when the Governor presented the golden key to the Prince, as a declaration that the exhibition was open, to the last hour of its official existence, the best of order was maintained throughout. Every exhibit was then found to be in place, and every detail of the plan elaborated in advance was adhered to.

Having generously contributed to other exhibitions in the past, Jamaica at last thought it time herself to act the part of hostess, and invite visitors to her beautiful shores. The proposition is said to have emanated from the Jamaica Institute, and when brought to the attention of the Governor, Sir H. E. Blake, it received not only his approval, but his cordial support. In an eloquent address at a public meeting in September, 1889, he set forth the many possible advantages likely to accrue to the island from an exhibition of her products, and added: "And let the venture succeed, as I believe it will, or let it fail to pay its way; at least it will show that Jamaica is up and doing, ready to stand in the forefront, and to take her natural position as the Queen of the British Antilles." This advanced position His Excellency from the first maintained, and it was admitted by many that his pluck and energy prevented the exhibition from becoming a failure.

The exhibition idea expanded beyond the original conception; the wealthy citizens subscribed freely, and a building was erected over five hundred feet in length and nearly two hundred in breadth. This structure was cruciform in shape, the main portion running east and west, with a dome in the center, which was one hundred feet from the ground to the lantern. The circular roof of the nave was supported on pillars, and there was a continuous gallery around the building, inside, over four hundred feet in length. Although built of wood and cheaply constructed, yet this main structure, with its commanding central dome, its minarets, and semi-Moorish ornamentation, presented an imposing appearance at a distance. From the sea it was even magnificent: situated over a mile and a half from the harbor, with a broad open space in front, and a background of blue and purple hills towering above the sloping Liguanea plains.

It is worthy of note that the material for the structure came from the States, but all the labor employed was native to the island.

The grounds attached to the exhibition, comprising

some fifty acres, were beautifully laid out, with fine effects, produced by the artistic grouping of palms, tree-ferns, bamboos, etc. The entire building and grounds were lighted by electric and colored lamps, while on certain evenings there were splendid displays of fireworks which it would be hard to excel; and on certain afternoons and evenings the famous black band of the 1st West India Regiment added the attraction of music. Invitations were sent to the different countries of the world, and the somewhat limited space was soon filled. Of the foreign exhibitors, the Dominion of Canada occupied the greatest space, and through her active commissioners made a desperate attempt to divert the trade of Jamaica to her shores. That these endeavors, though meriting success, will prove futile, a student of the situation must be convinced; for Jamaica, like most of the West Indies, will continue to trade with the nation nearest her that can take her products — and that nation is the United States.

To many observers this exhibition seemed a failure, it being specially urged that Jamaica herself did not exhibit half her products. While it may have been the original intention to have more fully developed the local resources, yet it finally came about that the foreign exhibits overtopped the home products, which proved eventually, the best thing for the island. Regarded merely as a financial risk, it was foredoomed to failure; yet that has been the fate of nearly every exhibition of the kind. But, considered in its higher aspects, it was certainly a success of the most far-reaching kind; for, if we consider its influence upon the people alone, with-

CARIB CARVINGS ON A ROCK IN THE ISLAND OF ST. JOHN'S.

out referring to the attention it has called to the island, one cannot but admit that it has been beneficial. Only those resident among the blacks of these islands can understand how it was that many of them refrained from visiting the exhibition at first, because they had been told, by some mischievous person, that the great building was a vast barracoon, into which the white men were desirous of enticing them, after which they would shackle them, and again sell them into slavery; they had been told this, and hundreds of them actually believed it.

The Jamaica exhibition was a success; but I assured the people that, to gain its full fruition, they must not stop at that one effort but must seek their reward at Chicago, in 1893.

Of the thousands of interesting things at the exhibition it will be impossible to speak; but there was one strange exhibit that particularly appealed to me, because of its wonderful history. It was a bundle of old and ragged papers, which, in the words of my friend, the Rev. J. B. Ellis, the author of "The Tourist's Guide to Jamaica," have "a history stranger than the most far-fetched conception of the most imaginative writer of fiction." I once wrote a story in which I made the plot hinge upon the finding of two leaves of an old book in the maw of a shark. The book had been brought from New England, and the shark was killed on the coast of Yucatan, the leaves so conveniently found in his stomach being necessary to the elaboration of the plot. They had been lost overboard a short time before. It is very comforting to an author, therefore, who gives free rein to the imaginative faculty, to happen upon such a find as the following. The old adage, "truth stranger than fiction," is wonderfully supporting. For these old papers exhibited in Jamaica, and of which I had never heard before, have a history which puts my invention to the blush. It seems that in the year 1799, a brig, the *Nancy*, was captured by a British cutter, the *Sparrow*, and brought into Port Royal, where her officers were put on trial for piracy. No papers, however, were found on her, and the prosecution was on the point of breaking down for want of evidence; but it was soon forthcoming from an unexpected quarter. About that time a British man-of-war was off the harbor of Jacmel, coast of Haiti, and one day the officers amused themselves by fishing for sharks. One of the sharks caught was drawn on deck and cut open, and in its belly the sailors found a bundle of papers. Sailing for Kingston soon after, the papers were sent on shore by the captain, who knew nothing of the capture of the *Nancy*. They arrived while the trial was going on, and an investigation showed them to be the missing papers of that vessel, which had been thrown overboard by her captain, but which were presented in court just in time to be used against him, and secured the conviction and subsequent hanging of the crew of the vessel as pirates. Can, indeed, any fiction be stranger than this truth?

The animating and supporting spirit of the exhibition was the Governor, Sir H. A. Blake, K. C. M. G., formerly executive of the Bahamas, whose administration in both the Bahamas and Jamaica has brought him prominently before the people of America. He has a worthy consort in his talented wife, and the varied accomplishments of Lady Blake have added luster to the achievements of the Governor. She is an artist of reputation, and her aquarelle of "the Landfall of Columbus," which was on exhibition at the Jamaica court, was but one of many meritorious works her genius has evoked. Possessed of a scientific and inquiring mind, Lady Blake has left the impress of her talent and industry wherever she has been. While Sir Henry was Governor of Newfoundland, she made a collection of water colors of the plants of that country; in the Bahamas, likewise, she reproduced in colors all, or nearly all, of the flowering plants of that chain, exhibiting at the Indian and Colonial Exhibition of 1886 a series of over one hundred. All were correct botanical studies, faithful representations of the plants illustrated, besides being artistically beautiful. She has commenced a series illustrating the flora of Jamaica; those that she was kind enough to show me having, besides the flowers, specimens of insects, such as butterflies and moths, and sometimes bits of characteristic landscape as a background. As to her indefatigable industry in ferreting out the remains of aboriginal occupation, especially in the Bahamas, I myself am an unwilling witness, having vainly sought for Indian relics in the region visited by her, and which I was desirous of finding.

With a salary of six thousand pounds per annum, and another thousand as allowance for entertainment, the Governor exercises a lavish hospitality, and the "King's House" is a most desirable place to visit.

From the delicate attentions of these gracious people of Kingston, who all contributed to make my short stay in the island so agreeable, I was obliged to tear myself away, after my duties to the Exposition were accomplished, and sail for other scenes.

But I have not forgotten that the great Navigator has not even been mentioned in this chapter. Having begun with the adventures of Columbus in Spain, on his first voyage, in the Bahamas; having seen the foundation of the first city; taken with him that eventful second voyage, and the equally adventurous third, we have only to trace out his fourth and last voyage, in which he coasted a second time along the shores of Jamaica, and explored the mainland from Yucatan to Darien. Thus we shall complete our investigations and be with him at his death. For that last voyage was nothing less than that: death to his hopes, death to his hitherto buoyant spirit.

It was on the ninth of May, 1502, that Columbus left Cadiz, Spain, on his fourth and last voyage to the New World, with four small vessels and one hundred and fifty men. He found land about midway the Caribbee chain of islands, and thence steered for Santo Domingo. The Governor refused him admittance to the harbor, and the Admiral was compelled to seek shelter from an impending storm in a small port on the south side of the island. The hurricane came, as Columbus had predicted, and a fleet of vessels, that was on the point of sailing for Spain, was destroyed, carrying down the old enemy of the Admiral, Bobadilla, who two years before had sent him to Spain in chains. With Bobadilla went to the bottom of the sea the largest nugget of gold ever found in Santo Domingo.

Continuing his course, Columbus coasted the south shore of Haiti, whence he was swept over to Cuba, thence across nearly to Yucatan, and southwardly to

DON CHRISTOPHER'S COVE, WHERE COLUMBUS'S CARAVELS WERE WRECKED, 1503.

Honduras. A landing was made at Cape Honduras, near the present town of Truxillo, where large numbers of Indians were seen, who gave the Spaniards provisions.

For several months after this the vessels were beating about the Mosquito coast, finding little gold, but learning of the rich province of Veragua, from which the grandson of Columbus, Don Luis, derived his title of Duke of Veragua, which is held by the only living descendant to-day.

The Admiral explored the coast as far south as Darien, vainly seeking for a strait or passage through to the Pacific, and at last, after repeated disaster and the loss of many men, he shaped his course northwardly. He was carried by the currents to the south coast of Cuba, and in an endeavor to regain the island of Hispaniola, was swept back to the north coast of Jamaica. Here he encountered a dreadful storm that nearly wrecked his ships, but finally reached a sheltering harbor, into which he ran, on the last of June, 1503.

His vessels, he wrote, were bored as full of holes as a honeycomb, he had lost nearly all his anchors, and his crews were worn out with constant watching and battling with the elements. Seeking a fit harbor for the purpose, the Admiral ran his sinking ships ashore, where the water soon filled them up to the decks; then he fastened them together, built thatched cabins at prow and stern, and resigned himself and men to a dreary waiting for rescue that lasted nearly a year.

Six months they waited, and then, weary of the restraint, many of the crew broke out in mutiny. Headed by one Francisco de Porras, they broke into the Admiral's cabin, where he was sick with the gout, and demanded permission to go on shore. Columbus and his brother, Don Bartholomew, were powerless to restrain them, and they departed, ranging the island, and eventually committing many dreadful excesses. The island of Jamaica swarmed with Indians, who at first brought provisions to the Spaniards, but after a while left them to their fate. Being in imminent danger of starvation, the Admiral had recourse to stratagem to obtain the needed supplies, and summoning the caciques of all the near tribes, he told them that unless they brought supplies to him as he wished, he should deprive them of the light of the moon. He had calculated a total eclipse of the moon, due to take place within a few days, and availed himself of his superior knowledge to impose upon the guileless aborigines.

True to his prediction, on the night in question, the lunar orb was shut out from their sight, and amidst howlings and supplications, they promised Columbus anything he wanted if he would only restore the light of the moon. The crafty old Admiral retired to the shelter of his cabin, and about the time the eclipse was to pass he emerged, and told them that his prayers had been heard, and that the light would be restored — but only on condition that they keep him supplied with provision during his stay. This they gladly did, and after that the sailors lacked for nothing which the Indians could supply.

Having in mind the connection of Jamaica with the most eventful episode in the later voyages of Columbus, I prepared to visit the north coast of the island — the scene of his shipwreck. I had identified the spot where occurred the disaster to the *Santa Maria*, on the coast of Haiti, in December, 1492; to conclude my investigations into the career of Columbus in America, it only remained for me to visit and determine the scene of his last shipwreck, in 1503. Constant demands upon my time prevented the consummation of my desires until the last week of my stay, when I broke away from town, and accomplished all that could be done.

The center of attraction, to one following in the footsteps of Columbus, is about St. Ann's bay, into which he sailed in June, 1503, and which was called by him Santa Gloria. The parish of St. Ann's is the most beautiful spot in Jamaica. Says an old writer: "Earth

THE BAY OF ST. ANN'S. — JAMAICA.

has nothing more lovely than the pastures and pimento groves of St. Ann's;" and so far as I could see, he was right.

This bay I visited and photographed; but the actual site of the wreck — or rather the spot where Columbus ran his vessels ashore, and was for a twelvemonth "castled in the sea" — is a mile to the south. It is called Don Christopher's Cove, never-varying tradition perpetuating the story of that event, how, the vessels of the Admiral being leaky and full of holes, he ordered them to be run aground, and finding them to be half-filled with water built thatched huts upon the decks. Don Christopher's Cove is a beautiful little bay, between walls of coral rock, with a beach of yellow sand overhung with thickets of sea-grapes. It seems just the place a mariner would choose in which to strand a sinking vessel, the sloping shore giving a secure resting-place, and the near coral ledges affording protection from stormy seas and the heaviest gales.

Here Columbus remained a year, until finally succored by a vessel sent from Santo Domingo. He might have perished had it not been for the brave action of one of his sailors, Diego Mendez, who, in an open canoe, with Indians to paddle it, crossed the broad channel between Jamaica and Haiti, and carried the news of his disaster to the Governor of Santo Domingo. About midway in the channel is the island of Navassa, at which Mendez landed, finding there a little water, but for which he and his men would have perished; and Columbus also might have died in Jamaica, instead of later expiring in Spain. He was rescued in May, 1504, and two years after he died at Valladolid, worn out with his arduous toils.

Having now followed in the wake of the Great Admiral in his various voyagings, visiting all the islands he discovered and the seas in which he sailed, we will leave him here, at the scene of his last and most unfortunate adventure. on the north coast of Jamaica.

# INDEX.

## A

ABORIGINAL Celts, 81, 82; seat of carved wood, 82.
Aborigines of the Bahamas, 74; extinction of, 84.
Acul, bay of, 219.
Acklin's Island, 90.
Admiral's landfall, where? 85.
Aguada, bay of, 392.
Agueynaba, Indian cacique, 392.
Aguadilla, bay of, 391.
Ajes, Haitien roots, 225.
Ajoupa, or Carib hut, 196.
Albert's town, Bahamas, 62.
Alhambra, palace of, 8; hall of justice in, 22.
Alix, Señor, 334.
Altars, Santo Domingo cathedral, 351-356.
Americapan, aboriginal word, 487.
Americus Vespucci, 487-489.
Anchor, ancient, from the Santa Maria, 230-234.
Anacaona, Indian princess, 363.
Anguilla, island of, 442.
Antigua, island of, 453.
Annexation, desired by West Indies, 139.
Antiquities, aboriginal, 78, 350.
Appleton, Captain N., 289.
Arenas, islas de, 101.
Arroyo of Chancleta, 318; port of Puerto Rico, 393.
Astrolabe, used by Columbus, 53.
Atalaya, Moorish watch-tower, 68.
Author's table of islands discovered by Columbus, 102.
Ave Maria, painting of, 361.

## B

BAHAMAS, when discovered, 55; aborigines of, 74; cruise through, 105-110; their lost opportunity, 111; travel in, 117; history and flora of, 118.
Babeque, aboriginal name, 217.
Balandra Head, 292.
Balboa, Marquis de, 132.
Bajo-Bonico, river of Santo Domingo, 262.
Bandits of Cuba, 140.
Banyan-tree, 460.
Baptismal book, Santo Domingo, 350, 378.
Basse terre, town of, 451, 457.
Basle, treaty of, 371.
Baracoa, port of, 162-166.
Barbuda, island of, 454.
Barcelona, 239.
Baird, Mr. Alexander, 299.
Bay of Samana, 293; of Arrows, 294.
Becher, Capt. A. B., 86.
Behechio, Indian cacique, 312.
Bell, ancient, of Santo Cerro, 316; of the fig-tree, 326; of Jacagua, 276.
Belem, church of, 143.
Bellini, Padre, 326, 374; General, 328.
Bellamar, caves of, 157.
Beasts of burden, 288.
Berezillo, famous bloodhound, 39.
Bimini, island of, 409.
Bird rock, Bahamas, 64, 96.
Birds of Bahamas, 97, 98.
Bird notes, 466.
Blaine, Hon. J. G., instructions from, 129.
Blake, Sir H., 76, 492, 508; Lady, 119, 509.
Boatmen of Santo Domingo, 278.
Boca del Serpiente, 484.

## INDEX.

Bog-walk (Boca del agua) river, 498.
Bohio (Haiti), 217.
Boveda (vault) of Columbus, 381.
Bottom, town of, 431–433.
Borinquen (Puerto Rico), 388.
Bread, native, 95.
Bread-fruit, 443.
Brazil-line steamers, 413.
Bridge of Pines, 18.
Briggs, Sir Graham, 451.
British consulate at Puerto Plata, 284.
Buccaneers, origin of the, 192, 196.
Bullocks and bull-carts of Santo Domingo, 279, 287.

### C

CACAO, fruit of, 442.
Cannon, ancient, from Santo Domingo, 345; from Tortola, 425.
Cathedral of Santo Domingo, 351, 356; chapels of, 356–360.
Cat Island, 107; caves of, 108.
Casa blanca, Puerto Rico, 407.
Castries, town of, 473.
Capesterre, Guadeloupe, 459.
"Camps in the Caribbees," 459.
Caonabo, Indian chieftain, 228, 271, 311.
Caciques of Española, 311.
Castle, oldest in America, 343.
Casa del Cordon, 353.
Caribs, incised figures of the, 424; first discovered, 456; homes of the, 462; speech of the, 465; islands of, 471; relics of, 477; black, 478; yellow, 482; present status of, 484.
Caribbee Islands, 461.
Caravels of Columbus, 217.
Cadiz, city of, 240.
Cathay, mention of, 103.
Carved seats of lignum vitæ, 82.
Cannibalism in Haiti, 190.
Captain-general of Cuba, 131.
Cattle, loading, coast of Cuba, 161.
Canary Islands, 54.
Caves, of Watling's Island, 76; of Cat Island, 77.
Casa de Colon, 344.
Cassava, native bread, 95.
Cambiaso, Mr., 374.

Castillo, Mr., 374.
Canoe, first seen by Europeans, 72; found in a cave, 89.
Cartman, encounter with a, 281.
Ceboyan (Indian of the Bahamas), 75.
Celts, Indian antiquities, 81, 274; of Bahamas, compared with others, 82.
Chateaubelair, town of, 476.
Chicago, commissioners meet in, 122; its spirit of enterprise, 123; *Herald's* expedition, 101.
Christmas, first American, 217.
Christophe, emperor of Haiti, 202; palace and castle of, 206–216.
Charlotte Amalia, St. Thomas, 415.
Cibao (land of gold), 225, 260; hotel, 282.
Cipango, 98.
Club del comercio, Santo Domingo, 283.
Cockburn town, Watling's Island, 64.
Coaling stations in the West Indies, 414, 416.
Codrington family and college, 454.
Colardeau, M. St. Felix, 459.
Cocoa palms, study of, 497.
Columbus, first appearance of, at Granada, 15; before Isabella, 17; at the Bridge of Pines, 18; birth and early years, 24; in Portugal, 24; arrival in Spain, 24; at Cordova and Salamanca, 24; at the Monastery of La Rabida, 25; signs capitulation with Spanish sovereigns, 26; sets out for Palos, 26; memorials of, 26; marble tablet to, 27; again at La Rabida, 38; departure on first voyage, 52; his discoveries at sea, 54; landfall of, 56; landing-place at Watling's Island, 69; journal of, 55; landing of, in the Bahamas, 71; description by, of the Indians, 71; aborigines discovered by, 73 et seq.; landfall of, critically examined, 85 et seq.; at Guanahani, 89; sails around Guanahani, 90; discovers other islands, 92–96; sails for Cuba, 101; statue of, at Nassau, 116; tablet-bust of, Havana, 121, 151; instructions to commissioner regarding relics of, 128; bust and statues of, Cuba, 149, 150; alleged remains of, Havana, 151; on coast of Cuba, 158–166; wreck of flag-ship, Santa Maria, 221; guest of Guacanagari, 222; builds fort

## INDEX.

at Navidad, 225; coasts shores of Santo Domingo, 235; discovers mermaids and gold, 236; enters Samana Bay, 294; first sheds Indian blood, 294; hears of the Amazon Island, 295; sails for Spain, 238; anchors at Palos, 239; is received at court, at Barcelona, 239; departs on second voyage, 240; founds town of Isabella, 241 et seq.; explores interior of Santo Domingo, 261; finds gold and erects fort, 267; views the Royal Plain, 308; subjugates the Indians, 312; makes slaves of Indians, 313; erects a cross at Santo Cerro, 314; builds forts in the mountains, 321; where were the bones of? 363-387; the tomb of, 363; statue of, Santo Domingo, 363, 369; duality of, 363; first burial-place, 364; second burial-place, 364; remains of, taken to Santo Domingo, 367; alleged transfer to Cuba, 371; boveda, or vault, of, Santo Domingo cathedral, 373, 384; recent discovery of remains, 373; casket containing ashes of, 375, 377; tablet above vault of, 384; author views remains of, 386; opinion as to last resting-place, 387; discovers Puerto Rico, 388; returns to Santo Domingo, 389; second voyage of, 455; third voyage of, 484; among the Pearl Islands, 486; imprisoned, 487; last voyage of, 510; on coast of Honduras and Veragua, 511; is driven by storm to Jamaica, 512; strands his vessels at Santa Gloria, 512; predicts an eclipse of the moon, 513; scene of shipwreck in Jamaica, 514; last venture of, 515; death of, 515; Bartholomew, brother of Christopher, 338; burial-place of, 353; Diego, son of Christopher, 345; house of, 344; in chains, 349; Don Luis, grandson of Christopher, 373.
Commissioners, appointed, 122; depart on their mission, 123; instructions to, 124; local, appointed in Cuba, 131.
Compass, variation of, noted by Columbus, 53.
Concepcion de la Vega, 321; fortress of, 323; relics from, 325.
Conquistadores, 27, 29, 276.
Cotton, first discovered by Columbus, 90.

Cotubanama, Indian cacique, 311.
Conchs of the Bahamas, 118.
Crania, Indian, 75, 77, 165.
Crooked Island, Bahamas, 60, 96.
Cross of Santo Domingo, 358; of Santo Cerro, 360.
Cuba, discovered, 101; circumnavigated, 103; the author in, 121; political state of, 137; bandits in, 140; outline of history of, 147; as a center of colonization, 153; along the north coast of, 159.
Curacao, island of, 487.
Curtis, Mr. W. E., 145.

### D

Dare, Virginia, birth of, 195.
Dessalines, Haitien general, 201.
Diamond Rock, 472.
Divers, black, at Nassau, 112.
Diaz, Miguel, discovers gold in Santo Domingo, 338.
Diego Columbus, son of Christopher, 345.
Dog, the dumb, 163.
Domingo Rubio, river of Spain, 40.
Dominicans, 297.
Dominica, island of, 462.
Don Christopher's Cove, Jamaica, 515.
Douglas, F., 168.
Drake, Sir F., 194, 195.
Duquesne, Marquis of, 132.
Durham, Mr., 348.

### E

Eco del Pueblo newspaper, 334.
Earthquake-buried cities, 321.
Ellis, Rev. J. B., 493.
English in West Indies, 111; first appearance in West Indies, 193.
Escudo (coat of arms), ancient, 354.
Española (Santo Domingo), 238.
Exposition, directions from executives of, 123; exploiting the, in Cuba, 135; in Haiti, 176; first foreign building at, 179; ancient relics for the, 276, 320; the Jamaica, 493 et seq.

# INDEX.

## F

FARM, a Bahaman, 66.
Fajardo, port of Puerto Rico, 393.
Fauna of Bahamas, 98.
Fawcett, Mr., Jamaica, 499.
Fernandina, Bahamas, 95.
Filibusters, their origin, 196.
Fort de France, Martinique, 469.
Fortune Island, Bahamas, 57; sharks of, 61.
Fountain of Youth, 409.
Fox, Capt. G. V., 86.
Frenchman's Wells, Bahamas, 98.
French, first voyages of, to West Indies, 193; planters in West Indies, 193; massacre of, in Haiti, 200.
Fruits of the West Indies, 461.

## G

GALLEONS, Spanish, 197.
Galvan, Señor, 326.
Game-cocks of Puerto Rico, 405.
Garcilasso de la Vega, 12.
Ghosts of Isabella, 258.
Gherardi, Admiral, 493.
Gibbs, George, paper on landfall of Columbus, 87.
Goat without horns, the, 190.
Gold, altar gilded with first, from America, 49; first seen in America, by Columbus, 72; discovered by Columbus, 237, 259; of the river Yanico, 267; dust and flakes from the Yanico, 274; of river Hayna, 339.
Golden sands, river of the, 275; grove estate of, 476.
Golfo de las Flechas, 294.
Gonaives, island of, 167.
Gosnold, B., in West Indies, 195.
Graham's Harbor, Bahamas, 91.
Granada, gardens of, 1; conquest of, 8, 15.
Grand Turk, island of, 83, 87.
Grand Khan, the, 163.
Green's Harbor, Bahamas, 93.
Guacanagari, Indian cacique, 219, 222, 227; possessions of, 311; ill-treatment and fate of, 390.

Guarico, Indian town, 222, 224, 227.
Guarionex, cacique, 311, 321; province of, taken by Columbus, 312.
Guadalquivir, river of, 30.
Guadeloupe, island of, 455-462.
Guanahani, first land discovered by Columbus, 72; described by Columbus, 90; author's departure from, 106.
Gundlach, Dr., of Cuba, 145.

## H

HAITI, derivation of the word, 218; author's arrival at, 167; foreigners and their rights in, 171; the president of, 175; resources of, 179; decadence of, 182; revolutions in, 182; description of, 186; martial law in, 187; massacre in, 200.
Haitien revolutionists, 183; civilization, the, 187; serpent worship, 188; independence, 201; Cape, 203-226.
Hammocks, when first seen by Columbus, 74.
Hatuey, Cuban cacique, 164.
Hawkins, Sir John, 194.
Hawk's bells, used in trade with Indians, 325.
Hayna, gold region of, 339.
Haynes-Smith, Sir W. F., 453.
Hamilton, Alexander, birthplace of, 451.
Havana, cathedral of, 130; author's arrival at, 131; a glance at, 136; newspapers of, 142, 148; art and literature of, 143; museums of, 144; the founding of, 149; captain-general's palace in, 150.
Henwood, Cornwall, 445.
Herrera, historian, 70.
Heureaux, President, of Santo Domingo, 391.
High woods, the, 459.
Holy hill, the, 302.
Horses, first used in America, 263.
Homenage, castle of the, 341, 362.
Hotels of Jamaica, 499.
Huelva, city of, 48.
Hungria, Señor, 268.
Hutia, or utia, animal of Cuba, 164.
Hyot, M. Charles, 460.

# INDEX.

## I

ICTERUS OBERI (a West Indian bird), 453.
Iguana, the, 101.
Imperial parrot, 466.
Inscriptions on Columbus casket, 375, 380.
Inagua, island of, 56.
Indians first seen by Columbus, 71; discovered by Columbus, 73; crania of Lucayan, 75; antiquities of the, 78; of Haiti, 217; of Santo Domingo, 263, 271; of Samana Bay, 294; Indian caciques of Santo Domingo, 311.
Invisible bird, the, 481.
Irving, Washington, references to, 55; theory of landfall, 87.
Isabella, queen, at Santa Fé, 15; island of, 101; town of, founded, 241–246; author's visit to, 243; relics and remains of, 248–250; abandonment of, 251; map of, 251; idols from, 256.

## J

JACAGUA, ancient city of, 275; view of, 329; ruins of, 334; history of, 336.
Jamaica, 492–515; author's visit to, 492; the Institute of, 494; newspapers of, 497; hotels of, 499; floral display of, 500; exposition of, 502; Columbus in, 512–515.
Jibara, Cuba, port entered by Columbus, 159.
Josephine, empress, birthplace of, 469.
Journal of Columbus, 71, 88, 89.

## K

King's House, Jamaica, 494.
Kingston, Jamaica, 492 et seq.
Kingstown, St. Vincent, 474, 476.

## L

Ladder, the, of Saba, 429.
Lake dwellers, of Venezuela, 488–490.
Landfall of Columbus, 55, 85, 90; authorities on, 87.
La Ferriere, castle of, 206, 216.
La Merced, church of, 355.
Las Casas, Bishop, 354.
Latin-American Department, Exposition, 122, 146.
Le Clerc, General, in Haiti, 201.
Lemonade, Count of, 202.
Llenas, Dr., 289.
Lombard, ancient, from Santo Domingo, 317.
Long Island, Bahamas, 95.
Lonja at Seville, archives of, 27.
Loup-garous, of Haiti, 189.
Lucayan Indians, of Bahamas, 74; skulls of, 75.
Luquillo, mountain of, 393.

## M

MACUQUINA (cut coins) of Puerto Rico, 407.
Mail, coat of, fragment found, 289.
Manatees of the Rio Yaqui, 236.
Madanino, island of, 295.
Manuscripts, ancient, 350.
Maracaibo, gulf of, 488.
Marmalade, Duke of, 202.
Martinique, island of, 466–470.
Marigalante, island of, 456.
McLelland, Mr., 298.
McLain, Mr., consul at Nassau, 115.
Matanzas, Cuba, 157; manchineel apples, 194.
Martyr, Petrus, old writer, 163.
Marco Polo, as read by Columbus, 163.
Mama-loi, Voudous priestess, 190.
Maysi, Cape of, Cuba, 165.
Melpomene, bust of, 216.
Mermaids, found by Columbus, 236.
Meriño, Monseñor, 350.
Mint, old, Santo Domingo, 356, 359.
Misery, Mount, 449.
Monument at Isabella, 289.
Montserrat, island of, 451.
Monte Cristi, Columbus at, 235.
Moclin, siege of, 21.
Moguer, and Palos, 33; church at, 36.
Monastery of La Rabida, 38–48.
Morgan, the pirate, 197.
Moreau de St. Mery, historian, 368.
Morro, of Havana, 133; of Puerto Rico, 406.

## INDEX.

Murdock, Lieutenant, 87.
Murillo, painting ascribed to, 358.
Myrtle-bank hotel, Jamaica, 497.
Millot, valley of, 208.

### N

NAIRN, Captain, 65.
Nassau, Bahamas, 109, 115.
Navarrete, historian, 89.
Navassa, island of, 515.
Navidad, fortress of, 226; site of, 227; massacre at, 228, 240.
Negroes, brought to Haiti, 198.
Nelson, Lord, at Nevis, 451.
Nevis, island of, 451.
New Providence, island of, 109.
Newport, Sir C., 195.
Nouet, Governor, 457.
Nuevitas, Cuba, 159.
Nuggets of gold, Santo Domingo, 267; large, from Santo Domingo, 340.

### O

O'BRIEN, Rev. Father, 289.
Ojeda, Alonzo de, 272; burial-place of, 353; in Guadeloupe, 456; voyage of, 487.
Ovies, Don Ricardo, 335.
Ozama River, 340.

### P

PADRE, the, of Santo Cerro, 316.
Palos, author's visit to, 31; Irving's journey to, 31; village and church of, 33, 34; to La Rabida, 37; return of Columbus to, 239.
Palms of Cuba, 125.
Papa-loi, priest of the Voudous, 190.
Papers, old, recovered from a shark, 508.
Paria, gulf of, 486.
Passailaigue, Mr., owner of Isabella, 289.
Parrots, seen by Columbus, 90.
Pearls, pink, 118.
Pearl islands, the, 486.
Petit Anse, Haiti, 227.
Petrifactions of Antigua, 454.
Peter the Great, a buccaneer, 197.
Piccolet, Point, Haiti, 226.

Phipps, Sir William, finds treasure, 198.
Pinzon, Martin Alonzo, 25, 71, 237.
Pitch Lake, of Trinidad, 485.
Pitons of St. Lucia, 473.
Plant Line steamers, to Havana, 131.
Poey, Don Felipe, 144.
Ponce de Leon, conquistador, 390; house of, 407; discovers Florida, 409; last resting-place, 410; epitaph on, 411.
Ponce, port of Puerto Rico, 394.
Pointe a pitre, Guadeloupe, 457.
Porte au Prince, Haiti, 167; streets of, 169; revolutions in, 170; newspapers of, 170; massacre in, 184.
Port Royal, Jamaica, 493.
Porvenir, el, newspaper, 288.
Privilegio (immunity), 357.
President of Santo Domingo, the, 285.
Puerta de Perdon, the, 357; bautismo, the, 361.
Puerto Plata, 238, 277 et seq.
Puerto de los Caballeros, the, 262.
Puerto Rico, island of, 388-412; when discovered, 388; arms of, 388; settlement of, 393; capital of, 394; captain-general of, 401; aborigines of, 402.

### Q

QUADRUPEDS seen by Columbus, 90; of Cuba, 164.
Quebec Line steamers, 453.
Quisqueya, native name of Santo Domingo, 218.

### R

RABIDA, La, monastery of, 38; Columbus at, 38; description of, 40; mirador of, 47.
Raleigh, Sir W., at Trinidad, 195.
Railroad in Santo Domingo, 286; from Samana to Santiago, 299, 301.
Reed, Don Juan, 348.
Repartimientos (apportionments of Indians), 392.
Riding Rocks, harbor of, 64.
Rio del Oro, 235, 263.
Rio Tinto, Spain, 31, 40.
Restos (remains) of Columbus, 363-387; "los, de Colon," 384.

# INDEX.

Roque Cocchia, Monseñor, 384.
Route of Columbus, map of, 99.
Royal Academy of Spain, 381.
Royal Plain, the, 308, 319.
Rum Cay, Bahamas, 92, 106.

## S

SABA, island of, 420–447.
Saints and Virgins, 413–425.
Saint Ann's, Jamaica, bay of, 514; Barts, island of, 442; Eustatius, 442, 449; John's, 413, 423; Kitt's, 448, 450; Martins, 442; Thomas, 414 et seq.; Ursula, 413; Vincent, 474–484.
Saint Vincent, volcano of, 481; Caribs of, 483.
Saint John, Sir Spencer, 185.
Saint Lucia, 472; Pierre, city of, 467.
Saint Nicolas, Mole, 218.
Saltes, bar of, Spain, 48.
Samana, bay of, 292, 296.
Sanchez, Santo Domingo, 298, 302
Sanctissima Trinidad, 357.
San-coche, native dish, 308.
San Antonio, church of, 355; Jose de las Matas, 272, 274; Juan de Puerto Rico, 395; Nicolas, church of, 354; Miguel, church of, 355; Francisco, convent of, 353.
Sans souci, palace of, 208.
Santa Barbara, church of, 355; town of, 296; Cruz, island of, 413; Fé, city of, Spain, 9, 10; Gloria, bay of, Jamaica, 514.
Santa Maria, flag-ship of Columbus, 220; wreck of the, 222; reliquia (holy relic), 357.
Santiago de los Caballeros, city, 268; road to, 331; description of, 332.
Santo Cerro, shrine of, 306–310; cross of, 357.
Santo Domingo, city of, 338–346; people of, 348; cathedral of, 350, 356–362; church of, 354; convents of, 356–362; island of, 259–387.
Sargasso Sea and weed, 52, 53, 70.
Saunders, Mr., vice-consul, U. S., Nassau, 115.
Savannas of Santo Domingo, 303.

Second voyage of Columbus, 240.
Sereno (night-watchman), 284.
Serpent-worship in Haiti, 188.
Seville, Spain, treasures of, 26–30.
Sharks, in the Bahamas, 61.
Shea, Sir Ambrose, 109.
Silk-cotton tree, 116.
Silver mountain-port of the, 277.
Silla (choir-stall), Santo Domingo, 357.
Skull, aboriginal, 75, 77.
Slave-trade, growth of, 198–300.
Smith, Captain John, in the West Indies, 195.
Spain, allusion to early history of, 5.
Soufriére of St. Lucia, 473; of St. Vincent, 481.
Stewart, Mr., consul at Puerto Rico, 398.
Swords of the conquistadores, 336.
Sun dial, old, Santo Domingo, 346.

## T

TEJERA, Sr., Emiliano, 384.
Templeté of Havana, 149.
"Thunderbolts" (Indian celts), 81.
Tobacco, first found, 95; seen in Cuba, by Columbus, 158; of Santo Domingo, 286.
Tomb of Columbus, 314.
Toledo swords, found in Santo Domingo, 336.
Tortola, old coins of, 425.
Tortuga, island of, 56, 193.
Torrecilla de Colon, 343.
Toussaint l'Ouverture, 200.
Trade winds, 53.
Tree of Columbus, 314.
Tree ferns, 440.
Trinidad, island of, 484–486.
Turk's Island, 82, 163.

## U

UNIVERSITY, the first in America, 354.
Utia, or dumb dog, 74, 164.

## V

VAN HORNE, Dutch privateer, 197.
Vega, the royal, Santo Domingo, 299, 305, 308.

## INDEX.

Vega Vieja (old vega), 321; church of, 325; bell obtained at, 326; excavations at, 329.
Veragua, Duke of, 372.
Verde, Rio, 330.
Velasquez, paintings ascribed to, 360.
Venezuela, discovery of, 489.
Vespucci, Americus, 487-489.
Virgin of Providencia, 398; Gorda, 423.
Voudouism, in Haiti, 189.

### W

WARD Line, steamers of, 109, 120.
Washerwomen of Haiti, 290; of Santo Domingo, 297.
Watling's Island, 56, 65; map of, 85; natives of, 105.

Wellman, Walter, explores Bahamas, 102.
Wilberforce's plea in House of Commons, 199.

### Y

YAGUA ("palm bark"), 308.
Yanico, Santo Tomas de, 264; first fort built at, 267, 272; author's visit to, 268.
Yaqui River, 236, 337; valley of the, 263.
Yumuri valley, Cuba, 155.
Yunque, Cuban mountain, 162; mountain of Puerto Rico, 411.

### Z

ZUBIA, crosses of, 21.

www.ingramcontent.com/pod-product-compliance
Lightning Source LLC
Chambersburg PA
CBHW031944290426
44108CB00011B/672